Voices of Experience

*Memorable Talks from the
National Institute on the
Teaching of Psychology*

VOLUME ONE

EDITED BY
Baron Perlman, Lee I. McCann, and
William Buskist

ASSOCIATION FOR PSYCHOLOGICAL SCIENCE

www.psychologicalscience.org

Published by
Association for Psychological Science
1010 Vermont Avenue, NW
11th Floor
Washington, DC 20005-4907

International Standard Book Number: 0-9626884-4-4
Library of Congress Catalog Number: 2005926638

To order copies of *Voices of Experience*
Call (202) 783-2077 or go to
www.psychologicalscience.org/teachpsych

FOREWORD

To some psychology faculty, it must seem that there has always been a National Institute on the Teaching of Psychology (NITOP). The rest of us, though, can clearly recall a time before NITOP, when there was absolutely no reason for any department head or dean to pay to send psychology teachers to Florida in January. Now, NITOP is the best place for a teacher of psychology to spend the first week of each new year.

NITOP met for the first time on October 9 to 11, 1978, on the campus of the University of Illinois at Urbana-Champaign (UIUC). Many people assume that NITOP was my idea, but it was actually the brainchild of Frank Costin, a fellow member of the UIUC psychology department in whose memory the Costin award is now given at NITOP. Frank's simple, but vital, idea was to give psychology faculty a chance to get together to exchange ideas and advice about the challenges, frustrations, problems, and pleasures of teaching psychology. To be honest, I don't recall if I attended the institute that first year. I don't think I did, because the first I remember hearing about it was when Frank asked me to be a speaker at the second annual meeting, in the fall of 1979. To me, the invitation to speak was just that. I had no idea at the time that the institute would become an institution or that I would become so involved in it, and I certainly had no inkling of the impact it would come to have on psychology teachers, on how and what they teach, and even on the growth of other teaching conferences.

I remember being struck by the intense interest the participants showed as they listened to their colleagues talk about teaching methods and ideas for updating course content, and how eager they were to talk to each other about student-faculty relationship issues, grading policies, ethical dilemmas, and the like. I had no idea that so many faculty in psychology cared so much about these things — because, frankly, most members of my research-oriented department did not talk much about teaching, especially undergraduate teaching, other than to complain about having to do it. As someone who loved teaching and who wanted to find out how to do it better, I had learned to keep my mouth shut about my nasty little secret and just do the best I could. (I remember being laughed at by a senior colleague when I told him how happy I was to have been "trusted" with a 350-student section of abnormal psychology in my very first semester at Illinois.) But now I wondered: If there were faculty who took the trouble to come to Champaign, Illinois, of all places, in an effort to improve their teaching, maybe there was a way I could help them, and improve my own teaching in the process.

Early in 1980, Frank Costin asked me to join the planning committee for the Third Annual NITOP, and it was at a meeting of that committee that we decided to try to broaden the appeal of the institute, and serve more people, by moving it to Florida in January, where it has been held ever since. At the Fifth Annual Institute, in 1983, we tried something else new: We included two roundtable discussion sessions that were suggested by previous participants. The format was popular enough that the following year we scheduled six roundtables. By 1988, at program committee member Bob Hendersen's suggestion, we began inviting all participants to submit topics for discussions that they themselves would lead during what came to be called Participant Idea Exchanges (PIE). That same year, we also invited participants to present posters on any topic related to the teaching of psychology. The response to these invitations was stunning, as dozens of participants submitted PIE topics, poster proposals, or both. No doubt they did so partly because giving a presentation at NITOP helped support requests for travel money, but years of touring crowded rows of posters and eavesdropping on packed PIE sessions has made it clear to me that these presentations and discussions are helping to meet much more fundamental needs. They actually give participants at our conference a chance to confer with one another, to tell interested colleagues about what they are doing in their classes, and to hear what those colleagues are doing, too. Perhaps even more important, these sessions provide participants with an opportunity to describe the problems they are having in their courses, and to get ideas for solving them. In the process, they discover they are not alone in having to face those problems, or in being perplexed, worried, and even frightened by them.

I am particularly proud of these features and of the stellar talks our distinguished speakers have delivered over the years, some of which are included in this volume.

They have helped to realize the vision that Frank Costin had for NITOP more than a quarter of a century ago: to get teachers of psychology together in a way that benefits their teaching and their lives as teachers. Past participants tell me that attending NITOP helps them to renew their enthusiasm for teaching, gives them new ideas for making their classes more interesting and up-to-date, and offers them fresh perspectives and strategies for dealing with the inevitable student–faculty problems they must face. I, too, am gratified that NITOP's impact has been amplified through its role in helping others who seek to promote the teaching of psychology. NITOP appears to have served as a stimulus and model for the many regional teaching conferences that have developed since 1984, and for the Association for Psychological Science's annual preconvention Insititute on the Teaching of Psychology, which is coordinated by the Society for the Teaching of Psychology (STP).

The NITOP program committee continues to look for new ways to improve our institute, and to expand its role in promoting excellence in the teaching of psychology. This book, which we hope will begin a continuing series, is one result of those efforts. We hope you enjoy reading this first volume, and that it will prompt you to attend a future NITOP meeting, where you can hear talks just as good as these, presented live in the warmth of a Florida winter.

Doug Bernstein
University of South Florida
Chair, NITOP Program Committee

PREFACE
AND
ACKNOWLEDGMENTS

The National Institute on the Teaching of Psychology (NITOP) draws teachers from far and wide each January. The *raison d'etre* of NITOP is the fire it lights or sustains for pedagogical excellence — commitment to students, and making courses and classes more relevant, exciting, and interesting. Simply put, the talks and workshops at NITOP are first-rate, loaded with useful pedagogical examples we can follow in the courses we teach, and with ideas on how best to present psychology to our students.

Until now, though, after the echoes of the last talk each January fade, NITOP is put away for another year. NITOP, because it lures attendees away from their home campuses, and because its setting is conducive to sitting, thinking, wondering, and relaxing, is a conference conducive to epiphanies. Our epiphany came in the form of a question: *Why? Why did the wonderful guidance, ideas, and experience of superb speakers and workshop facilitators have to be put away, sometimes seemingly forever?* The answer was, *they don't.*

We are pleased to include in this volume 13 superb talks and workshops from NITOP. The book begins with history and context, moves to themes important in any psychology course, follows with several chapters on teaching methods, presents issues on doing successful empirical scholarship of teaching and student learning, and ends with the lessons two long-time teachers believe form the essence of good teaching and of being an academic. For those of you who have not attended NITOP, we hope this book proves to be the next-best experience. Perhaps it will convince you to attend NITOP next year, or at some other time in the future. If you do, be sure to say hello to us. It is people that make NITOP so worthwhile and we would be interested in meeting you.

THE BOOK'S CONTENT

Teaching cannot take place in a vacuum, and what is new is often not as new as it seems. It is grounded, as it must be, in what went before. Psychologists are real people, who often lead interesting and curious lives. We found Sdorow's chapter on the people behind psychology (emphasizing biographical vignettes) and Benjamin's archival adventures enthralling, and hope that you do also.

Another theme evident in *Voices of Experience* is that as we mature and age, much of the material that was taught to us — and that seems to us so self-evident — has a way of entering the dustbin of brief mention in texts, if any mention is made at all. Gerow and Bordens present compelling tales of research that no longer finds its way into many of our textbooks — but probably should. Many of us simply assume that these findings are core psychological content. As Gerow and Bordens show us, though, such an assumption is mistaken. You may look at your texts, especially if you teach introductory psychology, and find that you have much more to add on these topics than your text has time to present.

Voices of Experience also presents important content that will enrich your teaching and your students' ability to think critically about psychology. First, whereas many teachers and students are unfamiliar with different cultures, Goldstein skillfully lays out the issues that arise when our research considers the complex and differing cultures that humans have created and in which they live. Second, Gray asks us to ponder evolutionary theory, perhaps the most important theory to which we will expose our students. Gray does a masterful job helping teachers appreciate and understand how relevant evolutionary theory is to the teaching of psychology. Third, it is possible, using dramatic and powerful examples, to convince students that neuroscience is relevant to their lives, and Kosslyn and Rosenberg do so beautifully.

Our mission as teachers is to profess psychology, and we can do so badly or well. We sometimes create boundaries between our students and ourselves: We are too formal, too stiff, and too boring. Berk, in describing storytelling as a teaching strategy, illustrates how all of us can weave tales that create an atmosphere of warmth in our classrooms and heighten our students' interest in our subject matter. Kassin's insightful theme is that commonsense knowledge and prediction of human behavior are not always supported by the science of our discipline. Showing the discrepancy between what students believe and what psychology knows is a powerful way to teach the relevance and utility of science in students' lives.

Bernstein shows us how to maintain our enthusiasm for the classroom, underscoring how important energy and positive affect are to our teaching. Daniel's chapter is a morality tale: a caution to us all that the god or goddess of technology can create but often destroys — a Shakespearian theme.

Of course in addition to the content of our courses, we also must consider how well we are teaching and what our students are learning, and share these findings with colleagues. Perlman and McCann present ideas on doing successful, empirical scholarship of teaching and learning (SoTL). They believe that this type of SoTL best fits the expertise of psychologists, and has the best chance of counting as scholarship at one's home institution and the best chance of entering the public domain.

Lastly, Lefton and Myers present their collective wisdom, both for teaching and for leading an academic life. These are the musings and lessons of two psychologists who have taught for a "lifetime." Both essays are informative and insightful.

ACKNOWLEDGMENTS

We thank our authors for the superb jobs they did in converting the spoken to the written word. Preparing a written message demands different organizational and communication skills than preparing a spoken one. We truly appreciate their work in formalizing and updating their talks. Their willingness to share their knowledge with us, and their commitment to making this book a success, deserves our sincere *thank you.*

We also thank the Association for Psychological Science, a longtime supporter of NITOP and the publisher of this volume. APS prizes good teaching. Its ongoing support of NITOP has been above and beyond the call of professional duty. In particular, we wish to thank Alan Kraut, Brian Weaver, Eric Jaffe, and Eric Wargo for their indefatigable behind-the-scenes support that made it possible to bring this volume to fruition.

One more group deserves our appreciation. The NITOP Planning Committee, both past and present, which has overseen NITOP for the last decade, during which our authors presented: Bill Buskist, Frank Costin, Jane Halonen, Robert Hendersen, Sandra Goss Lucas, Louis Penner, Ed Roy, and Carol Wade. These teachers serve behind the scenes to make NITOP a worthwhile venue and destination year after year.

Once one arrives at NITOP, Joanne Fetzner makes the Institute the wonderful experience it is. *Thank you!* Of course, Doug Bernstein has kept NITOP alive and vibrant over the years. We do not want to say too much about Doug lest his hat size increase. He, with Joanne Fetzner, provides the consistent solidity that any institute like NITOP needs in order to maintain its unparalled excellence in the world of teaching conferences.

We hope you enjoy what you are about to read and find it useful and thought-provoking in your teaching. We dedicate this volume to good pedagogy and enlightened students. Enjoy!

Baron Perlman, Lee I. McCann, and William Buskist

CONTENTS

CHAPTER ONE

THE PEOPLE BEHIND PSYCHOLOGY

Enliven Your Lectures With Biographical Vignettes

Lester M. Sdorow

Arcadia University

DURING MY FIRST 2 years as an undergraduate, I majored in English and was particularly enthralled by biographies and autobiographies of eminent people in all fields of endeavor. Reading their life stories, I learned the essentials of their accomplishments and contributions in a more lively way than by simply reading textbook presentations of what they did.

My particular interest in reading biographies and autobiographies of contributors to psychology came about when I was perusing Freud's *The Interpretation of Dreams* (Freud, 1900/1990) and came across a footnote mentioning empirical dream research done in the 1890s by Mary Whiton Calkins. I was surprised that anyone had conducted dream research before Freud — let alone empirical research, by a woman whose name I recognized but about whom I knew little. I proceeded to ask a librarian at the school where I was teaching, Lafayette College (which proudly displayed a photograph of its eminent alumnus, James McKeen Cattell, in its psychology wing), to brave the musty basement where it keeps its old journals. She returned with an ancient but intact volume of the *American Journal of Psychology* with a long article by Calkins (1893) describing dream research she had conducted with one of her mentors, Edmund Clark Sanford. I was impressed by her cleverness: She had done a substantial empirical study of the content of dreams using only a pencil, a pad of paper, and an alarm clock. Much of what she discovered (such as our tendency to dream more during the second half of the night) was only verified many decades later by sophisticated research done with modern physiological recording equipment.

I became intrigued by Calkins herself, so I proceeded to read everything I could about her, beginning with her contribution to *A History of Psychology in Autobiography* (Calkins, 1930). In it, she remarked that she could not understand why Freud believed there were deep meanings in dreams, given that she had found

1

that dreams typically were connected to mundane daily experiences. I proceeded to read brief biographies of Calkins in journal articles and collections of biographies, most notably those written by Laurel Furumoto, the leading Calkins scholar (Furumoto, 1979, 1980, 1990).

Becoming a fan of Mary Whiton Calkins also inspired me to read biographies of other eminent early female psychologists. I made periodic presentations about them at professional meetings, including the *National Institute on the Teaching of Psychology*'s annual conference. Soon my interest broadened from the lives of female psychologists to the lives of male contributors to the field too. I felt compelled to incorporate what I was learning into my courses, and found that doing so enriched the material significantly, making it more interesting to my students and to me. This positive effect on my teaching inspired me to begin collecting biographies and autobiographies of psychology's guiding lights.

Over the years, I have acquired dozens of collections of biographies or autobiographies and hundreds of individual biographies and autobiographies of major contributors to psychology — some of which I have listed in Appendix B to this chapter. A few examples drawn from this material should illustrate the benefits of talking about the lives of psychologists in your courses.

WHERE IDEAS AND RESEARCH INTERESTS COME FROM

Students love learning about the unexpected origins of the great ideas and research projects in psychology. One of my students' favorites is the story of how Hans Berger originally developed his electroencephalograph (EEG) to study telepathic communication. When he was 19 years old and serving in the German army, Berger received a telegram informing him that his sister had been overcome by the feeling that he was in trouble. He received the telegram the evening of the day that he and his horse had slid down an embankment into the path of an oncoming piece of horse-drawn artillery and had narrowly missed being crushed to death. The scientist wondered if he and his sister — who were extremely close — had communicated by mental telepathy, so he set off to measure the energy that he believed might be passing between them (Stevens, 1971).

Students also enjoy hearing how in 1921 Otto Loewi was directed to conduct his crucial experiment on the chemical nature of neural transmission by a repeated dream. In accordance with the dream, Loewi placed the beating heart of a frog, along with a portion of the vagus nerve still attached to the heart, into a saline solution. By electrically stimulating the vagus nerve, he made the heart beat slower. He then put another beating frog heart into the same solution. Even though he did not stimulate its vagus nerve, the second heart immediately began to beat slower. Loewi concluded that stimulation of the vagus nerve of the first heart had released a chemical into the solution. It was this chemical, which he later identified as acetylcholine, that slowed the beating of the hearts (Loewi, 1960).

More recently, there is the example of Elaine Hatfield, a leading researcher on interpersonal attraction — particularly romantic love. Her interest in the subject was born during late-night conversations with other graduate students at Stanford University. She found that, almost without exception, her colleagues were distressed about their romantic lives — either finding it impossible to meet a romantic partner, having problems with their current romantic partner, or trying to deal with an impending divorce. She met resistance to her research ideas from professors at Stanford because of the popular belief at the time that passionate love was a taboo and trivial topic, but her mentor, Leon Festinger, who was a prominent social psychologist, insisted that she be permitted to conduct her research (Hatfield, 2001).

Developmental psychology researchers likewise may get their ideas from everyday sources. Eleanor J. Gibson had several experiences that stimulated her interest in conducting research on depth perception using the visual cliff. As a child, she had developed a fear of heights after visiting the Grand Canyon and looking down from some of its steep overlooks. Later her colleague Richard Walk at Cornell University related his experiences working with parachutists learning to overcome their natural fear of jumping from heights by being trained to jump off the edges of high platforms. At Cornell, Gibson and Walk also were intrigued by the tendency of newborn goats to avoid walking over the edges of platforms (Gibson, 1980).

Consider, too, the story of Hans J. Eysenck. He got his inspiration to turn against psychoanalysis in favor of behavior therapy from an unknown psychoanalyst named Alexander Herzberg. Herzberg told Eysenck that he had been successful in directly removing patients' symptoms rather than relying on prolonged attempts to psychoanalyze them. One of Herzberg's favorite techniques was to expose fear-ridden patients to increasingly anxiety-inducing situations, which he found alleviated their fears (Eysenck, 1990). Years later, Joseph Wolpe formalized and publicized this technique as a component of systematic desensitization. As a result, Wolpe — and not Herzberg, who was simply an obscure refugee from Germany — received credit as its creator.

INFLUENTIAL LIFE EXPERIENCES

Students are always interested in the possible role of life experiences, particularly childhood experiences, in shaping the views and careers of giants in the field. An amusing example is that of Hermann Rorschach. During his childhood, he was given the nickname Klecks (from the German for "inkblot") because he enjoyed Klecksography, a game in which children would drip ink on a piece of paper, fold it, and tell each other the things they saw in the inkblot ("Who Named It?: Hermann Rorschach," 2001).

Then there's Eleanor Maccoby, best known for her research on child development and gender differences, who, growing up in Tacoma, Washington, had one of the most unusual childhoods of any psychologist. Her parents, vegetarian Theosophist folksingers who were interested in Eastern religions and philosophies as well as ESP, astrology, and the supernatural, were part of what we would call the alternative culture of the early 20th century. Given this, as a teenager in the 1930s Maccoby felt free to write to leading parapsychologist J. B. Rhine, who corresponded with her and sent her Zener cards so she and her friends could conduct their own research. After finding that she could see the symbols through the backs of the Zener cards, she lost faith in ESP and decided that a skeptical, scientific approach was essential in assessing all claims (Maccoby, 1989).

Many contributors to psychology have been influenced by emotionally painful experiences too. After watching his kindly mother die an agonizing death from cancer, William McDougall, best known for championing instincts as factors in human behavior and for trying to make parapsychology a legitimate field of scientific research, lost his faith in God and insisted that only science can help improve the lot of human beings (McDougall, 1930). Ernest Hilgard, who later became a leading hypnosis researcher and psychology textbook writer, intended to become a physician, but recoiled from it after his physician father was killed while serving during World War I (Hilgard, 1974). Wilder Penfield, after being grievously wounded when a U-boat attacked and sunk his ship during World War I, believed that God had permitted him to survive in order to serve humanity. This event led him to become a physician and physiology researcher; he developed a surgical technique for treating intractable epilepsy and mapped the sensory and motor areas of the cerebral cortex (Lewis, 1981).

Erik H. Erikson, famous for his theory of life-span development, suffered a powerful identity crisis of his own while growing up in Germany. Erikson, blonde and blue eyed and decidedly Nordic looking, was reared by Jewish parents and felt that he did not fit in with either Jewish or Christian children. In school, many of the other students considered him a Jew. In synagogue, many in the congregation considered him a Gentile. His confusion was heightened when, before reaching adolescence, he learned that his father, whom he believed throughout childhood was his biological father, was actually his stepfather and that his probable biological father was a Danish Christian (Friedman, 1999). This probably contributed to the emphasis that Erikson put, in his theory of psychosocial development, on the individual's search for an identity during adolescence.

Perhaps the most powerful example of the relationship between a psychologist's life and professional outlook can be gleaned from the painful early life and war experiences of Frederick "Fritz" Perls, the founder of Gestalt therapy (Shepard, 1975). Perls was reared in a Jewish ghetto in Germany. His father was a wine salesman who rarely came home and often cheated on his wife. When he was home, he belittled Fritz unmercifully. (Years later Perls refused to attend his funeral.) After Perls had enrolled at the University of Berlin to study medicine, World War I intervened and he became a medical volunteer for the Red Cross, later enlisting in a Zeppelin battalion. He won a medal for continuing to unload ammunition while under intense Allied bombardment. On another occasion he was wounded when a shell exploded near him during trench warfare. On still another occasion he suffered lung damage from a gas attack. Throughout his adulthood, Perls was haunted by the memory of a gas attack during which many of the gas masks failed and suffocating soldiers clung to him, begging for air as he passed the few functioning gas masks from one soldier to another.

One evening while on furlough, Perls attended the opera *Figaro*. The stark contrast between the beauty of the opera and the horror of the trenches made him run out of the theater and burst into tears. During this period of his life, Perls also was overcome by the loss of his closest friend, Ferdinand Knopf, who was killed in action.

After the war, Perls became emotionally numb and socially detached for years, apparently suffering from what we now call posttraumatic stress disorder. His experiences with the ugly underbelly of humanity during his childhood and in WWI led him to spend a lifetime supporting humanitarian causes and opposing senseless wars. However, his experiences also made him wary of getting too close to people, which might account in part for his rather callous "Gestalt prayer" — which appalled even his own children:

> I do my thing and you do your thing. I am not in this world to live up to your expectations, and you are not in this world to live up to mine. You are you and I am I and if by chance we find each other, it's beautiful.

WHO INFLUENCED WHOM?

During the more than a century of psychology's existence as an independent intellectual discipline, major contributors have been influenced by other individuals — sometimes psychologists themselves. Some of these relationships are obvious, given their mutual interests. Others are not obvious — or are even surprising. William James was so impressed with Clifford Beers, for example, that he urged him to publish a book about his experiences in Connecticut mental institutions and even helped secure him a publisher (Dain, 1980). This relationship led to the publication of one of the bestselling autobiographies ever, *A Mind that Found Itself* (Beers, 1908/1981). G. Stanley Hall, a protégé of James, convinced African American Francis Sumner to pursue his PhD at Clark University. Sumner went on to develop the psychology program at Howard University and write abstracts in English of more than 3,000 articles written in French, German, and Spanish for the *Psychological Bulletin* and the *Journal of Social Psychology* (Guthrie, 2000). Sumner, in turn, influenced the careers of Kenneth B. Clark and Mamie Phipps Clark, who majored in psychology at Howard and conducted research on African American children's self-esteem — research that influenced the landmark 1954 U.S. Supreme Court decision in Brown v. Board of Education of Topeka, Kansas (Guthrie, 1990).

Clark Hull, a prominent learning researcher, welcomed Eleanor J. Gibson as his doctoral student at a time when women found it difficult to find a mentor. She recalled him as a kindly man who reminded her of her father (Gibson, 1980). William Dement served as an assistant in Nathaniel Kleitman's sleep research laboratory and went on to become an eminent sleep researcher himself (Dement, 1974). The year that Stanley Milgram spent with Solomon Asch doing postdoctoral research is clearly shown in his classic research on obedience. (In fact, Milgram initially wanted simply to replicate Asch's line judgment study with a more socially meaningful design; Evans, 1980). More recently, Richard Davidson's undergraduate advisor at New York University, Judith Rodin, who became a leading researcher on eating and obesity, convinced him that it was possible to use the experimental method to study cognitive processes. He went on to become the leading researcher on hemispheric differences in emotional processing ("Distinguished Scientific Contributions: Richard J. Davidson," 2000).

PSYCHOLOGISTS' OTHER LIVES

Many famous contributors to psychology led lives outside of the laboratory that never make it into textbooks but that students love hearing about. Consider Wilder Penfield, perhaps the giant of 20th-century neuroscientists. He was an imposing person — personally, intellectually, and physically. An athlete, he played varsity football while at Princeton and then worked as an assistant coach. Princeton lost a potential head coach and the world gained a prominent brain researcher when he turned down a coaching promotion to accept a Rhodes Scholarship. Less well-known than his work on the brain is his work on motion sickness. During World War II, the Canadian government called upon him to run a crash program to find a treatment to aid sailors and soldiers on voyages to Europe. So, with the help of his associates, Penfield went on various rides at a Montreal amusement park to find the ones that best mimicked the nausea-inducing movements of a ship at sea, and then built a "ride" that best replicated that motion in a squash court at McGill University. He tested the effects of various drugs on riders until he found one that worked: thiobarbiturate (Lewis, 1981).

Santiago Ramón y Cajal, Penfield's scientific hero, is now best known for demonstrating that neurons had gaps between them rather than being physically connected in a network. However, he also was one of science's true Renaissance men. For one thing, he was an outstanding gymnast and an early proponent of bodybuilding. In fact, his stimulating autobiography, *Recollections of My Life* (Ramón y Cajal, 1937/1989), includes a photo of the author posing shirtless and flexing his biceps. His strong — yet extremely appealing — ego is revealed in the caption: "The photo does not do justice to my monstrous development." Cajal also was an accomplished artist who drew beautiful pen-and-ink drawings of the nervous system that are still used in textbooks today. On top of this, he was an expert photographer who wrote one of the first books on the subject, and a wonderful writer who produced eloquent poetry. He also was a championship chess player. But it almost ruined Cajal's life when, for a period, he began to devote more time to reading and playing chess than to his professional and personal commitments.

Even statistics can be made less dry by presenting aspects of the unusual lives of its major figures. Consider the story of William Sealy Gosset (1876-1937), also known as "Student," who invented the *t* test. Students are surprised to hear that Gosset was not only an eminent statistician but a career brewmaster for the Guinness brewery in Dublin. He created the *t* test to help him improve the ability of Guinness Stout to retain its taste after being shipped. Gosset would compare several batches of stout treated one way to several batches treated another way, using the *t* test to determine whether there was any statistically significant difference in quantitative measures related to the taste of the beer (Pearson, 1990).

A number of more recent contributors to the field of psychology have led interesting lives too. Love researcher Elaine Hatfield has become a successful novelist (Hatfield, 2001) whose works include *Rosie* (with Richard Rapson) and *Darwin's Law*. Sandra Scarr, a well-known psychologist who pursued diverse research interests in human development and behavioral genetics, retired to a beach house in Hawaii, where she grows orchids and even became a rescue scuba diver (Scarr, 2001). Like Cajal, Leon Festinger became so engrossed in chess that his academics suffered, as he haunted chess clubs instead of studying (Cohen, 1977). Howard Gardner was such an outstanding musician (relevant to one of his multiple intelligences) that he gave music lessons while still a child, and toyed with the idea of becoming a professional pianist (Doorey, 2004). Paul Ekman and Richard Davidson have been befriended by the Dalai Lama, who asked Davidson to help create a dialog between Buddhism and neuroscience and Ekman to do research on the effects of meditation on emotion (Kreisler, 2004).

Perhaps the most bizarre anecdote about the "dark side" of eminent psychologists concerns the possible role of Henry Murray in provoking Ted Kaczynski, the so-called Unabomber, to go on his 17-year vendetta against scientists and modern technology. During World War II, Murray had worked for the OSS, running its assessment program for selecting spies. From 1959 to 1962, Kaczynski had participated in a study of personality manipulation that Murray conducted at Harvard University — a study that involved the use of techniques similar to those used in brainwashing, including repeated personal humiliation. Some observers wonder if this traumatic experience contributed to Kaczynski's murderous rage against academic researchers (Chase, 2003). In all, he planted 16 bombs that killed three people and wounded 23.

APPRECIATING PSYCHOLOGY'S CULTURAL CONTEXT

Another interesting aspect of psychologists' biographies is how many of them have been affected — often negatively — by their political and cultural situation. As with other sciences, racism, anti-Semitism, and sexism have affected our field. For many decades, for example, few African Americans pursued careers in psychology because they could not get the necessary education, and academic positions were not available outside of traditionally Black colleges. Robert Guthrie's book, *Even the Rat was White*, presents the stories of major African American contributors to psychology during the 20th century (Guthrie, 1998).

Anti-Semitism has also played a role. Wolfgang Köhler, a Christian and known for his research in Gestalt psychology, regularly stood up for his Jewish colleagues against the Nazis even after they invaded his classroom to intimidate him. After refusing to sign an oath of allegiance to Hitler, he fled to the United States in 1935 and took a position at Swarthmore College (Sherrill, 1991). In 1938, Otto Loewi, who shared the Nobel Prize for his discovery of the chemical basis of neural transmission, was arrested with two of his sons and imprisoned with hundreds of Jews. As ransom for their being permitted to leave Germany, he had to give up all of his possessions — including the money he received from his Nobel Prize, which he had to send to a Nazi bank in Stockholm ("Nobelprize.org: Otto Loewi," 2004). Also in 1938, the Nazis removed EEG inventor Hans Berger from his post as head of his academic department for being a Jew. He fell into a deep depression and eventually hung himself ("Who Named It?: Hans Berger," 2001).

For decades, anti-Semitism also was pervasive in the lives of American Jewish psychologists. For example, as a young man, Edwin Shneidman — who later became the world's foremost suicidologist — wanted to enroll in UCLA's doctoral program in clinical psychology. His hopes were dashed when the openly anti-Semitic chairman of the department refused to accept him, claiming that he would not be able to find an academic position for a Jewish graduate. Ironically, many years later, Shneidman was actively recruited by the same university to be a professor of suicidology in its Neuropsychiatric Institute (Shneidman, 1991).

Perhaps the oddest example of the role of anti-Semitism in the lives of eminent psychologists is that of Harry Israel — better known to the world as Harry

Harlow. Though Israel was a protestant, he changed his name at the suggestion of Lewis Terman, one of the pioneers in intelligence testing, whose associate Walter Miles informed him that Israel would be unlikely to find a faculty position with such a Jewish-sounding last name (LeRoy & Kimble, 2003).

Another theme throughout the first century of psychology was male antipathy toward women psychologists. The case of Mary Whiton Calkins is worthy of a full-length biography, and is probably the best known. Her contemporary, Margaret Floy Washburn, was told by James McKeen Cattell that, as a woman, she would have a better chance of receiving a PhD at Cornell University than at Columbia University, so she enrolled in Edward Titchener's graduate program and earned her doctorate there. Yet, Titchener, whose graduate psychology program was perhaps the most open to female students, banned female psychologists from his Society of Experimental Psychologists — allegedly because of "man talk" and cigar smoking (Benjamin, 2005).

Christine Ladd-Franklin, a well-known color vision researcher, became Titchener's nemesis, accosting him at professional meetings and accusing him of hypocrisy for admitting men who were not experimentalists and excluding women who were. She also noted that she could handle man talk and enjoyed an occasional cigar. Titchener vowed to her that a woman would be admitted to his society only over his dead body. He was correct. Shortly after his death, Washburn became the first woman to gain admission (Scarborough & Furumoto, 1987).

In more contemporary examples, Eleanor J. Gibson recalled her distasteful experience at Yale University when she asked Robert Yerkes if she could be a research assistant, only to have him abruptly show her to the door, saying he did not accept women in his laboratory (Gibson, 1980). More recently, prominent personality researcher Gordon Allport told Sandra Scarr that he opposed her being in the graduate program at Harvard (where she obtained her PhD in 1965) because she would probably get married, stay home to raise children, and never pursue an academic career (Scarr, 2001). Scarr went on to become an influential researcher on the effects of daycare on children and the relative influence of heredity and life experiences on intellectual development. Linda Bartoshuk turned to psychology after being dissuaded from pursuing her first love, astronomy, because she was a woman. Even so, Carl Pfaffman, the prominent chemical senses researcher, told her that he did not accept women in his laboratory at Brown University. But Bartoshuk persevered, Pfaffman became her mentor and friend (Bartoshuk, 2001), and she went on to become a noted chemical senses researcher in her own right.

A tragic story is that of Christiana Morgan, who co-created the Thematic Apperception Test with Henry Murray. Her tale is told in the eye-opening biography, *Translate This Darkness* (Douglas, 1993). Morgan was known for both her great beauty and her great intellect. Eminent philosopher Alfred North Whitehead called a statue of Morgan the most magnificent one he had ever seen of a woman. The famous critic Lewis Mumford, who socialized with the best and the brightest, noted that Morgan had one of the three greatest minds he had ever encountered. (After Murray's death, his manuscripts were found to contain Morgan's comments throughout them.) But she became an alcoholic and spent her life as little more than Henry Murray's intellectual helper and mistress. After his wife's death, Murray promised Morgan he would marry her if she stopped drinking. She did so, but he chose to be with a woman 20 years younger than her instead. In deep emotional pain, Morgan then committed suicide. She went to a beach, neatly folded her clothes, removed the ring that Murray had given her years earlier, wrapped it in a small beach bag, and placed it on the sand — and walked out into the sea and drowned herself.

Some contributors to our field, like Harry Stack Sullivan, bore the brunt of several social stigmas. Sullivan was born to poverty-stricken parents who had emigrated from Ireland to escape the devastating potato famine. They had lost their other two children during childbirth. Sullivan endured a lonely, unhappy childhood, continually faced with his father's aloofness and his mother's criticisms. These stressful experiences were compounded by the anti-Catholic hostility he encountered in his largely Protestant hometown. In adulthood, many of Sullivan's friends and colleagues knew that he was gay but the times in which he lived forced him to hide his sexual orientation. Though Sullivan became a renowned psychiatrist who helped many people, he lived his own life in chaos, drinking too much and finding himself in constant financial trouble. Sullivan fought a constant battle against depression, and his longtime colleague, psychoanalyst Edith Weigert, recalled an occasion when Sullivan suddenly put a hand on her shoulder and said, "Edith, you do not know how lonely I am" (Chatelaine, 1991, p. 340).

SERENDIPITY

Albert Bandura (1982) has noted that many of our life choices are governed by serendipity involving chance events and chance encounters. He recalled that the primary reason he changed from majoring in biology to majoring in psychology was that an introductory psychology course fit perfectly in his schedule one semester. Among many other examples of the role of serendipity in career choices is that of Hermann Ebbinghaus, who accidentally came upon a used copy of Fechner's *Elements of Psychophysics* while working in a Paris bookshop. Reading it inspired him to apply the scientific method to the study of memory (Boneau, 1998). Hans J. Eysenck, who became one of the most influential psychologists of the late 20th century, intended to major in physics at the University of London but lacked the prerequisite courses, so he majored in psychology instead, simply because it was the only science major that did not have those prerequisites (Eysenck, 1990). Donald O. Hebb, who became a renowned brain researcher, didn't know what course of study to pursue in graduate school. But when his sister Catherine, who just happened to be a doctoral student in physiology at McGill University, informed him of a graduate fellowship there, he applied for it and wound up studying under the neuroscience giant, Wilder Penfield (Hebb, 1980).

One day, while attending Vassar College, Mary Cover (later Mary Cover Jones) was preparing to go to a play, when a friend convinced her to attend a lecture at Columbia University instead. The speaker, John B. Watson, discussed research that he and his graduate student Rosalie Rayner had conducted on conditioning fear in their child test subject, Little Albert (Jones, 1975). Cover became interested in psychology after attending the lecture, going on to do an experiment in which she used a similar approach to alleviate the fear of rabbits in a little boy named Peter. (One also wonders whether her friendship with Rayner, when they were students together at Vassar, influenced her becoming a psychologist.) In another case, one of young Roger Sperry's parents returned from the local public library with a copy of William James's *Principles of Psychology*, intending to read it. Roger spied the book and, though he was only 12 years old, read it from cover to cover. This stimulated his lifelong interest in the relationship between mind and brain (Puente, 2000).

PUTTING LIFE INTO LECTURES

Why spend any of your valuable time hunting down biographical information on eminent contributors to psychology and reading it? And why include such material in your lectures when it will necessarily reduce coverage of the "content" of psychology? By carefully integrating a modest amount of material about the lives of the field's eminent figures — both historical and contemporary — you can make your courses more engaging and rewarding, both to your students and to you. Life stories make lectures richer than when they are limited to the communication of facts, theories, and research studies. You might even find yourself becoming more enthusiastic about the course content you present when you can tie it to interesting information about relevant contributors. This would be particularly beneficial when you find yourself covering the same dry topic for the umpteenth time.

Also, biographical material gives necessary context to the material you are teaching. The June 1991 issue of *American Psychologist*, which was devoted to undergraduate education, noted that psychology students should be provided with an appreciation of the historical context of their field. They should also come to realize that psychology was not developed by intellectuals working in ivory towers isolated from outside influences. Students become more appreciative of the human context of psychology by learning about contributors' other interests and the intimate relationship between their life experiences and their professional work. Even great scientists are not immune from the vagaries of life. Their life experiences might make them gravitate to certain intellectual pursuits or affect their ability to conduct their work. Their childhoods, relationships, educational background, culture, gender, religion, and ethnicity — as well as just plain serendipity — each can play a role in their work. Many intellectuals have persevered despite awful childhoods, emotional difficulties, relationship problems, or prejudice directed at them. Vivid anecdotes about the lives and struggles of contributors to our field not only give historical context, they connect the course content to more distinctive and easily recalled information, helping your student remember it better.

REFERENCES

Bandura, A. (1982). The psychology of chance encounters and life paths. *American Psychologist, 37,* 747-755.

Bartoshuk, L. M. (2001). Linda M. Bartoshuk. In A. N. O'Connell (Ed.), *Models of achievement: Reflections of eminent women in psychology* (Vol. 3, pp. 171-183). Mahwah, NJ: Erlbaum.

Beers, C. W. (1908/1981). *A mind that found itself.* Pittsburgh: University of Pittsburgh Press.

Benjamin, L. (2005). Archival adventures: History lessons from reading other people's mail. In B. Perlman, L. I. McCann, & W. Buskist (Eds.), *Voices of Experience: Memorable talks from the National Institute on the Teaching of Psychology* (Vol. 1, pp. 17-32). Washington, DC: Association for Psychological Science.

Boneau, C. A. (1998). Hermann Ebbinghaus: On the road to progress or down the garden path? In G. A. Kimble & M. Wertheimer (Eds.), *Portraits of pioneers in psychology* (Vol. 3, pp. 51-64). Washington, DC: American Psychological Association.

Calkins, M. W. (1893). Statistics of dreams. *American Journal of Psychology*, 5, 311-341.

Calkins, M. W. (1930). Mary Whiton Calkins. In C. Murchison (Ed.), *A history of psychology in auto-biography* (Vol. 1, pp. 31-62). New York: Russell & Russell.

Chase, A. (2003). *Harvard and the Unabomber: The education of an American terrorist*. New York: Norton.

Chatelaine, K. L. (1991). Harry Stack Sullivan: The clinician and the man. In G. A. Kimble, M. Wertheimer, & C. L. White (Eds.), *Portraits of pioneers in psychology* (pp. 325-340). Washington, DC: American Psychological Association.

Cohen, D. (1977). Leon Festinger. In *Psychologists on psychology* (pp. 126-144). New York: Taplinger.

Dain, N. (1980). *Clifford Beers: Advocate for the insane*. Pittsburgh: University of Pittsburgh Press.

Dement, W. C. (1974). *Some must watch while some must sleep*. San Francisco: Freeman.

Distinguished Scientific Contributions. (2000). Richard J. Davidson. *American Psychologist*, 55, 1193-1106.

Doorey, M. (2004). Howard Earl Gardner (1943-). In *Gale encyclopedia of psychology*. Retrieved November 23, 2004, from http://www.findarticles.com/p/articles/mi_g2699/is_0004/ai_2699000478

Douglas, C. (1993). *Translate this darkness: The life of Christiana Morgan*. New York: Simon & Schuster.

Evans, R. I. (1980). Stanley Milgram (1933-). In *The making of social psychology: Discussions with creative contributors* (pp. 187-198). New York: Gardner Press.

Eysenck, H. J. (1990). Maverick psychologist. In C. E. Walker (Ed.), *The history of clinical psychology in autobiography* (Vol. 1, pp. 39-86). Pacific Grove, CA: Brooks/Cole.

Freud, S. (1900/1990). *The interpretation of dreams*. New York: Basic Books.

Friedman, L. J. (1999). *Identity's architect: A biography of Erik H. Erikson*. New York: Scribner.

Furumoto, L. (1979). Mary Whiton Calkins (1863-1930): Fourteenth president of the American Psychological Association. *Journal of the History of the Behavioral Sciences*, 15, 346-356.

Furumoto, L. (1980). Mary Whiton Calkins (1863-1930). *Psychology of Women Quarterly*, 5, 55-68.

Furumoto, L. (1990). Mary Whiton Calkins (1863-1930). In A. N. O'Connell & N. F. Russo (Eds.), *Women in psychology: A bio-bibliographic sourcebook* (pp. 57-65). Westport, CT: Greenwood.

Gibson, E. J. (1980). Eleanor J. Gibson. In G. Lindzey (Ed.), *A history of psychology in autobiography* (Vol. 7, pp. 239-271). San Francisco: Freeman.

Guthrie, R. V. (1990). Mamie Phipps Clark (1917-1983). In A. N. O'Connell & N. F. Russo (Eds.) *Women in psychology: A bio-bibliographic sourcebook* (pp. 66-74). Westport, CT: Greenwood.

Guthrie, R. V. (1998). *Even the rat was white: A historical view of psychology* (2nd ed.). Newton, MA: Allyn & Bacon.

Guthrie, R. V. (2000). Francis Cecil Sumner: The first African American pioneer in psychology. In G. A. Kimble & M. Wertheimer (Eds.), *Portraits of pioneers in psychology* (Vol. 4, pp.181-193). Washington, DC: American Psychological Association.

Hatfield, E. (2001). Elaine Hatfield. In A. N. O'Connell (Ed.), *Models of achievement: Reflections of eminent women in psychology* (Vol. 3, pp. 137-147). Mahwah, NJ: Erlbaum.

Hebb, D. O. (1980). D. O. Hebb. In G. Lindzey (Ed.), *A history of psychology in autobiography* (Vol. 7, pp. 273-303). San Francisco: Freeman.

Hilgard, E. R. (1974). Ernest Ropiequet Hilgard. In G. Lindzey (Ed.), *A history of psychology in autobiography* (Vol. 6, pp. 131-182). Englewood Cliffs, NJ: Prentice-Hall.

Jones, M. C. (1975). A 1924 pioneer looks at behavior therapy. *Journal of Behavior Therapy and Experimental Psychiatry*, 6, 181-187.

Kreisler, H. (2004). Face to face: The science of reading faces: Conversation with Paul Ekman. Retrieved on December 1, 2004, from http://globetrotter.berkeley.edu/people4/Ekman/ekman-con0.html

LeRoy, H. A., & Kimble, G. A. (2003). Harry Frederick Harlow: And one thing led to another . . . In G. A. Kimble & M. Wertheimer (Eds.), *Portraits of pioneers in psychology* (Vol. 5, pp. 279-297). Washington, DC: American Psychological Association.

Lewis, J. (1981). *Something hidden: A biography of Wilder Penfield*. Garden City, NY: Doubleday.

Loewi, O. (1960). An autobiographical sketch. *Perspectives in Biology and Medicine*, 3, 3-25.

Maccoby, E. E. (1989). Eleanor E. Maccoby. In G. Lindzey (Ed.), *A history of psychology in autobiography* (Vol. 8, pp. 291-335). Stanford, CA: Stanford University Press.

McDougall, W. (1930). William McDougall. In C. Murchison (Ed.), *A history of psychology in autobiography* (Vol. 1, pp. 191-223). Worcester, MA: Clark University Press.

Nobelprize.org: Otto Loewi (2004). Otto Loewi. Retrieved on November 23, 2004, from http://nobelprize.org/medicine/laureates/1936/loewi-bio.html

Pearson, E. S. (1990). *"Student": A statistical biography of William Sealy Gosset*. New York: Oxford University Press.

Puente, A. E. (2000). Roger W. Sperry: Nobel Laureate, neuroscientist, and psychologist. In G. A. Kimble & M. Wertheimer (Eds.), *Portraits of pioneers in psychology* (Vol. 4, pp. 321-336). Washington, DC: American Psychological Association.

Ramön y Cajal, S. (1937/1989). *Recollections of my life.* Cambridge, MA: MIT Press.

Scarborough, E., & Furumoto, L. (1987). "A little hard on ladies": Christine Ladd-Franklin's challenge to collegial exclusion. In *Untold lives: The first generation of American women psychologists* (pp. 109-129). New York: Columbia University Press.

Scarr, S.W. (2001). Sandra Wood Scarr. In A. N. O'Connell (Ed.), *Models of achievement: Reflections of eminent women in psychology* (Vol. 3, pp. 99-112). Mahwah, NJ: Erlbaum.

Shepard, M. (1975). *Fritz: An intimate portrait of Fritz Perls and Gestalt therapy.* New York: Dutton.

Sherrill, R., Jr. (1991). Natural wholes: Wolfgang Köhler and Gestalt theory. In G. A. Kimble, M. Wertheimer, & C. L. White (Eds.), *Portraits of pioneers in psychology.* Washington, DC: American Psychological Association.

Shneidman, E. (1991). A life in death: Notes of a committed suicidologist — An epistolary autobiography. In C. E. Walker (Ed.), *A history of clinical psychology in autobiography* (Vol. 1, pp. 225–292). Pacific Grove, CA: Brooks/Cole.

Stevens, L. A. (1971). *Explorers of the brain.* New York: Knopf.

Who Named It?: Hans Berger (2001). Hans Berger. Retrieved on December 1, 2004, from http://www.whonamedit.com/doctor.cfm/845.html

Who Named It?: Hermann Rorschach (2001). Hermann Rorschach. Retrieved on December 1, 2004, from http://www.whonamedit.com/doctor.cfm/1232.html

APPENDIX A: TRIVIAL PURSUIT SCAVENGER HUNT

Biographical material can enliven your lectures, but a more interactive way to work it into your courses is to conduct "trivial pursuit scavenger hunts." Make a deck of index cards, each one containing a question about an eminent psychologist — a question that can't be answered without obscure information your students won't find in their textbook. Have students blindly select a card, and give them a time limit (whether hours or days) in which to find the answers and share their answers in class. The exercise provides a welcome break from academic routine for students and helps hone their library and Internet research skills. The following are some possible psychology trivia questions, with the answers given in brackets. (A longer list of questions is available from the author.)

1. Which psychologist became the first female president of an Ivy League school when she assumed that position at the University of Pennsylvania in 1994? [*Judith Rodin*] (Dube & Sherman, 2003)

2. What eminent 19th-century German physicist-physiologist's mother, Caroline Penne, was a descendant of William Penn? [*Hermann von Helmholtz*] (Adler, 2000)

3. What giant of 20th-century neuroscience was nicknamed "Ramón" by his colleagues because of his great admiration for Santiago Ramón y Cajal? [*Wilder Penfield*] (Lewis, 1981)

4. Which pioneer in intelligence research conducted research on projective tests long before Hermann Rorschach, conservation of number long before Piaget, and conformity to line-length judgments long before Solomon Asch? [*Alfred Binet*] (Fancher, 1991)

5. Which leading researcher in the psychology of love had ancestors who were on one side of the violent Hatfields versus McCoys feud? [*Elaine Hatfield*] (Hatfield, 2001)

6. Which prominent neuroscientist criticized Pavlov's theory at the 1929 International Congress of Psychology in New Haven, as Pavlov fumed in the audience? [*Karl Lashley*] (Bruce, 1991)

7. Who won a Nobel Prize that recognized his invention of prefrontal lobotomy to treat mental illness while ignoring his invention of brain angiography, which revolutionized the detection of brain abnormalities? [*Egas Moniz*] ("Nobelprize. org: Egas Moniz," 2004)

REFERENCES

Adler, H. E. (2000). Hermann Ludwig Ferdinand von Helmholtz: Physicist as psychologist. In G. A. Kimble & M. Wertheimer (Eds.), *Portraits of pioneers in psychology* (Vol. 4, pp. 15-31). Washington, DC: American Psychological Association.

Bruce, D. (1991). Integrations of Lashley. In G. A. Kimble, M. Wertheimer, & C. L. White (Eds.), *Portraits of pioneers in psychology* (pp. 307-323). Washington, DC: American Psychological Association.

Dube, C., & Sherman, E. (2003). Judith Rodin to step down after decade as university president. Retrieved December 1, 2004 from http://www.dailypennsylvanian.com/vnews/display.v/ART/2003/06/26/3efaaafca6078?in_archive=1

Fancher, R. E. (1991). Alfred Binet, general psychologist. In G. A. Kimble & M. Wertheimer (Eds.), *Portraits of pioneers in psychology* (Vol. 3, pp. 67-83). Washington, DC: American Psychological Association.

Hatfield, E. (2001). Elaine Hatfield. In A. N. O'Connell (Ed.), *Models of achievement: Reflections of eminent women in psychology* (Vol. 3, pp. 137-147). Mahwah, NJ: Erlbaum.

Lewis, J. (1981). *Something hidden: A biography of Wilder Penfield.* Garden City, NY: Doubleday.

Nobelprize.org: Egas Moniz (2004). Egas Moniz. Retrieved on November 23, 2004, from http://nobelprize.org/medicine/laureates/1949/moniz-bio.html

APPENDIX B: FINDING THE INFORMATION

My first years as a collector of psychologists' biographies came before the advent of sophisticated computer search engines for used and antiquarian books. So I haunted used bookstores and enlisted the aid of a crack book finder who lived in Queens, New York, to track down volumes for me that I could not locate myself. Now I search for my own books on the Internet, which is more efficient — but much less sociable!

To make sure that I don't miss anything, I periodically search the Library of Congress online catalog for all books, Barnes and Noble (www.bn.com) for new books, and AddALL (www.addall.com) for used and antiquarian books. (AddALL is a metasearch site that combines the power of a number of powerful book-search engines that can comb the holdings of thousands of book dealers. You can search AddALL in a variety of ways, including by author, by title, by price, and by publication date. AddALL's listings also describe the condition of the books. I have found remarkable bargains in which a book in near fine condition is priced much lower than the same title in merely good condition.)

To avoid doing the same work over and over, I keep a master list of major contributors to the field that I continually update. There is no foolproof way to identify all of the relevant books, given that their titles often do not provide a clue to their subject. Nonetheless, I rarely find that I miss an important book. Once I obtain a book, I peruse its bibliography for relevant biographical or autobiographical books that I might have missed. I generally do a complete book search during the summer and in January, when teaching responsibilities do not overwhelm me.

I have learned to refrain from trying to collect all of the biographical works about the few major figures, such as Sigmund Freud and Carl Jung, who continue to have book after book written about them. In those cases, I try to make sure that I find the most important ones. Here is a list of collections of biographies and autobiographies that are not included in this chapter's reference list, followed by a list of useful individual biographical and autobiographical works.

ADDITIONAL BIOGRAPHICAL AND AUTOBIOGRAPHICAL COLLECTIONS

Boring, E. G., Langfeld, H. S., Werner, H., & Yerkes, R. M. (Eds.). (1952). *A history of psychology in autobiography* (Vol. 4). Worcester, MA: Clark University Press.

Boring, E. G., & Lindzey, G. (Eds.). (1967). *A history of psychology in autobiography* (Vol. 5). New York: Appleton-Century-Crofts.

Kimble, G. A., Boneau, C. A., & Wertheimer, M. (Eds.). (1996). *Portraits of pioneers in psychology* (Vol. 2). Washington, DC: American Psychological Association.

Kimble, G. A., & Wertheimer, M. (Eds.). (1998). *Portraits of pioneers in psychology* (Vol. 3). Washington, DC: American Psychological Association.

Kimble, G. A., & Wertheimer, M. (Eds.). (2000). *Portraits of pioneers in psychology* (Vol. 4). Washington, DC: American Psychological Association.

Kimble, G. A., & Wertheimer, M. (Eds.). (2003). *Portraits of pioneers in psychology* (Vol. 5). Washington, DC: American Psychological Association.

Kimble, G. A., Wertheimer, M., & White, C. L. (Eds.). (1991). *Portraits of pioneers in psychology* (Vol. 1). Washington, DC: American Psychological Association.

Lindzey, G. (Ed.). (1974). *A history of psychology in autobiography* (Vol. 6). Englewood Cliffs, NJ: Prentice-Hall.

Lindzey, G. (Ed.). (1980). *A history of psychology in autobiography* (Vol. 7). San Francisco: Freeman.

Lindzey, G. (Ed.). (1989). *A history of psychology in autobiography* (Vol. 8). Palo Alto, CA: Stanford University Press.

Murchison, C. (Ed.). (1930). *A history of psychology in autobiography* (Vol. 1). Worcester, MA: Clark University Press.

Murchison, C. (Ed.). (1932). *A history of psychology in autobiography* (Vol. 2). Worcester, MA: Clark University Press.

Murchison, C. (Ed.). (1936). *A history of psychology in autobiography* (Vol. 3). Worcester, MA: Clark University Press.

O'Connell, A. N. (2001). *Models of achievement: Reflections of eminent women in psychology* (Vol. 3). Mahwah, NJ: Erlbaum.

O'Connell, A. N., & Russo, N. F. (1983). *Models of achievement: Reflections of eminent women in psychology*. New York: Columbia University Press.

O'Connell, A. N., & Russo, N. F. (1988). *Models of achievement: Reflections of eminent women in psychology* (Vol. 2). Hillsdale, NJ: Erlbaum.

O'Connell, A. N., & Russo, N. F. (Eds.). (1990). *Women in psychology: A bio-bibliographic sourcebook*. Westport, CT: Greenwood.

Scarborough, E., & Furumoto, L. (1987). *Untold lives: The first generation of American women psychologists*. New York: Columbia University Press.

Tankard, J. W. (1984). *The statistical pioneers*. Cambridge, MA: Schenkman.

Walker, C. E. (1991). *The history of clinical psychology in autobiography* (Vol. 1). Pacific Grove, CA: Brooks/Cole.

Walker, C. E. (1992). *The history of clinical psychology in autobiography* (Vol. 2). Pacific Grove, CA: Brooks/Cole.

ADDITIONAL INDIVIDUAL BIOGRAPHIES AND AUTOBIOGRAPHIES

Barsky, N. (1997). *Noam Chomsky: A life of dissent*. Cambridge, MA: MIT Press.

Benjamin, L. T., Jr. (1991). *Harry Kirke Wolfe: Pioneer in psychology*. Lincoln: University of Nebraska Press.

Bjork, D. W. (1993). *B. F. Skinner: A life*. New York: Basic Books.

Blass, T. (2004). *The man who shocked the world: The life and legacy of Stanley Milgram*. New York: Basic Books.

Blum, D. (2002). *Love at Goon Park: Harry Harlow and the science of affection*. Cambridge, MA: Perseus.

du Boulay, S. (1984). *Cicely Saunders: The founder of the modern hospice movement*. New York: Amaryllis Press.

Brodsky, A. (2004). *Benjamin Rush: Patriot and physician*. New York: St. Martin's Press.

Brown, R. (1996). *Against my better judgment: An intimate memoir of an eminent gay psychologist*. Binghamton, NY: Haworth Press.

Bruner, J. (1983). *In search of mind: Essays in autobiography*. New York: Harper & Row.

Buckley, K. W. (1989). *Mechanical man: John Broadus Watson and the beginnings of behaviorism*. New York: Guilford.

Burston, D. (1991). *The legacy of Erich Fromm*. Cambridge, MA: Harvard University Press.

Burston, D. (1996). *The wing of madness: The life and work of R. D. Laing*. Cambridge, MA: Harvard University Press.

Carmichael, A. (1833). *A memoir of the life and philosophy of Spurzheim*. Boston: Marsh, Capen, & Lyon.

Cannon, W. B. (1945). *The way of an investigator: A scientist's experiences in medical research*. New York: W. W. Norton.

Cattell, J. M. (1980). *An education in psychology: James McKeen Cattell's journal and letters from Germany and England, 1880-1888* (M. M. Sokal, Ed.). Cambridge, MA: MIT Press.

van Dijken, S. (1998). *John Bowlby: His early life — A biographical journey into the roots of attachment theory*. New York: Free Association Books.

Eccles, J. C., & Gibson, W. C. (1979). *Sherrington: His life and thought*. New York: Springer-Verlag.

Erdmann, E., & Stover, D. (1991). *Beyond a world divided: The brain-mind science of Roger Sperry*. Boston: Shambhala.

Eysenck, H. J. (1990). *Rebel with a cause: The autobiography of Hans Eysenck*. London: W. H. Allen.

Fisher-Box, J. (1978). *R. A. Fisher: The life of a scientist*. New York: Wiley.

Frankl, V. (1997). *Viktor Frankl: Recollections — An autobiography*. New York: Plenum.

Fransella, F. (1995). *George Kelly*. Thousand Oaks, CA: Sage.

Freeman, L. (1972/1994). *The story of Anna O: The woman who led Freud to psychoanalysis*. New York: Aronson.

Gathorne-Hardy, J. (1998). *Sex the measure of all things: A life of Alfred C. Kinsey*. Bloomington: Indiana University Press.

Gay, P. (1988). *Freud: A life for our time*. New York: W. W. Norton.

Gibson, E. J. (2001). *Perceiving the affordances: A portrait of two psychologists*. Mahwah, NJ: Erlbaum.

Gillham, N. W. (2001). *A life of Sir Francis Galton: From African exploration to the birth of eugenics*. New York: Oxford University Press.

Goetz, C. G., Bonduelle, M., & Gelfand, T. (1995). *Charcot: Constructing neurology*. New York: Oxford University Press.

Goodall, J. (1990). *Through a window: My 30 years with the chimpanzees of Gombe*. Boston: Houghton Mifflin.

Grosskurth, P. (1986). *Melanie Klein: Her world and her work*. New York: Knopf.

Hale, M., Jr. (1980). *Human science and the social order: Hugo Münsterberg and the origins of applied psychology*. Philadelphia: Temple University Press.

Hare, A. P., & Hare, J. R. (1996). *J. L. Moreno*. Thousand Oaks, CA: Sage.

Harrower, M. (1983). *Kurt Koffka: An unwitting self-portrait*. Gainesville: University Presses of Florida.

Hearnshaw, L. S. (1979). *Cyril Burt, psychologist*. Ithaca, NY: Cornell University Press.

Heidelberger, M. (2004). *Nature from within: Gustav Fechner and his psychophysical world view*. Pittsburgh, PA: University of Pittsburgh Press.

Heider, F. (1983). *The life of a psychologist: An autobiography*. Lawrence, KS: University of Kansas Press.

Higgins, F. C. (1918). *The life of Naomi Norsworthy*. Boston: Houghton Mifflin.

Hoffman, E. (1988). *The right to be human: A biography of Abraham Maslow*. Los Angeles: Tarcher.

Hoffman, E. (1994). *The drive for self: Alfred Adler and the founding of individual psychology*. Reading, MA: Addison-Wesley.

Hollingworth, H. L. (1943/1990). *Leta Stetter Hollingworth: A biography by Harry Hollingworth*. Bolton, MA: Anker.

Joncich, G. (1968). *The sane positivist: A biography of Edward L. Thorndike*. Middletown, CT: Wesleyan University Press.

Jung, C. G. (1963). *Memories, dreams, reflections*. New York: Random House.

Koenigsberger, L. (1906). *Hermann von Helmholtz*. Oxford, England: Clarendon.

Kraepelin, E. (1987). *Memoirs* (H. Hippius, G. Petters, & D. Ploog, Eds.). New York: Springer-Verlag.

Lazarus, R. S. (1998). *The life and work of an eminent psychologist: Autobiography of Richard S. Lazarus*. New York: Springer.

Mackler, B. (1969). *Philippe Pinel, unchainer of the insane.* New York: Watts.

Macmillan, M. (2000). *An odd kind of fame: Stories of Phineas Gage.* Cambridge, MA: MIT Press.

Marrow, A. J. (1969). *The practical theorist: The life and work of Kurt Lewin.* New York: Basic Books.

Markowitz, G. & Rosner, D. (1996). *Children, race, and power: Kenneth and Mamie Clark's Northside Center.* Charlottesville: University of Virginia Press.

McReynolds, P. (1994). *Lightner Witmer: His life and times.* Washington, DC: American Psychological Association.

Minton, H. L. (1988). *Lewis M. Terman: Pioneer in psychological testing.* New York: New York University Press.

Muckenhoupt, M. (2003). *Dorothea Dix: Champion for the mentally ill.* New York: Oxford University Press.

Murphy, L. B. (1990). *Gardner Murphy: Integrating, expanding, and humanizing psychology.* Jefferson, NC: McFarland.

Myers, G. E. (1986). *William James: His life and thought.* New Haven, CT: Yale University Press.

Nicholson, I. A. (2003). *Inventing personality: Gordon Allport and the science of selfhood.* Washington, DC: American Psychological Association.

Penfield, W. (1977). *No man alone: A neurosurgeon's life.* Boston: Little, Brown.

Perry, H. S. (1982). *Psychiatrist of America: The life of Harry Stack Sullivan.* Cambridge, MA: Harvard University Press.

Poppen, R. (1995). *Joseph Wolpe.* Thousand Oaks, CA: Sage.

Porter, T. M. (2004). *Karl Pearson: The scientific life in a statistical age.* Princeton, NJ: Princeton University Press.

Quinn, S. (1987). *A mind of her own: The life of Karen Horney.* New York: Summit.

Reed, E. S. (1988). *James J. Gibson and the psychology of perception.* New Haven, CT: Yale University Press.

Rhine, L. E. (1983). *Something hidden.* Jefferson, NC: McFarland.

Rieber, R. W., & Robinson, D. K. (Eds.). (2001). *Wilhelm Wundt in history: The making of a scientific psychology.* Dordrecht, Netherlands: Kluwer Academic.

Robinson, F. G. (1992). *Love's story told: A life of Henry A. Murray.* Cambridge, MA: Harvard University Press.

Ross, D. (1972). *G. Stanley Hall: The psychologist as prophet.* Chicago: University of Chicago Press.

Sarason, S. B. (1988). *The making of an American psychologist: An autobiography.* San Francisco: Jossey-Bass.

Schiller, F. (1979). *Paul Broca: Founder of French anthropology, explorer of the brain.* Berkeley: University of California Press.

Selye, H. (1979). *The stress of my life: A scientist's memoirs.* New York: Van Nostrand Reinhold.

Sharaf, M. (1983). *Fury on earth: A biography of Wilhelm Reich.* New York: St. Martin's Press/Marek.

Simon, H. A. (1991). *Models of my life.* New York: Basic Books.

Stern, M. B. (1971). *Heads and headliners: The phrenological Fowlers.* Norman, OK: University of Oklahoma Press.

Suhd, M. M., Dodson, L., & Gomori, M. (Eds.). (2001). *Virginia Satir: Her life and circle of influence.* Palo Alto, CA: Science and Behavior Books.

Thorne, B. (2003). *Carl Rogers* (2nd ed.). Thousand Oaks, CA: Sage.

Todes, D. (2000). *Pavlov: Exploring the animal machine.* New York: Oxford University Press.

Van Over, R., & Oteri, L. (1967). *William McDougall: Explorer of the mind —Studies in psychical research.* New York: Helix Press.

Velten, E. (2005). *The lives of Albert Ellis: The authorized biography.* Tucson, AZ: See Sharp Press.

Vidal, F. (1994). *Piaget before Piaget.* Cambridge, MA: Harvard University Press.

Weidman, N. M. (1999). *Constructing scientific psychology: Karl Lashley's mind-brain debates.* New York: Cambridge University Press.

Wilson, E. O. (1990). *Edward O. Wilson: A life in science.* Cambridge, MA: Harvard University Press.

Wolf, T. H. (1973). *Alfred Binet.* Chicago: University of Chicago Press.

Wyckoff, J. (1975). *Franz Anton Mesmer: Between God and devil.* Englewood Cliffs, NJ: Prentice-Hall

Young-Bruehl, E. (1988). *Anna Freud.* New York: Summit.

Zenderland, L. (1998). *Measuring minds: Henry Herbert Goddard and the origins of American intelligence testing.* New York: Cambridge University Press.

CHAPTER TWO

ARCHIVAL ADVENTURES

History Lessons From Reading Other People's Mail

Ludy T. Benjamin, Jr.

Texas A&M University

I WILL BEGIN this chapter with what must truly be a heretical statement, given that this book consists of addresses from a national conference dedicated to the improvement of teaching. In my professional life, my most enjoyable moments are not those spent in the classroom. Nor are they the meetings I have with my students. The best times for me professionally are the hours I spend in archives. I never have enough such opportunities, so I treasure every one. I feel like I ought to start this chapter by saying, "My name is Ben, and I'm an archive addict."

I look forward to my archival visits with the anticipation that I once held for the arrival of Santa Claus. Sometimes I have trouble sleeping the night before, just imagining what I might discover in the papers I am about to explore. On the day the archival work begins, I am there 15 minutes before the door opens, sometimes standing in the cold winds outside the Boston Public Library, or in the snow on the steps of the archives at Carnegie Mellon University. During the course of the day, other researchers will wander in and out, spending an hour or so in a particular collection. Not me; I am there for the duration, leaving only when one of the archivists says to me, "we really have to close now." Back in my hotel room I rework the notes I have taken on my laptop and I study the documents I have photocopied that day and I wonder what I will find tomorrow.

This behavior may seem bizarre, so I want to try to explain the fascination archives hold for me. What I want to do is share a little bit of what I have learned from my own archival work as well as the archival work of others. I want to describe some of the joys and some of the discoveries in what is admittedly a very personal account. I hope after reading this chapter, readers may be inclined to explore archives on their own and involve their students in archival research.

The Nature of Archives

I should begin by saying a few things about what archives are, because I imagine few readers will have experienced such places.

Archives are collections of unique materials, usually unpublished documents that do not exist anywhere else. Archives may contain the papers of large corporations like the Coca-Cola Company, or organizations like the Association for Psychological Science, or more commonly the papers of individuals like Thomas Edison (1847-1931), Zelda (1900-1948) and Scott Fitzgerald (1896-1940), William James (1842-1910), or Mary Whiton Calkins (1863-1930). In psychology, the papers of individuals — called manuscript collections — consist mostly of correspondence, but may also contain documents like lecture notes, unpublished manuscripts, research notebooks, lab protocols, cases histories, grant proposals, and a multitude of other written material such as reprint request cards, birth certificates, college transcripts, Christmas cards, newspaper clippings, hotel receipts, love letters, and book royalty statements.

Such collections are typically housed in rooms that are temperature and humidity controlled, with the papers stored in acid-free boxes — steps that are taken to preserve the life of the documents. Archival staff prepare *finding aids* for scholars to use that will give an idea of what the collections contain and where particular items can be found in the collection. Some collections may be quite small, only a file folder or two. Others are massive. The papers of James McKeen Cattell (1860-1944), in the Library of Congress, include more than 50,000 items and take up more than 120 linear feet of shelf space.

Finding aids differ from archive to archive. The Archives of the History of American Psychology at the University of Akron — the largest collection of historical documents in psychology anywhere in the world — has many item-by-item inventories of its collections. Thus, if you wanted to work in the papers of Walter Miles (1885-1978), an important experimental psychologist in the first half of this century, you could start with the 700-page inventory that lists every single letter in the collection with a (usually) one-sentence description of the letter's main content. The inventories for the more recently processed collections in Akron's archives are not nearly so detailed — in keeping with archival practices at most other archives as well as growing demands on staff time for processing collections. (Go to http://www3.uakron.edu/ahap to visit Akron's psychology archives online.)

Archives also differ in their user policies. Most will not allow pens to be brought into their reading rooms. Pencils are okay, and most archives now let you bring your laptop. But purses, briefcases, coats, and other items are typically checked outside the reading room. If you are using paper to take notes, some archives will provide that, allowing them to keep better control over the paper that enters and leaves the archives. Most archives allow photocopying of their documents, but some restrict the number of copies you can make per visit. My strategy is usually to photocopy as much as I can, which saves me a lot of valuable time on the archival visit. Then I can study the documents in more detail back home. What do you do if you photocopy more documents than you can fit in your suitcase? That's a no-brainer. Pack the documents in your suitcase and mail your underwear home.

There's much more I could tell you about the nature of archives, but I have other ground to cover. For one thing I must mention, briefly, one of the common diseases associated with archival work. Arguably the most serious problem in archival research is perversely one of its joys. I call the disorder *Documentia Distracta*: the continual distraction from materials not related to the research purposes at hand. This condition produces disorientation and distortions in time perception. The affected researcher begins to read documents that are wholly irrelevant to the research effort. In its acute form, this disease greatly prolongs the time required for completion of the intended project. The more serious chronic form typically causes the researcher to abandon one project for a new one that is subsequently abandoned for another one, and so forth and so on. Although the disease uses up valuable time in the archives intended for use on the target project, the experienced archival researcher learns to accept it, and accordingly, to budget twice the time for a project than should be required.

Archival research is detective work. Sometimes you find what you hoped to find; sometimes you don't. Sometimes you make an unexpected discovery. Consider this example from historian Gloria Urch, who was searching the records in a county historical society when she discovered Rachel Harris, who she describes as perhaps the only African American nurse during the Civil War era. Urch wrote:

> I was looking for something else when I found her photo. … I held it for a moment and studied it. … I put her photo aside and continued my research. A few minutes later the photo — which I thought I had placed securely on the shelf above me — fell into my lap, and those same eyes were gazing up into mine again. Before I left that day I made a copy of Rachel's photo and obituary and tucked it away. (Hill, 1993, p. 81)

Because of that photo falling into Gloria Urch's lap, we now know about the life and career of a very interesting person, previously lost to history.

TITCHENER'S EXPERIMENTALISTS

I have a discovery of my own to describe, but first I need to discuss the work of other researchers that relates to my story. This work concerns the papers of Christine Ladd-Franklin (1847-1930), which are housed in the archives at Columbia University, and the papers of Edward Bradford Titchener (1867-1927), which are located in the archives of Cornell University. Titchener, a graduate of Wilhelm Wundt's (1832-1920) program at the University of Leipzig, came to Cornell in 1892 and remained there until his death in 1927. His structural approach to the study of consciousness had a significant impact on American psychology during his lifetime.

Ladd-Franklin was an early experimental psychologist who produced an evolutionary-based theory of color vision that is still cited in color vision texts today. Five years before Titchener arrived in America, Ladd-Franklin had already published an article on vision in the 1887 inaugural issue of the *American Journal of Psychology*, the first psychology journal in the United States. Over the next 20 years she published numerous experimental studies in professional journals, including more than 20 articles in the *Psychological Review* alone.

The story of Ladd-Franklin and Titchener begins in 1904, when Titchener formed his private club of experimental psychologists. He wrote to about 20 of his colleagues that he wanted to found a new society that confined its membership to men who were working in that field. The Experimentalists, as they were usually called, began meeting in 1904, and met annually thereafter, as an all-male society. The membership consisted of most of the prominent psychologists in the Northeast — at least, the male ones. Not everyone agreed with Titchener's desire to exclude women. August Kirschmann (1860-1932), a psychologist at the University of Toronto, wrote to Titchener: "I find it a little hard on the ladies, who take an interest in Experimental Psychology if we exclude them altogether" (Scarborough & Furumoto, 1987, p. 117).

Ladd-Franklin was shocked at Titchener's exclusion of women from his meetings and exchanged a number of letters with him, arguing her case. In 1912 she wrote:

I am particularly anxious to bring my views up, once in a while, for hand-to-hand discussion before experts, and just now I have especially a paper that I should like very much to read before your meeting of experimental psychologists. I hope you will not say nay! (Scarborough & Furumoto, 1987, p. 125)

Titchener apparently did say nay, and Ladd-Franklin replied:

I am shocked to know that you are still — at this year — excluding women from your meeting of experimental psychologists. It is such a very old-fashioned standpoint! (Scarborough & Furumoto, 1987, p. 125)

One of the reasons that Titchener had given as an objection to women in attendance was that the men needed to be able to smoke their cigars without fear of offending the women. Ladd-Franklin wrote:

Have your smokers separated if you like (tho I for one always smoke when I am in fashionable society), but a scientific meeting (however personal) is a public affair, and it is not open to you to leave out a class of fellow workers without extreme discourtesy. (Scarborough & Furumoto, 1987, p. 125)

In 1914 the meeting of the Experimentalists was to be at Columbia University in New York City, where Ladd-Franklin lived. She wrote to Titchener once more and was told that she would not be invited. She replied:

Is this then a good time, my dear Professor Titchener, for you to hold to the mediaeval attitude of not admitting me to your coming psychological conference in New York — at my very door? So unconscientious, so immoral, — worse than that — so unscientific! (Scarborough & Furumoto, 1987, p. 126)

This prompted Titchener to write to Harvard psychologist Robert Yerkes (1876-1956):

I am not sure that we had better not disintegrate! I have been pestered by abuse by Mrs. Ladd-Franklin for not having women at the meetings, and she threatens to make various scenes in person and in print. Possibly she will succeed in breaking us up, and forcing us to meet — like rabbits — in some dark place underground. (Scarborough & Furumoto, 1987, p. 126)

Titchener managed to keep his club exclusively male during his lifetime. After his death in 1927, the society was reorganized. It got a new name, the Society of Experimental Psychologists, limited itself to a maximum of 50 members, and in 1929, invited two women to its meeting. Ladd-Franklin, who died in 1930, was never invited (Furumoto, 1988; Goodwin, 1985).

The Society of Experimental Psychologists, or SEP, still exists today as a very prestigious organization. It has long been the major feeder group for psychologists who are elected to the National Academy of Sciences. Women, although admitted now, have always been small in number within the organization. It continues to be selective, having only about 200 members today.

THE PSYCHOLOGICAL ROUND TABLE

Now for the related story from my own work. I was doing research at the Psychology Archives in Akron in the summer of 1975. I pulled a folder from a manuscript box, but accidentally pulled a second, very thin folder as well. This folder was marked with the initials "PRT." It contained only a few documents, unrelated to my research project, but I glanced at them before putting the folder back. What I read was most interesting. It was clear that the PRT was some kind of secret society in psychology that existed in the late 1930s. There were four psychologists involved in the brief correspondence, three of them still alive. So when I returned home to Nebraska I wrote to those three asking about the PRT. I received replies from two of them, both offering fascinating details about this clandestine organization. One told me that he was pretty sure that the organization still existed. Thus began my hunt to see what I could find out about this secretive society.

The PRT began in 1936 as a result of discussions among several younger psychologists in the Northeast. They lamented the fact that some of their elders were going off each year to the SEP meetings to discuss experimental psychology when (in their younger colleagues' view) these older folks were not doing all that much interesting research anymore. So the young psychologists decided to start their own organization. They would meet annually like the SEP, they would limit invitations to 40 people or less, and such persons could attend the meetings by invitation only until they reached their 40th birthday. At that point they became superannuated — tossed out, because intellectually they must clearly be over the hill! They chose to call their new group the Society of Experimenting Psychologists — but when Harvard's E. G. Boring, one of the senior members of the older SEP, heard about the name of the new group, he threatened his younger Harvard colleagues with Saturday classes if they persisted with the name. So the young upstarts changed it to the Psychological Round Table, or PRT.

The PRT began meeting in December 1936 and has not missed an annual meeting since, not even during the war years. In fact the 1941 meeting had just ended on Sunday, December 7, when many members learned about the attack on

Pearl Harbor on their way home. In its early years, the PRT was run by a group known as the *Secret Six*, or the *Brethren*. These six decided on the meeting place and on who would be invited. The meetings occurred on a weekend, usually at an inn or small hotel in New England. The days were occupied by research presentations that were unusual. These presentations, called "revelations," were sometimes about research just completed, but more often they were about research being planned. The discussion that followed was frequently as long as the presentation itself — a no-holds-barred critique that often led to significant improvements in the research, or perhaps a whole new approach that the researcher hadn't even considered. Evenings were filled with dinner, drinking, and socializing, and an annual humorous (typically scatological) address called the William A. Hunt "Memorial" Lecture. (Hunt, one of the Secret Six, was born in 1903 and lived until 1986.) In many ways the PRT had a format similar to the SEP, including the exclusion of women (until 1971).

When I had received the first few replies to my inquiries, it was clear to me that this was an interesting story and one I wanted to learn more about. I never imagined at that time how difficult it would be to get the information that I needed. I asked my correspondents to remember as many names as they could of people who had attended meetings with them. Little by little, my list expanded to more than 150 people. The list read like a who's who of psychology: Frank Beach, Jerome Bruner, Eugene Galanter, James Gibson, Harry Harlow, Joseph McVicker Hunt, David Krech, David McClelland, Neal Miller, Clifford Morgan, Robert Sears, S. S. Stevens, and many others.

Most who replied to my requests for information were quite helpful. But some clearly thought I was up to no good. One replied, "I feel that I cannot honorably respond to your letter concerning the Psychological Round Table … I sincerely hope that you will desist in your efforts. …" Another wrote that the PRT was a non-organization of non-members, and that the best he could do was provide some non-memories. Another said that my probe would only bring harm to those currently involved, and encouraged me to abandon the inquiries. I continued the work, partly because the story was so interesting, but also because most of the former PRT attendees were very happy to help in my project. For the next year I wrote hundreds of letters, sometimes exchanging as many as five letters with a particular correspondent. Two of the original Secret Six were still alive, one of those being the famous Hunt of the annual Hunt Memorial Lecture, and I was able to interview him in Chicago in 1976. I interviewed others as well, and some sent me audiotapes.

I tried to get copies of early PRT documents, but this was a group that did not put much on paper. It truly was a non-organization of non-members. Those invited were called invitees. They were cautioned not to list PRT on their vita, and they were warned about declaring expenses as a tax deduction. They were also cautioned about mentioning the society to other colleagues. Thus paper records were minimal. Eventually I turned up a few documents, including mimeographed programs for several meetings, a few Hunt Lectures, and some interesting notes from a member of the Secret Six regarding the acceptability or unacceptability of prospective invitees.

I must confess to a little paranoia during this project. My search for the PRT history occurred just a few years after Watergate, so I was aware that treachery existed at the highest levels of government. Surely I could expect some of that kind of behavior in a secret psychological society. So certain events took on a new meaning. For example, two former PRT invitees died shortly before interviews I had scheduled with them, one from injuries sustained in an automobile accident. Another person called to cancel our interview, saying that he was just too busy and that he did not have time to make a tape or write out his memories. Thinking about those events, and the letters I had received asking me to cease and desist, I wondered if there were forces trying to stop me. I worried that my PRT correspondence file might be stolen, so I copied all the letters and kept one set in my home and the other in my office. In case I was killed, I told my wife where the letters were and encouraged her to take them to the FBI explaining that I was likely murdered by this secret society of experimental psychologists. I admit to exaggerating my fear here, but I did wonder if all of those events were coincidences or if there might be some conspiracy afoot.

Then in October of 1976 I got a call from someone who identified himself as a current member of the Secret Six. He told me that he and other PRTers had heard that I was researching their history, and that because this was their 40th anniversary, the Secret Six had decided to invite me to their upcoming meeting to tell them what I had learned. He told me two other things that I remember: (a) that not everyone on the Secret Six approved of what I was doing and some had objected to my being invited, and (b) that I should consider myself a one-time special invitee. (He was wrong, as it turned out: I was invited again, to the 60th meeting in 1996.) So I went to that meeting in Philadelphia, where I joined the regular invitees, including Marty Seligman, Linda Bartoshuk, Judith Rodin, Howard Egeth, Norma Graham, Jerre Levy, John Darley, Jr., and about 30 others — all of us in our late twenties or thirties at that time.

To illustrate the importance of these meetings, consider the following comments from former PRT attendees about what those meetings meant to them. One biopsychologist wrote:

> One of the things that was most fun about this meeting was that this was the place where everyone felt free to ridicule anyone else's work … It was a very exhilarating experience and sometimes gave one much food for thought. (Benjamin, 1977, p. 545)

From another:

> PRT was a great experience. It allowed us to develop close friendships with the people who turned out to be the leaders of American psychology. PRT represented that kind of ideal intellectual and social interaction that can only take place when groups are small and interests are held in common. (Benjamin, 1977, p. 549)

Finally:

> PRT was of great value to me as a young scientist because it was viewed as a rough and tumble club of "intrepid investigators" who could be as caustic

in their criticisms and as high in their standards as they were creative in their own research. For the young investigator it had all the value of initiation into maturity in science and all the rewards of give and take relationships with peers, no holds barred. (Benjamin, 1977, p. 549)

Reading that last quotation helps me understand what Christine Ladd-Franklin missed, and what she realized she was missing. Her contributions were substantial as they stand, but what might they have been had she and the other women psychologists of her day been permitted the same kind of intellectual and social exchanges enjoyed by their male colleagues? Certainly her exclusion was a detriment to her research and intellectual development. The research of her male colleagues suffered too, because they did not have the benefit of her mind in critiquing their own studies.

If you want to read more about Ladd-Franklin and the subject of collegial exclusion, you will find it in an excellent book by Elizabeth Scarborough and Laurel Furumoto (1987) entitled *Untold Lives: The First Generation of American Women Psychologists*. My history of the early years of the PRT was published in the *American Psychologist* (Benjamin, 1977), and you can find a later account by Gary Hardcastle (2000).

APA AND BROWN V. BOARD OF EDUCATION

The second archival project of mine that I want to describe is more recent. It involves psychology's role in the famous 1954 Supreme Court decision, *Brown v. the Board of Education* of Topeka, Kansas. It is likely that many American historians would argue that it was the most important Supreme Court decision of the 20th century (see Patterson, 2001). On May 17, 1954, the justices unanimously declared school segregation illegal, ending the "separate but equal" doctrine of the 1896 decision, *Plessy v. Ferguson*. Not only was *Brown v. Board* a great victory for those who opposed racial segregation in the schools, but it was a great victory for psychology. It marked the first time that psychological research had been cited in a written decision of the Supreme Court. Indeed, the research was more than just cited; the decision read by Chief Justice Earl Warren noted that the research was compelling evidence of the dangers of segregation. Some of the research the court referred to was, of course, the early 1940s studies by Kenneth B. (1914-) and Mamie Phipps Clark (1917-1983) on racial identification and preference in black children (Clark, 1950; Clark & Clark, 1939a, 1939b, 1940).

A longstanding interest for me, and a theme of much of my historical research over the past 25 years, has been the nature of psychology's public image. I wondered how psychologists might have responded to and used such national recognition. Specifically, I wondered how the American Psychological Association (APA) would have reacted to psychology's prominent role in such a historic moment? What accolades might have been bestowed on the several psychologists involved in preparing the brief for the Court? Might there have been press releases from APA to celebrate the role of psychological science in a legal decision? I could not find answers to those questions in any published accounts, so I took the next step to see what the archival records held. I started at the Library of Congress, which holds the APA Archives, the NAACP (National Association for the Advancement of Colored People) Archives, the Thurgood Marshall Papers, and the Kenneth B. Clark Papers. Marshall was the lead attorney in the case, working for the Legal Defense Fund of the NAACP, and Clark was the chief author of the social science brief filed with the Court.

All in one place — the Library of Congress — were the records of most of the principal players in this story. That is unusual in historical research. More typical is archive-hopping all over the country, tracking down the papers of the various actors in the story (that is, assuming the papers exist at all or that they can be located). I began my search by looking at the Clark Papers, focusing my attention on the records of the early to mid 1950s — that is, from a few years before the trial to a few years after the Court's decision. I found a most interesting folder of letters congratulating Clark on the victory. Gordon Allport (1897-1967) of Harvard University, whose classic book on prejudice was published that same year (Allport, 1954), wrote:

> You are probably receiving congratulations on all sides. Let me add my word of admiration for your Herculean labors and adroit handling of social science evidence for proper presentation to the Supreme Court. The happy outcome marks an epoch in the development of social science, in the history of the Negro race, and in the improvement of American foreign relations. Since you had a large part to play in all these achievements I congratulate you with all my heart. (Benjamin & Crouse, 2002, p. 41)

Otto Klineberg (1899-1992), author of *Race Differences* (1935) and Clark's mentor when he earned his doctorate at Columbia University, wrote:

> The great news has just reached me, and I am writing immediately because I know how you must be feeling, and because I want to take this occasion to congratulate you personally for the wonderful job that you have done. Although a number of social scientists did work with you, I have always felt that without your leadership and enthusiasm the task would not have been accomplished nearly so well. (Benjamin & Crouse, 2002, p. 41)

A third letter is from Buell Gallagher, President of City College in New York City, where Clark was a faculty member. He wrote:

> Dear Ken, … With you, I am proud, deeply moved, and humbly grateful. That the real task is now before us is the sobering meaning of the hour. But I cannot let the moment of rejoicing pass without entering in the record my profound appreciation of your part in setting straight the course of American history. (Benjamin & Crouse, 2002, p. 41)

I have tried to imagine what Kenneth Clark must have felt like in the immediate aftermath of the decision. What must it be like in your lifetime to realize that you have changed the course of American history, to have righted a great social wrong? Clark gave some indication of that in his letters to friends shortly after the decision. There is clear joy in his voice, some expressions of relief after a long legal battle, and concern over how long it will take the law to become reality. Several weeks after the court decision, he wrote to Klineberg:

> These three weeks since the Court's decision have been in many respects the most exciting period of my life. Starting from about 2:00 p.m. on May 17th, Mamie, Thurgood, Bob Carter and the entire staff of the Legal Defense and Educational Division of the NAACP and all of our friends have been celebrating. The first three or four days we were in the clouds and refused to be brought down to earth by a consideration of the really serious problems that we must now all face. (Benjamin & Crouse, 2002, p. 41)

In reading the letters in the Clark Papers, I have thought to myself: How many of us will ever know the feeling that would derive from the realization that our research had been used for some great national good? Of the thousands of research articles published in psychology every year, which of those will one day prove to benefit humanity in some significant way? Clearly such studies are incredibly rare.

When I was looking through Clark's papers, I was particularly interested in correspondence from APA. What was the nature of APA's response to the decision, both in public and in private? I was looking for a letter from the then APA executive secretary Fillmore Sanford (1914-1967) congratulating Clark, or a letter from the APA Board of Directors saying how proud they were of his accomplishments and of the recognition he had brought to psychology as a science. What I found were two letters from APA in 1954. One was from Fillmore Sanford, informing him that his dues were in arrears. The other was from APA staff member Lorraine Bouthilet telling Clark that he was scheduled to make two presentations at the 1954 APA meeting, and that APA rules limited members to one presentation. I searched the folders once more, just in case I had missed the congratulatory letter, but it wasn't there.

Next I went to the APA Papers. I started with Fillmore Sanford's correspondence folders but found no letters to Clark. I then went to the minutes of the meetings of the Board of Directors in 1954 and 1955. I thought, maybe the Board issued some kind of a commendation. But nowhere was there any mention of Clark or of the *Brown v. Board* decision.

What about recognition in APA's publications? Of course the *APA Monitor* did not exist then; the official communication device for all APA members was the *American Psychologist*. The most logical place for its appearance in that journal was a regular column entitled "Across the Secretary's Desk," a column authored by Sanford as executive secretary. That column often reported on Washington events related to psychology, such as federal funding of psychological research or support by the Veteran's Administration for training of clinical psychologists. But in looking at all of the *American Psychologist* issues in the years surrounding the historic case, there was not a single mention of Clark or the Court's decision. The closest thing I found was a comment by Robert Perloff in a 1955 issue of the *American Psychologist*, encouraging psychologists to use their science to end racial discrimination.

My search widened to the Stuart Cook Papers in the Psychology Archives at Akron; the records of the Society for the Psychological Study of Social Issues

(SPSSI), also at Akron; and to the Michael Amrine Papers at Georgetown University. Amrine was the public information officer for APA for a while during the mid 1950s; Stuart Cook (1913-1993) had testified on behalf of the plaintiffs in some of the lower court cases that led to *Brown v. Board* and was one of the three principal co-authors (with Kenneth Clark and Isidor Chein) on the social science brief for *Brown v. Board.* SPSSI had been the guiding force in mobilizing the psychologists to create the brief. These searches, however, failed to find evidence of any attention being paid to Clark or the others.

On a later visit to the Library of Congress I worked once more in the Clark Papers. My previous search had focused on all of the folders marked *Brown v. Board* and Clark's general correspondence folders for 1951-1957. I had missed seeing a folder marked "APA Business." In that folder were several letters related to routine APA business. There was also a letter written in March 1955 from Fillmore Sanford, approximately a year after the Court's decision, inviting Clark to consider writing an article for the *American Psychologist* on the subject of psychological research and segregation. Apparently, Stuart Cook made the suggestion to Sanford to invite such a contribution from Clark. So Clark's accomplishment did not go totally unnoticed. But what recognition did he receive from organized psychology? The answer appears to be, none.

Was the lack of response from APA due to the fact that the significance of the court decision was not understood at the time? No. The decision had been much anticipated and was hailed by *Time* magazine in 1954 as the landmark decision of the court. Historian Ben Keppel (1995) wrote, "From the moment of its announcement, the *Brown* decision became a sacred and redemptive chapter in the history of American democracy" (p. 115). APA leadership was clearly aware of its members' work on behalf of the plaintiffs in the various lower court cases and in preparation of the social science brief for the Supreme Court.

Was the lack of response due to the fact that APA did not make public commendations or public statements on social issues? No. The APA took a number of political stands in the 1940s and 1950s issuing statements and passing resolutions on such issues as academic freedom, mandatory oaths, legal discrimination against immigrants and international visitors to the United States, and loyalty investigations that were part of McCarthyism in the late 1940s and early 1950s.

Was the lack of response due to APA's concerns that there might be Communist ties to the social activism of the psychologists involved in *Brown v. Board*, specifically the organization known as SPSSI? There were those inside and outside of psychology who suspected SPSSI of Communist sympathies. For example, when the organization was formed during the Great Depression of the 1930s, George Estabrooks (1885-1973) of Colgate University responded as follows to the invitation to join:

> With reference to your mimeographed sheets concerning the participation of psychologists in the contemporary political world, allow me to register my hearty dissent with approximately everything contained therein. If psychologists, as individuals wish to make themselves politically vocal on any topic — white, red, or pink — it seems to me that is wholly up to them. … It seems to me that, as psychologists, our duties are pretty clear cut. If any group of us

wish (sic) to organize as a "Committee for the Propagation of Mild Pinkism," for goodness sakes let us organize ourselves as such and not in camouflage under the protecting skirts of the American Psychological Association. (Benjamin, 1993, pp. 174-175)

Indeed, the FBI had established a file on SPSSI in the 1930s because of its perceived leftist agenda (Harris, 1980). Thus it is possible that APA's silence on *Brown* may have had to do with potential fallout from supporting the activities of what was perceived as a leftist organization or, worse, an organization involved in school desegregation efforts that many believed were Communist inspired.

Was APA's reluctance to celebrate or congratulate related in any way to a perception that the social science evidence cited by the court was "flawed" data, and thus not good science? After the decision there were numerous attacks on psychology as a legitimate science, for example a 1956 *Newsweek* article in which the author, Raymond Moley, stated, "The assumption by the court that these psychological writings constitute firm and lasting facts determined by scientific methods is nonsense" (p. 104). There were also attacks on the studies of the Clarks that had used black and white dolls to assess racial identification and prejudice in African American preschool children. (See Jackson, 2000, for an excellent treatment of the criticisms of the research in the social science brief.) It is possible that APA had concerns about the research, but if so, there is no information in the published or archival record that would support such a conclusion.

There is another possible explanation about why APA chose not to celebrate or congratulate. In 1954, racially segregated schools existed by law in 17 states and the District of Columbia and were permitted in four other states. Other forms of segregation existed in churches, theaters, trains, buses, restaurants, housing, work settings, mental institutions, prisons, restrooms, drinking fountains, and polling booths. Racism was present everywhere in America and psychology was no exception. A president of APA and chair of the psychology department at Columbia University from 1941 to 1955, Henry Garrett (1894-1973), was one of the principal spokespersons for maintenance of racial segregation. He testified in several of the lower court cases leading to *Brown* and was especially critical of the psychological evidence presented in those cases, even though both Kenneth and Mamie Clark had studied with him. Although racial attitudes in America were undergoing changes in the 1950s, racial questions continued to divide psychology's house. Such a division made it difficult for APA to speak on racial issues without offending many members. That race was a very sensitive issue is evidenced by a 1954 survey of social attitudes of leading psychologists that avoided any question of race altogether, focusing instead on attitudes about divorce, the death penalty, euthanasia, and religion (Keehn, 1955). In short, I believe that the divided opinions on race among psychologists in the 1950s prevented APA from seeing *Brown v. Board* as a triumph for psychology or for America.

The story of these research questions regarding APA and *Brown v. Board* can be found in Benjamin and Crouse (2002). For the most comprehensive account of the story of *Brown*, see Kluger (1975), the biography of Thurgood Marshall by Juan Williams (1998), and, for the role of the social scientists in the desegregation court cases, see Jackson (2001).

CONCLUSION

In conclusion, let me return briefly to the nature of archival research. Historian of psychology Josef Brozek (1975) has described archival research as a high-risk, high-gain operation. It is difficult to predict what you will find. Days may be spent where you turn up nothing. Indeed, an entire archival trip may produce little of value for a project — although I would say that has never happened for me. This high-risk, high-gain nature of archival work is no doubt part of the drama that makes it so exciting. There is intrigue in every visit. Every folder to be opened has the possibility of yielding important secrets that have remained hidden since those words were put on paper. Diligence of research strategy is important, but so is luck. When serendipity strikes, the researcher needs to recognize the value of what is there. Remember that archival work is *unique* because the materials are themselves unique.

In this type of research, one typically begins in one archival collection and then pursues related materials through other archives, following wherever the leads suggest going. Collections are rarely, if ever, complete. Some documents relating to important questions are almost always missing. Survivors who will ultimately deposit the person's papers may go through them, discarding documents that seem unimportant or ones that might cast the individual in a negative light. Archivists and historians don't like such pre-selection, but it is a fact of archival life. Occasionally, documents that were once part of the collection are missing — occasionally because they have been stolen by an unscrupulous researcher (thankfully, a rare event) but more commonly because a scholar at some point has refiled the document in a wrong folder or, worse, a wrong box. Often we find one side of the correspondence but not the other, a problem that was made better in the 1920s with the invention of carbon paper.

Here is how Michael Hill has summarized the joys of this work in his book on archival strategies. Hill (1993) wrote:

> Archival work appears bookish and commonplace to the uninitiated, but this mundane simplicity is deceptive. It bears repeating that events and materials in archives are not always what they seem on the surface. There are perpetual surprises, intrigues, and apprehensions. … Suffice it to say that it is a rare treat to visit an archive, to hold in one's hand the priceless and irreplaceable documents of our unfolding human drama. Each new box of archival material presents opportunities for discovery as well as obligations to treat the subjects of your … research with candor, theoretical sophistication, and a sense of fair play. Each archival visit is a journey into an unknown realm that rewards its visitors with challenging puzzles and unexpected revelations. (pp. 6-7)

I hope I have explained some of the fascination that this work holds for me and why those all too few days each year that I get to spend in archives are so enjoyable. I should add that this kind of work is there for you as well and for your students. So if you have a few spare hours one afternoon, you might just wander in and read somebody else's mail. I warn you, though, that the high may be something that you find you cannot do without.

You don't have to go to the Archives of the History of American Psychology in Akron, Ohio or to the Manuscript Division of the Library of Congress in Washington, DC to do archival research, although if you are within easy driving distance of those places then an abundance of treasures awaits you. One important source for locating archives is an annotated listing of more than 500 manuscript collections in the United States related to psychology, compiled by Sokal and Rafail (1982). Some of those may be near you. Regardless, archival records exist virtually everywhere, including in your own back yard, or at least in your own community. You might find interesting historical records in your college or university, in your local historical society, in a state hospital, in a city hall, in a municipal court, in the YMCA, in your public library, in a regional office for Girl Scouts or Boy Scouts, and so forth. Most communities have some psychology-related agencies, past or present, such as phrenological societies, mental health advocacy groups, or mental healing societies. Discovering or recognizing their existence greatly expands the historical research opportunities for your students. Searching the paper or microfilm records of old newspapers in the public library is one way to get some ideas about psychology in your community in the past.

Has a history of psychology on your campus been written? If not, you might consider involving your students in the research and writing of such a history (see Benjamin, 1990). Research might include questions like: Has the name of the psychology department changed over time? When were the first psychology courses offered on your campus and in what department? What were the titles of these courses? Their content? What texts did they use? How has the psychology curriculum changed over time? When did specific courses appear and disappear, and can you account for those changes? What have been the requirements for the psychology major and how have those changed over time? When did laboratory instruction begin? What was the nature of the laboratory? Did any published research come out of the laboratory? What faculty members have taught psychology? Where did they receive their training and in what fields? What faculty titles did they hold? Can you locate former faculty members for oral histories (see Hoopes, 1979)? Can you locate publications by former faculty members? Did student psychology clubs exist? Was there a Psi Chi chapter? Can you locate former students in the program for oral histories? Might they have notes from their student days of their psychology classes? Did famous psychologists speak on your campus at some time? Can you locate information about their visits? These are just some of the questions that could make for interesting student/faculty research.

For a start on this kind of work, begin in your college library or archives, looking at old yearbooks, college catalogs, student newspapers, and departmental records. (For many schools, department heads were expected to file an annual report on the activities of the department, and these reports, if they exist, will likely be in the college archives.) Other sources might be a state historical society or state education agency (or a church archive, if your college has a religious affiliation). Psi Chi's National Office in Chattanooga, Tennessee, which has old records for many chapters dating to the 1930s, might be willing to copy those for you if you have or had a Psi Chi chapter. Your alumni office can sometimes provide information on oldest living alums who were psychology majors. Don't think of these projects as one-semester endeavors. Most of them, if done well, will take longer. You can break the tasks into smaller units that can be accomplished by students in a smaller time frame, with the idea that other students will pick up other parts of the project as subsequent classes work toward a finished history.

I hope you will consider involving your students in some kind of archival history. In addition to gaining knowledge, rediscovered or new, students enhance their library skills (and yes, libraries are still important), learn about important resources in historical research, learn about historical research techniques and issues of interpretation, acquire some group cooperation skills, and develop a better appreciation of the past and the personal and contextual issues that shaped it.

REFERENCES

Allport, G. W. (1954). *The nature of prejudice*. Cambridge, MA: Addison Wesley.

Benjamin, L. T., Jr. (1977). The Psychological Round Table: Revolution of 1936. *American Psychologist*, *32*, 542-549.

Benjamin, L. T., Jr. (1990). Involving students and faculty in preparing a departmental history. *Teaching of Psychology*, *17*, 97-100.

Benjamin, L. T., Jr. (1993). *A history of psychology in letters*. New York: McGraw-Hill.

Benjamin, L. T., Jr., & Crouse, E. M. (2002). The American Psychological Association's response to *Brown v. Board of Education*: The case of Kenneth B. Clark. *American Psychologist*, *57*, 38-50.

Brozek, J. (1975). Irons in the fire: Introduction to a symposium on archival research. *Journal of the History of the Behavioral Sciences*, *11*, 15-19.

Clark, K. B. (1950). *The effects of prejudice and discrimination on personality development (Midcentury White House Conference on Children and Youth)*. Washington, DC: Federal Security Agency, Children's Bureau.

Clark, K. B., & Clark, M. K. (1939a). Segregation as a factor in the racial identification of Negro preschool children: A preliminary report. *Journal of Experimental Education*, *8*, 161-163.

Clark, K. B., & Clark, M. K. (1939b). The development of consciousness of self and the emergence of racial identification in Negro preschool children. *Journal of Social Psychology*, *10*, 591-599.

Clark, K. B., & Clark, M. K. (1940). Skin color as a factor in racial identification of Negro preschool children. *Journal of Social Psychology*, *11*, 159-169.

Furumoto, L. (1988). Shared knowledge: The Experimentalists, 1904-1929. In J. G. Morawski (Ed.), *The rise of experimentation in American psychology* (pp. 94-113). New Haven: Yale University Press.

Goodwin, C. J. (1985). On the origins of Titchener's experimentalists. *Journal of the History of the Behavioral Sciences*, *21*, 383-389.

Hardcastle, G. (2000). The cult of experiment: The Psychological Round Table, 1936-1941. *History of Psychology*, *3*, 344-370.

Harris, B. (1980). The FBI's files on APA and SPSSI: Description and implications. *American Psychologist*, *35*, 1141-1144.

Hill, M. R. (1993). *Archival strategies and techniques*. Newbury Park, CA: Sage.

Hoopes, J. (1979). *Oral history: An introduction for students*. Chapel Hill: University of North Carolina Press.

Jackson, J. P., Jr. (2000). The triumph of the segregationists? A historiographical inquiry into psychology and the *Brown* litigation. *History of Psychology*, *3*, 239-261.

Jackson, J. P., Jr. (2001). *Social scientists for social justice: Making the case against segregation*. New York: New York University Press.

Keehn, J. D. (1955). The expressed social attitudes of leading psychologists. *American Psychologist*, *10*, 208-210.

Keppel, B. (1995). *The work of democracy: Ralph Bunche, Kenneth B. Clark, Lorraine Hansberry, and the cultural politics of race*. Cambridge, MA: Harvard University Press.

Klineberg, O. (1935). *Race differences*. New York: Harper & Row.

Kluger, R. (1975). *Simple justice: The history of Brown v. Board of Education and Black America's struggle for equality*. New York: Random House.

Ladd-Franklin, C. (1887). A method for the experimental determination of the horopter. *American Journal of Psychology*, *1*, 99-111.

Moley, R. (1956, June 4). Psychosocial law. *Newsweek*, *47*, 104.

Patterson, J. T. (2001). *Brown v. Board of Education: A civil rights milestone and its legacy*. New York: Oxford University Press.

Perloff, R. (1955). Desegregation and psychology. *American Psychologist, 10*, 42-43.

Scarborough, E., & Furumoto, L. (1987). *Untold lives: The first generation of American women psychologists*. New York: Columbia University Press.

Sokal, M. M., & Rafail, P. A. (1982). *A guide to manuscript collections in the history of psychology and related areas*. New York: Kraus International.

Williams, J. (1998). *Thurgood Marshall: American revolutionary*. New York: Times Books.

CHAPTER THREE

WHATEVER HAPPENED TO ... ?

*Psychological Research That Introductory Psychology
Students Don't Hear Much About Anymore*

Josh R. Gerow
Kenneth S. Bordens

Indiana University-Purdue University Fort Wayne

TEACHERS OF PSYCHOLOGY have always shared a common goal: to present the content of psychology from a scientific perspective. This goal could be seen both in the classroom, where early psychologists used myriad scientific demonstrations, and in textbooks. Regardless of the era in which they were published or the specific approach taken, authors of bona fide psychology textbooks tried to present their discipline as a true science, one worthy of being included in the company of other sciences like biology or chemistry.

Of course, psychology textbooks have changed a lot over the past century. Early texts by pioneers like Wundt, Titchener, Carr, and Baldwin gave the author's particular theoretical position. These "monolithic" texts nevertheless aimed to present students with an introduction to the science of psychology as a whole. During the 1920s and 1930s, monolithic texts gave way to a new generation of textbooks with a more varied content (Weiten & Wright, 1992). The 1930s also witnessed another change: a shift to a more student-oriented book exemplified by Ruch's (1937) *Psychology and Life*. This book was market driven — material that students found interesting was highlighted and moved to the early chapters (Weiten & Wright, 1992).

The 1950s brought us the "encyclopedic text," with its emphasis on extensive coverage of contemporary research coming out of psychology laboratories and other venues. These books attempted to present cutting-edge research on popular topics of the day. They gave way in the 1970s to a new generation of textbooks — books designed to appeal to students by using lots of pictures, slick graphics, and glossy paper. Content was distilled down to the most elementary level.

The 1980s and 1990s saw a return to a more encyclopedic approach. However, some of the features evident in the artsy books of the 1970s were retained.

Most books used a four-color format and included many photographs and illustrations. Many of the pedagogical features pioneered in the 1970s also were retained: Running glossaries, interim summaries, and extensive chapter summaries were common. However, content was beefed up so that there is now a better balance between substance and pedagogical appeal.

Not only did the content and focus of psychology textbooks change over the decades, so too did the publication process. Until the mid-1980s, publishers produced revisions of their introductory psychology textbooks about every 5 years. Within a decade, a 4-year revision cycle became a 3-year cycle. Of course, there are many reasons for increasing the pace of textbook revisions. Most are economic, and reflect the skills of companies that manage the used textbook market.

Another reason for the truncated publication cycle is the desire by publishers to provide the most up-to-date material possible. The benefit of this strategy is obvious: students are presented with cutting edge research and timely topics. However, an unintended consequence has been a reduction in the amount of coverage of some of the classic studies in psychology. Pavlov's dogs are still in there, along with Watson and Rayner's little Albert and Milgram's studies of obedience — but many other timeless classics have lost their places in our introductory textbooks.

Most textbook authors agree that writing a 1,500-page text is far, far easier than writing a 700-page text. The difficulty is in choosing what gets added, what stays, and what goes. Even in the 1880s, William James complained to his publisher, Henry Holt, that to condense what he knew about psychology to only two volumes and 1,377 pages, plus end matter, was a terrific struggle (James, 1920, p. 294). We believe that in the effort to be timely, classic and important studies that were once commonplace in our introductory texts have been discarded and that they should be reintegrated into psychology classes. Teachers should talk about them. And our textbooks should start including them again.

It is important for several reasons:

♦ Many of these studies still have relevance for students today.
♦ In a student population that is increasingly ignorant of history, it is important to put new research into its historical context.
♦ Many of the classic studies in psychology used imaginative and innovative research methodologies and attempted to answer big questions about human behavior.
♦ The innovative but often simplistic, and occasionally unethical, methods of the classic studies can be contrasted with today's more sophisticated methods.
♦ The classic studies in psychology are just plain interesting.

Our purpose in this chapter is to inspire you to think back to some of those classic stories of earlier days, to skim through some older texts and bring those stories into your classroom today. We include here a brief synopsis of just a few studies that piqued our imaginations when were students, or that we took joy in teaching in our younger days. Each exemplifies all of the above five reasons for reviewing classic studies.

MAN SWALLOWS BALLOON TO MEASURE FEELING HUNGRY

Man feels hungry, swallows balloon. The tale is as harrowing as any in recorded history. It all started when the Nantucket whaling ship *Essex* set sail on August 12, 1819, on what should have been a 2- or 3-year whaling voyage. In a strange twist of fate, the hunter *Essex* became the hunted on November 16 of the following year, while she was over 1,000 miles west of the coast of South America. While two of the three smaller whaleboats were out hunting whales, a huge Sperm Whale (witnesses aboard the *Essex* put the whale at 85 feet long and weighing around 80 tons) attacked the *Essex*. Its first attack did some damage, but it was the second attack that eventually breached the ship's hull and caused her to begin sinking. The crew of the *Essex* salvaged as much food and fresh water as they could from the doomed ship and divided the provisions among the ship's three small whaleboats.

The crew rigged the whaleboats with sails and began a trek across the Pacific Ocean that killed most of the crew. After 18 days at sea and severe rationing of the scant provisions, the crew began to experience extreme hunger. Even the normally stoic first mate, Owen Chase, thought about breaking into the stores of food and distributing all that remained to the men (Philbrick, 2000). The ordeal of the crew of the *Essex* would last for another nearly 50 days. They ate the barnacles off the bottoms of their boats, and eventually resorted to cannibalism to survive.

Although few have experienced the kind of starvation the crew of the *Essex* suffered, we have all been hungry at one time or another and experienced those familiar hunger pangs. When we feel those hunger pangs we know instinctively that we need to eat. However, do those pangs cause the hunger, or, are they merely a signal that our bodies need nourishment?

Over 100 years later, Walter Cannon (1934) weighed in on this issue. He noted that, "A person who has gone without food for some hours does not feel hungry all the time. The aching and gnawing feeling described as hunger pangs occur irregularly" (pp. 248-249). Cannon designed a unique experiment to investigate the nature of hunger.

Cannon himself (and later others) swallowed a balloon and inflated it until it was firmly pressed against the walls of his stomach. A small tube was attached to the balloon, which was attached at the other end to an instrument that made a record of each time Cannon's stomach contracted. A telegraph key also was attached to the recording device. Each time Cannon felt a hunger pang he would press the key.

Cannon found that his subjective feelings of hunger correlated closely with stomach contractions. This finding led him to conclude that his stomach contractions were the motivators for eating.

The relationship between stomach contractions and hunger turned out not to be so simple. Hunger easily can occur in the absence of stomach contractions. For example, a man whose stomach has been removed surgically and whose esophagus was then connected to his intestine reported periodic desires for food much the same as those of persons with stomachs. Even earlier arguments were being made that the experience of hunger is "central" in origin, having more to do with the brain than with the stomach (Hoelzel, 1927). But the fact that Cannon — who is better known for his work on homeostasis (the natural tendency of the body to maintain a state of balance or equilibrium of internal physiological processing) might have been wrong about the role of the stomach in the hunger drive is not the point. The notion of the scientist acting as his own subject in what has to be a discomforting exercise gets students' attention. Cannon's experiment provides a lovely way to begin a discussion of what we now know about hunger and eating behaviors.

NAKED PHOTOS PROVE FAT PEOPLE ARE JOLLY

The search for a relationship between body shape and behavior has a long tradition in the behavioral sciences, going as far back as the Roman physician Galen. Galen believed that one's behavioral predispositions depended on the mix of four body humours (blood, black bile, yellow bile, and phlegm). In the late 1700s, Johannes Caspar Lavater (1789) argued that physiognomy was a true science, and proposed that different facial profiles correlated with different temperaments. Elements of physiognomy can be found in Franz Gall's work in phrenology, which maintained that there was a relationship between the morphology of one's skull and a variety of mental faculties.

The tradition of the physiognomists was carried on with William Sheldon's (1954) work relating body morphology to personality. Much of it can be found in his edited work, *Atlas of Men: A Guide for Somatotyping the Adult Male of All Ages*. Getting a copy of Sheldon's *Atlas* is well worth the effort.

Sheldon analyzed approximately 4,000 photographs of nude young men with regard to their dominant physical characteristics. (He later did the same for young women.) Based on his analysis, Sheldon identified three basic body types, and classified the men accordingly. *Endomorphs* displayed a "round" body style with a predominant visceral region. *Mesomorphs* had well-defined muscles and large chests. *Ectomorphs* presented skinny body morphology with a predominance of skin and neural tissue. But it was possible to fall in-between categories. Sheldon evaluated each individual on a 7-point scale, resulting in a three-digit representation of his body type. For example, someone who was average in endomorphy, high in mesomorphy, and low in ectomorphy would be somatotyped as 4-7-1.

The next step was to rate subjects for temperament. (Note that in those days there was no hesitation in referring to research participants as "subjects.") Sheldon rated them on emotional dimensions such as joviality, moodiness, tenseness, and activity level. He used a statistical analysis to reduce the various temperaments to three types: *viscerotonia*, characterized by comforts such as eating, joviality, and relaxation; *somatotonia*, involving competitiveness, aggressiveness, and movement; and *cerebrotonia*, characterized by restraint, thoughtfulness, and unusual sensitivity. Again, ratings were made on a 7-point scale, and a 2-7-1, for example, was characterized as boiling over with energy, while a 1-3-7 was thoughtful and apprehensive.

Not surprisingly, Sheldon found a strong correlation between body type and temperament ($r = .80$). Individuals rated high on endomorphy tended to receive high ratings on viscerotonia. Mesomorphs tended to be rated as somatotonic.

The clarity of hindsight reveals several problems with Sheldon's work, namely that the same investigators made both the physique and temperament ratings. "Studies using tests [instead of ratings] in which bias is excluded, have found few, if any, significant correlations between body build and personality" (Tyler, 1956, p. 444). But what better way to introduce students to the issue of single- and double-blind controls, or the difficulties inherent in trying to oversimplify so complex an issue as human personality?

WIRE-MESH MOMMIES DRIVE BABY MONKEYS CRAZY

The time was 1940, the place, England. The circumstance was the increasingly severe bombings of southern England by the German Air Force. A decision was made to relocate children to "residential nurseries" in the north of England. The plan necessitated separating children (some in infancy) from their parents.

Prominent psychologists of the day, including Anna Freud and Rene Spitz, sounded dire warnings about the effects of separating young children from their mothers (McCall, 2004). The contemporary wisdom was that the children would suffer psychologically because of maternal separation, even though they were provided with adequate physical and social care (McCall, 2004). The case was bolstered by Spitz's film called *Grief*, which graphically showed the plight of infants deprived of maternal care in an orphanage.

A debate raged over the psychological harm that maternal deprivation could cause. Books were written on the subject (e.g., Freud & Burlingham, 1943) and case studies were published. However, there was no hard empirical evidence for the effects of maternal deprivation on psychological adjustment. The classic experiments conducted by Harry Harlow (1958) provided some interesting insights into the effects of early social isolation and maternal deprivation. Harlow's research provides us with some of the most enduring images in the history of experimental psychology: Baby rhesus monkeys clinging to terrycloth models or cowering in the corner of their cages without a source of warmth and comfort.

In one of his experiments, Harlow (1958) separated infant monkeys from their mothers and reared them in isolation. The infants ate an adequate diet and showed no negative physical effects. Harlow noticed, though, that the isolated monkeys became strongly attached to the cloth diapers used to cover the floors of their cages. Harlow observed that the infants clung to the pieces of cloth and went into tantrums when the pieces of cloth were removed. He also noted that during the first 5 days of life, infants that did not have the cloths struggled to survive while those provided with the cloth tended to thrive.

These observations led Harlow to what is perhaps his most famous experiment. He constructed two "surrogate mothers" and made them available in the cages of infant monkeys removed from their mothers (Harlow, 1958). Harlow manipulated which of the mothers provided food. In some instances food was only available on the wire mother and in others only on the cloth mother. Harlow found that regardless of which mother provided food, the infant monkeys preferred the cloth mother. More hours per day were spent on the cloth mother, even if the wire mother provided food. Harlow also found that when placed in an unfamiliar environment, the infant monkeys ran to and clung to the cloth mother. If the wire mother was present, the infant monkey virtually ignored it and huddled in the corner of the room or lay motionless on the floor. Interestingly, this difference became more pronounced as the infant monkeys got older and had more experience with the cloth and wire mothers.

Harlow concluded that because the cloth mother provided "contact comfort" the infant monkey's instinctive need to cling and cuddle was met. Harlow maintained that the infants developed a love for the cloth mothers, a love that was not evident for the wire mothers. He claimed that contact comfort was an essential, although perhaps not the only, component in the development of an affectional relationship between an infant and its mother. Perhaps those who voiced concerns about the children relocated in England had a point.

It is worth noting that the question of whether there truly is a universal primate need for "contact comfort" has never quite been resolved. Given the active field of research in developmental psychology commonly referred to as "attachment theory," it seems a shame that Harlow's work gets so little mention these days.

Ducklings Follow Man Into Pond for Daily Swim

Attachment between an offspring and its caregiver is a process essential to the healthy development of the offspring. For humans and other primates who are born relatively immature, the attachment process ensures that the offspring will be cared for until it is capable of taking care of itself. There are some species of animals, such as precocial birds (e.g., ducks) that are born in a more developed state. Ducks can walk almost immediately after birth. In order to survive, ducklings need to become attached to their mother very quickly.

Fortunately, such an attachment does occur. It is called *imprinting*, and is best illustrated with fowl, most commonly chicks, goslings, and ducklings. If baby chicks are born in an incubator, they will follow any moving object. When guided by sight alone, they seem to have no more disposition to follow a hen than to follow a duck or a human being. In short, the first large moving object a chick sees becomes its "mother," and the chick will follow it wherever it goes.

Imprinting is instinctive; it requires no learning. It is usually the parent of the offspring that provides this stimulus. However, a member of some other species, or even an inanimate object, may happen to be the first moving object the young animal sees (Munn, Fernald, & Fernald, 1974). This phenomenon was first discovered and reported in the 19th century by Spaulding (1873) and noted by William James (1890) in his classic text *Principles of Psychology*. Spaulding also recognized that imprinting only occurs during a *critical period* early in the life of the chick (usually at or about 13-16 hours after hatching and hardly ever following 30-33 hours after hatching).

Hess (1958), using ducklings as subjects, showed that it was easy to imprint them on decoys. Other investigators, using other species, have shown that even a cardboard cube or cylinder is an adequate imprinting object. Studies of this behavior have shown that (a) the duckling is easily imprinted on the decoy; (b) when subsequently placed between a male decoy and female duck, the tendency is to follow the decoy; (c) in a pond, the imprinted ducklings congregate around the decoy in preference to a live adult duck; and (d) the duckling will overcome obstacles in order to remain near the object on which it is imprinted, suggesting that the relationship has motivational properties (Munn et al., 1974).

In truth, several contemporary textbooks *do* mention imprinting, if only in passing. As biopsychology and evolutionary psychology become increasingly popular topics, even in the introductory course, we suspect that we may be seeing more references to these charming and groundbreaking studies.

Leaders Cause Laziness, Aggressiveness, or Dedication in Children

In the 1930s, the world was experiencing monumental changes in how governments related to their peoples. In the United States, democracy was firmly entrenched as the political system although there were those who questioned whether democracy was the best form of government. In Germany, the Weimar Republic installed after World War I was being scrapped in favor of the authoritarian National Socialist Party headed by Adolph Hitler. In Italy, a parliamentary, multiparty system was being replaced by the Fascists, also an authoritarian party, headed by Benito Mussolini.

The world seemed to be in the midst of a great social experiment. At the root of this experiment was the question of which political system would ultimately prove to be the best. Would it be democracy, as championed by the United States and Great Britain? Or, would it be one of the authoritarian systems becoming so popular in Germany and Italy? Humankind was at the crossroads of history and people were looking for answers. Kurt Lewin, Ronald Lippitt, and Ralph White were determined to help find those answers.

Against this backdrop, Lewin and his colleagues decided to address these pressing questions by designing an experiment to test the relative merits of different leadership styles. They noted that there were several important questions that needed to be addressed. Among them was, "Is not democratic group life more pleasant, but authoritarianism more efficient?" (Lewin, Lippitt, & White, 1939, p. 271). Acknowledging the difficulties inherent in studying such issues experimentally, Lewin and his colleagues designed an imaginative experiment to test the relative efficacy of different forms of group leadership.

Lewin et al. (1939) studied three leadership styles: Democratic, Autocratic, and *Laissez-faire*, using 10-year-old boys as participants. The democratic leader left many decisions up to the group members and provided them considerable freedom concerning the group's activity. He provided guidance when needed and was fair-minded in his criticism and praise. In contrast, the autocratic leader exercised almost complete control over the group. He determined how the group would operate, with whom each child would work, how tasks were to be done, and was more personal in his praise and criticism. Finally, the *Laissez-faire* leader took a hands-off approach and allowed the group to do as they wished, with little or no direction from the leader.

During the course of the 5-month experiment, each group experienced each of the different leadership styles. At 6-week intervals each group got a new leader with a new leadership style (each leader was trained in all leadership styles). Researchers placed participants into five-person "clubs," and these met in special "clubrooms" that allowed two clubs to meet simultaneously in adjacent rooms. Observers watched the boys during club meetings and recorded several behaviors. Additionally, "extra-club" information was gathered including interviews with each child by a "non-club" interviewer, interviews with parents, talks with teachers, administration of the Rorschach test to each child, and conversations with the children on two hikes done after the experiment was completed.

The experiment's main focus was the amount of aggressive behavior shown by the boys under the different leadership styles. Lewin et al. (1939) did not specify precisely what constituted an aggressive act. Observers made records of the social behaviors shown by the boys, including "all social actions, both verbal and physical which [the observer] designated as 'hostile' or 'joking hostile'" (p. 278). Based on information provided throughout the article, we can conclude that aggressive behavior included "dominating behaviors" (p. 277) directed at one or more members of a group and overt acts of physical and verbal aggression.

Lewin et al. (1939) reported a moderate amount of aggression under the democratic leader. In four out of five groups under the autocratic leader, the children showed an "abnormally small" amount of aggression. In the fifth autocratic group, there was an extremely high level of aggression. Under the *Laissez-faire* leader, there was a very high level of aggressive behavior.

Under the autocratic leader, several group dynamics emerged. First, during the transition from the autocratic to the other leadership conditions children showed "sudden outbursts" of aggression once the repressive autocratic leader was removed. Second, during the periods when the leader left the room, children in the autocratic leadership condition showed levels of aggression that reached 10 times the amount displayed when the leader was present and also showed a concomitant drop in group productive behavior. Third, interviews with the boys prior to transitions and after the experiment showed clearly that the autocratic leader was disliked by a majority of the children and the democratic leader was liked (even if it was the same person playing the autocratic and democratic leadership roles). Generally, the autocratic leader created an atmosphere that was repressive, restrictive, rigid, and unpleasant. This atmosphere led to high levels of tension among the children, resulting in aggression and low levels of productivity when the autocratic leader was absent.

Under the democratic leadership style, the children were the most productive. Even when the democratic leader was late or left the room, the children engaged in task-relevant behavior. In contrast, children under the autocratic leader showed high levels of productivity only when the leader was present (Lippitt & White, 1965).

MAZE-BRIGHT AND MAZE-DULL RATS

On April 20, 1999, Eric Harris and Dylan Klebold entered Columbine High School in Littleton, Colorado and killed 12 of their fellow students and one teacher. In the aftermath of the tragedy it was natural that people offered speculations about why Harris and Klebold would commit such a crime. Were they "bad seeds" like the character Rhoda Penmark in the classic film *The Bad Seed*, genetically programmed to commit murder? Or were they products of their environment, driven to murder by circumstances? These questions go to the heart of a controversy that is older than the science of psychology: nature versus nurture.

When Richard Mulcaster (1582), musing over the contributions of nature and nurture to human abilities, wrote, "whereto nature makes him toward, but that nurture sets him forward" (p. 35), he could not have envisioned the controversy that would ensue. Embodied in Mulcaster's statement is the idea that nature puts us on a certain growth and development path, but it is nurture that sets the course. Over 300 years later, Sir Francis Galton (1875) would be among the first to attempt to "weigh in just scales the effects of Nature and Nurture" (p. 155) by studying the similarities and differences between twins.

In modern psychology, the study of the nature-nurture issue has fallen to behavior geneticists. These scientists try to determine the relative contributions of nature and nurture to a variety of psychological processes (e.g., intelligence and schizophrenia). Selective breeding studies are one of the major lines of research attempting to sort out the relative contributions of nature and nurture.

Robert C. Tryon (1942) conducted one of the seminal selective breeding studies. Tryon selected a random sample of rats from a heterogeneous colony and ran the rats in two complex T-mazes with 17 and 20 blind alleys, respectively. Correctly running the maze resulted in a food reward. Based on their performance, Tryon divided the rates into two groups: bright and dull. He then bred bright rats with other bright rats and dull rats with other dull rats producing "maze bright" and "maze dull" offspring. Tryon continued breeding maze-bright and maze-dull rats over several generations. Each generation of rats was tested in the complex mazes and number of errors (blind alleys entered) was recorded.

Tryon found that selective breeding over eight generations produced progressively large differences between the maze-bright and maze-dull rats. The first generation of maze-bright and maze-dull rats did not differ in their maze learning ability. However, by the second and third generations, Tryon observed significant separation between the maze-bright and maze-dull rats, with the dull rats becoming more and more poor at running the maze. By the eighth generation, there was almost complete separation between the bright and dull rats in their performance in the maze.

Tryon also reported on studies relating to the issue of whether the differences between the maze-bright and the maze-dull rats were due to a specific learning ability or to a general learning ability (i.e., "intelligence") that would apply in a variety of learning situations. He concluded that the superior performance of the maze-bright rats was *not* the result of an increase in general learning ability: "there is no such fact as *general* learning ability, but rather there are *numerous learning abilities*" (p. 236). Indeed, later studies showed that most of the differences between the two groups could be accounted for by differences in sensitivity or responsiveness to food — particularly food as a reward — and had little to do with the common notion of intelligence.

Tryon's results suggest that biological factors do play a role in the learning process. They also bear on the age-old controversy surrounding the relative contributions of nature and nurture. For the better part of the 20th century, psychologists favored nurture explanations for individual differences. Toward the end of the century, some psychologists (e.g., behavior geneticists and evolutionary psychologists) began making the case that nature played a greater role than previously acknowledged.

PING-PONG GOGGLES CAUSE MENTAL PROBLEMS

In the aftermath of the September 11, 2001 attacks within the United States, the question of how best to gather quality intelligence to help prevent future attacks has concerned everyone. One source of such intelligence is the interrogation of terror suspects or enemy combatants. Interrogators apply a variety of techniques designed to extract information that can be used to prevent future attacks, including physical and sensory isolation.

In fact, *Kubark* (1963), the recently declassified interrogation manual used by the CIA, lists "deprivation of sensory stimuli" among the interrogation techniques that can be used to obtain intelligence information. The section on sensory deprivation explains, "The chief effect of arrest and detention, and particularly of solitary confinement, is to deprive the subject of many or most of the sights, sounds, tastes, smells, and tactile sensations to which he has grown accustomed" (p. 86). The net effect, according to the manual, is to put the target under stress and create significant levels of anxiety. A skilled interrogator can use this anxiety by providing human contact and reducing the target's anxiety. Anxiety reduction is rewarding to the target and the interrogator becomes positively associated with those rewards.

A key assumption underlying the use of sensory deprivation as an interrogation technique is that it is aversive and alters the way the person being interrogated thinks about and perceives the world. Is this the case? Fortunately, psychology has provided an answer to this question.

Leo Goldberger and Robert Holt (1961) conducted a now-classic experiment on the effects of sensory deprivation. They subjected 14 male college students to a sensory deprivation procedure. Participants wore ping-pong balls (cut in half) over their eyes and experienced a constant flow of white noise to mask any auditory stimulation. The researchers subjected participants to this treatment for an entire day and instructed them to report on their feelings anytime they wished.

Goldberger and Holt's participants reported "a general feeling of decreased efficiency, and lack of continuity in thought; affective disturbances ... disturbances in time sense and miscellaneous other effects ... including depersonalization, body image disturbances, and creative activity" (pp. 136-137). The disturbances were so severe that 3 of 14 participants quit the experiment between 50 minutes and 3.5 hours into it! Not all participants reacted in the same way. Some participants handled the deprivation better than others and adapted to the deprivation.

Heron (1961) had male college students lie on a comfortable bed, 24 hours per day, for as long as they could — usually 2 to 3 days. While in bed, participants wore light-diffusing goggles and cotton gloves (to reduce tactile stimulation) and had auditory stimulation masked by the noise made by an air conditioner. In an interesting twist, Heron subjected participants to "propaganda" material during the period of isolation. The propaganda advocated the existence of various psychic phenomena. Heron gave participants a variety of tests, including items from an intelligence test and other tests of cognitive functioning, before, during, and after the isolation period. Attitude questionnaires concerning the topic of the propaganda were given before and after the period of isolation. What made Heron's experiment particularly compelling is that he had a control group that was not isolated, but was also exposed to the propaganda, take the same tests as the isolated participants.

Heron found that the isolated participants did significantly poorer than control participants on six of seven cognitive tests. Isolated participants were also more susceptible to the propaganda manipulation. Although both groups showed some attitude change in the direction advocated in the propaganda material, the isolated participants showed a larger effect. Heron also found that 25 of the 29 isolates reported visual hallucinations.

How did the isolates respond mentally to their isolation? Heron reported that participants moved from mental activity involving organized thought (e.g., reviewing work) to an inability to think of anything. Participants reported that it became increasingly difficult to concentrate on anything meaningful, because of boredom, and that "blank periods," during which no thoughts occurred, became more and more frequent. Some participants even reported having a hard time telling when they were awake or asleep!

These two experiments confirmed the assumptions made in the *Kubark*: Sensory deprivation disorients individuals and creates a mental state that may be conducive to the interrogation process. Whether these techniques amount to torture, as some allege, is debatable. What is not open to debate, however, is the knowledge that sensory deprivation is a highly aversive state that takes its toll very quickly.

IMPLICATIONS FOR STUDENTS AND TEACHERS

We have presented examples of several classic studies that you can use in your introductory psychology classes. Of course, there are scores of other studies, favorites from the past that are seldom talked about anymore. Please make no mistake: Overlooking interesting, valuable, instructive research from the past is not just a phenomenon of the introductory course. Classic studies in mental hygiene (*there's a term you don't see anymore*), biological bases of behavior, I/O psychology, sensation and perception, learning, memory, and cognition often are overlooked. Whatever happened to *transfer of training* as studied by Woodworth or Osgood, for example? Are these concepts no longer useful? Has something better come along to describe, explain, and predict behavior?

One of the great joys of teaching a course on the history of psychology (which we both do) is watching students — who usually enroll in the class reluctantly at best — come to the realization that "everything old is new again." Fearful that all they will hear about is ancient dead men — and perchance a few women — students soon come to realize the timelessness of psychology's earlier efforts to study behavior and mental processes using scientific methods. Appreciative of the reality that time is short when trying to cover the breadth of general psychology in but 16 weeks or so, we nonetheless make the appeal to look beyond the headlines and the most recent journal articles.

Consider this chapter our way of urging you to bring some of your own favorites back into your teaching of psychology. Your students will undoubtedly find them interesting and find their curiosity sparked — not only about classic research, but also the history of the field. They may come to appreciate the stepwise fashion in which most progress occurs in science. A major insight that we would like students to develop is the notion that (constant marketing efforts to the contrary notwithstanding) newer is not necessarily better. Perhaps the most important implication for students in any of our classes is that what they are getting from us and from our textbooks is but a sample of the content to which they could be exposed, given more time. When James wrote his two-volume *Principles*, he could pretty much cover all there was to know about psychology in 1890. To even pretend to do the same thing now would be hopeless, and that reality should be shared with our students in the classes we teach.

REFERENCES

Cannon, W. B. (1934). Hunger and thirst. In Murchison, C. (Ed.), *Handbook of experimental psychology* (pp. 247-263). Worcester, MA: Clark University Press.

Freud, A., & Burlingham, D. T. (1943). *War and children*. New York: Medical War Books.

Galton, F. (1875). History of twins. Retrieved July 21, 2004, from http://psychclassics.yorku.ca/Galton/twins.htm

Goldberger, L., & Holt, R. R. (1961). Experimental interference with reality contact: Individual differences. In P. Solomon, P. E. Kubzansky, P. H., Leiderman, J. H. Mendelsen, R. Trumbull, & D. Wexler (Eds.), *Sensory deprivation* (pp. 130-142). Cambridge, MA: Harvard University Press.

Harlow, H. F. (1958). The nature of love. *American psychologist, 13*, 673-685.

Heron, W. (1961). Cognitive and physiological effects of perceptual isolation. In P. Solomon, P. E. Kubzansky, P. H. Leiderman, J. H. Mendelsen, R. Trumbull, & D. Wexler (Eds.), *Sensory deprivation* (pp. 6-33). Cambridge, MA: Harvard University Press.

Hess, E. H. (1958). "Imprinting" in animals. *Scientific American, 198*, 81-90.

Hoelzel, F. (1927). Central factors in hunger. *American Journal of Physiology, 82*, 665-671.

James, W. (1920). *Letters of William James, Vol. I*. Boston: Atlantic Monthly Press.

James, W. (1890). *The principles of psychology*. New York: Henry Holt and Company.

Kubark: Counterintelligence interrogation (1963). Retrieved July 25, 2004, from http://www.mindcontrolforums.com/kubark.htm#I

Lavater, J. C. (1789). *Essays on physiognomy: For the promotion of knowledge and the love of mankind*. London: G.G.J. and J. Robinson.

Lewin, K., Lippitt, R., & White, R. K. (1939). Patterns of aggressive behavior in experimentally created "social climates." *Journal of Social Psychology, 10*, 271-299.

Lippitt, R., & White, R. K. (1965). An experimental study of leadership and group life. In H. Proshansky and B. Seidenberg (Eds.), *Basic studies in social psychology* (pp. 523-537). New York: Holt, Rinehart and Winston.

McCall, J. (2004). Research on the psychological effects of orphanage care: A critical review. Retrieved July 24, 2004, from http://www.gsm.uci.edu/~mckenzie/rethink/mck97-ch8.htm

Mulcaster, R. (1582). *Mulcaster's "Elementarie": Electronic edition*. Retrieved July 21, 2004, from http://www.hti.umich.edu/cgi/p/pd-modeng/pd-modeng-idx?type=HTML&rgn=TEI.2&byte=51422083

Munn, N. L., Fernald, L. D., & Fernald, P. S. (1974). *Introduction to psychology* (3rd ed.). Boston: Houghton Mifflin.

Philbrick, N. (2000). *In the heart of the sea: The tragedy of the whaleship Essex*. New York: Penguin Books.

Ruch, F. L. (1937). *Psychology and life*. New York: Scott Foresman.

Sheldon, W. H. (1954). *Atlas of men: A guide for somatotyping the adult male of all ages*. New York: Harper.

Spaulding, D. A. (1873). Instinct: With original observations on young animals. *McMillans Magazine, 27*, 282-293.

Tryon, R. C. (1942). Individual differences. In F. A. Moss (Ed.). *Comparative psychology: Revised edition* (pp. 330-365). Englewood Cliffs, NJ: Prentice Hall.

Tyler, L.E. (1956). *The psychology of human differences* (2nd ed.). New York: Appleton-Century-Crofts.

Weiten, W., & Wright, R. D. (1992). Portraits of a discipline: An examination of introductory psychology textbooks in America. In A. E. Puente, J. R. Matthews, & C. L. Brewer (Eds.), *Teaching psychology in America: A history* (pp.453-504). Washington, DC: American Psychological Association.

CROSS-CULTURAL PERSPECTIVES IN THE PSYCHOLOGY CURRICULUM

Moving Beyond "Add Culture and Stir"

Susan B. Goldstein

University of Redlands

Ultimately if the curriculum is centered in truth, it will be pluralistic.
— Hilliard (1991/1992, p. 13)

TWO DECADES AGO, scholars first identified cross-cultural psychology as a key resource for addressing a lack of cultural diversity in the psychology curriculum (e.g., Torney-Purta, 1984; Triandis & Brislin, 1984). In the years since, two main strategies for utilizing this resource have emerged. The first and most common approach has been to develop separate multicultural psychology courses or courses focused on the experiences of specific social groups (e.g., African American Psychology; Gloria, Rieckmann, & Rush, 2000). Although it has yielded a wide variety of innovative and valuable courses, this approach has done little to make the psychology curriculum as a whole more inclusive. A second, more recent strategy involves attempting to integrate diverse perspectives throughout the psychology curriculum. Yet such efforts tend to be superficial in terms of content, and they generally fail to address the culture-bound nature of psychology as a discipline or the pedagogical implications of an integrated curriculum, such as the need to facilitate inclusivity and minimize stereotyping. This latter approach, perhaps best described as "add culture and stir,"[1] may even fuel prejudices and silence diverse student perspectives (Goldstein, 1995).

The urgency of recent curriculum-transformation[2] efforts stems in part from significant changes in student demographics. With greater diversity on college

---

[1] Bohan (1992, p. 10) used the term "add women and stir" to refer to superficial attempts to integrate the contributions and experiences of women into historical accounts.

[2] The terms curriculum integration and curriculum transformation are used across disciplines to refer to efforts to produce course content and pedagogy that are more inclusive of traditionally marginalized groups.

campuses, much of the material taught in psychology courses has been criticized as being irrelevant to the student population (Guzman, Schiavo, & Puente, 1992; Hall, 1997; Levine & Cureton, 1998; Puente et al., 1993). But in addition, curriculum-transformation advocates recognize that all students require a multicultural education to prepare them for citizenship in an increasingly diverse and global society. Without integrating cultural perspectives into the psychology curriculum, students are given a view of human behavior that is incomplete and inaccurate.

Lonner (2003, p. 169) described the psychology taught in the United States as "culture bound" and "culture blind." It is culture bound in that it disregards research conducted outside of the United States or other primarily English-speaking countries (Sexton & Hogan, 1992), and it is culture blind in that it assumes its limited view of psychological processes to be universal (Mays, Rubin, Sabourin, & Walker, 1996). This form of psychology overemphasizes behavior and cognition rooted in individualist values (Hull, 2001), presents individual behavior patterns as isolated from the sociocultural context (Cole, 1996; Dunn, 2004), and underemphasizes the potential application of international perspectives to domestic problems (Mays et al., 1996). Hall (1997) has argued that if psychology as a discipline fails to make significant changes in terms of addressing cultural diversity, it risks obsolescence in its teaching, research, and practice.

In psychology there is a growing awareness that the existing body of literature in the field is limited and flawed in its understanding and representation of human experience (Enns, 1994). A recent survey of teaching psychologists indicated that, while some still viewed diversity as irrelevant to their courses, most were interested in moving toward a more integrated curriculum, prompting the authors to write, "the field has clearly moved from asking whether to asking how to incorporate issues of diversity into the psychology classroom" (Simoni, Sexton-Radek, Yescavage, Richard, & Lundquist, 1999, p. 94).

Those teachers who do not actively seek to include a cross-cultural dimension in their courses are increasingly likely to find such issues addressed in their textbooks (Cush & Buskist, 1997). Many recently published introductory psychology texts, for example, have been advertised as including a significant cross-cultural or diversity component. In addition, this past decade has seen the publication of several articles (e.g., Kowalski, 2000; Ocampo et al., 2003) and books (e.g., Bronstein & Quina, 1988, 2003; Davis-Russell, 2002; Enns & Sinacore, 2004) that provide guidance on addressing issues of diversity across the psychology curriculum.

Psychology teachers may find efforts to transform their curricula daunting. It is likely that most psychology faculty have received little training in issues of diversity and have only experienced Eurocentric models of curriculum design themselves. They may feel unqualified to locate or evaluate diversity-related resources or to handle the changes in classroom dynamics that often accompany discussions of diversity. Finally, in an already compressed semester, teachers of psychology may wonder how they can find the time to treat diversity issues and still meet their existing curricular goals without moving cultural perspectives into the margins of their courses. This chapter provides strategies that deal with (a) identifying sources on culture and human behavior; (b) avoiding the marginalization of cross-cultural perspectives; (c) identifying bias within the cross-cultural literature; and (d) creating a classroom environment conducive to exploring issues of diversity.

It should be noted at the outset that culture is but one dimension of a multicultural psychology curriculum. In fact, "sexual identity, socioeconomic level, physical and mental (dis)abilities, size, age, and religion, to name a few, are now being incorporated into contemporary multicultural definitions" (Quina & Bronstein, 2003, p. 4). These dimensions should not be viewed in isolation; they are interconnected aspects of identity and human experience. Although the focus of this chapter is cross-cultural perspectives, the strategies outlined here can and should be applied to the full spectrum of multicultural curriculum transformation.

IDENTIFYING SOURCES FOR CROSS-CULTURAL PERSPECTIVES

During the past decade, research on culture and cross-cultural differences has proliferated in such areas as motivation, emotion, perception, cognition, human development, and interpersonal processes (Lehman, Chiu, & Schaller, 2004). These studies fall under the disciplinary heading of cross-cultural psychology as well as a variety of related fields, including cultural psychology, indigenous psychology, ethnic psychology, and psychological anthropology. These areas serve as key sources for teachers seeking to bring diverse cultural perspectives to their psychology courses.

Cross-Cultural Psychology

Cross-cultural psychology focuses on comparing specific behaviors across cultures. For example, González, Moreno, and Schneider (2004) examined differences between Cuban and Canadian adolescents in expectations of friendship ties. Cross-cultural psychologists work within a wide variety of research areas including social, developmental, cognitive, clinical, and organizational psychology, with the ultimate goal of identifying universal principles of human behavior. For the most part, cross-cultural psychology is not characterized by a distinct content area, but by the specific methods used to make equivalent comparisons across cultures.

Cultural Psychology

Cultural psychology focuses on detailing the interrelationships among forms of behavior within a specific culture and is generally less concerned with cross-cultural comparisons or the use of quantitative research methods. Ye (2004), for example, conducted a culture-specific case study of Chinese linguistic representations of facial expressions.

Indigenous Psychology

The indigenous-psychologies approach utilizes concepts and methods that arise from within the culture of interest (Kim & Berry, 1993). Enriquez (1997), for example, described a form of indigenous psychology in the Philippines that has arisen from the colonial history of that nation. Yang (2000), suggested that cross-cultural and cultural psychology could be best conceptualized as forms of indigenous psychology provided that appropriate measures are taken to assure congruity of the researcher's theory, methods, and results with the sociocultural context.

Ethnic Psychology

Ethnic psychology is concerned with the use of culturally appropriate methods to understand the behavior and experiences of members of specific ethnic groups, focusing primarily on historically marginalized groups in North America. For example, Bowleg, Craig, and Burkholder (2004) tested a conceptual model of active coping among middle-class Black lesbians to assess the extent to which specific individual and environmental factors predicted psychosocial competence. Recently, cross-cultural psychologists have begun to conceptualize culture more broadly to include studies previously categorized as "ethnic minority research."

Psychological Anthropology

Psychological anthropology involves anthropological studies that make explicit and systematic use of psychological methods and concepts (Bock, 1995). Rabain-Jamin, Maynard, & Greenfield (2003), for example, analyzed ethnographic video data to examine the social and cognitive implications of sibling caregiving for cultural transmission among the Zinacantec Maya of Mexico and the Wolof of Senegal.

These areas of inquiry collectively provide research that serves to (a) identify culture-specific values, experiences, cognitive categories, and forms of behavior; (b) unconfound variables that are linked in one culture but may be unrelated in another culture; (c) expand the range of variables beyond those existing in any specific culture; (d) detail relationships between ecological and psychological variables; (e) identify human universals; (f) test the generality of psychological models or theories; (g) study the effects of cultural change; and (h) identify processes involved in effective intercultural interaction. Due to the wide variety of approaches to culture and human behavior, not only will teachers need to take a more interdisciplinary approach to developing their curricula, but students must also be given greater freedom in seeking resources for projects and assignments. Although teachers may wish to set criteria for selecting sources (for example, limiting articles to those published in peer-reviewed journals), if psychology as a discipline has been limited in cultural inclusivity, then it makes no sense to require that students refer only to the traditional works in the field. A list of specific journals, texts, reference materials, activity/simulation books, and Web sites on culture and psychology appears at the end of this chapter.

AVOIDING THE MARGINALIZATION OF CROSS-CULTURAL PERSPECTIVES

McIntosh (1983) outlined five phases of curriculum "re-vision" based on an analysis of history curricula. These phases provide a useful framework for assessing curriculum-transformation efforts and avoiding the marginalization of cross-cultural perspectives in psychology courses. Although the focus of the present discussion is culture, McIntosh's model may also be used to explore the exclusion of women and other groups historically underrepresented in the psychology curriculum.

In McIntosh's first phase, cultural diversity is virtually absent and its absence goes unacknowledged. In the second phase, culture is discussed in conjunction with a few well-known individuals or cases — such as Kenneth and Mamie Clark's (1939, 1947, 1950) doll studies of children's racial identification

— but does not challenge traditional notions of what constitutes psychology. The third phase of curriculum revision characterizes the current use of cross-cultural research by teachers of psychology. In this add-culture-and-stir phase, diversity enters our courses in the form of isolated issues, typically involving the portrayal of individuals or groups as problems or aberrations.

In this third phase, marginalization of cultural diversity is manifested not only in terms of course content, but also by the structure of the course and its placement within the psychology curriculum. Information on culture that appears only in supplementary materials, in the "boxes" of primary texts, or in a separate diversity chapter, may lead students to conclude that culture is not central to an understanding of human behavior and that members of various cultural groups are exotic "others" to be contrasted with what is portrayed as typical or normal. Exam questions, class discussions, and key assignments that exclude cultural factors also reinforce this message of marginality. Cultural perspectives are further devalued when departments fail to require courses addressing culture or fail to assign them a regular course number, list them in the course catalog, schedule them regularly, or include them in the criteria for evaluating student and instructor performance.

McIntosh's fourth phase requires that psychologists and students question the universality of psychological thought and produce a body of literature that is more inclusive and accurate. There would be no need for a separate cross-cultural psychology course or cross-cultural units in other psychology courses when all courses fully integrate a cultural dimension into various content areas.

Reaching the fifth phase would require the redefinition of psychology as a discipline, including a restructuring of psychology's topics and methods of inquiry. To move toward Phase 5, it is helpful to take a functional equivalence perspective in curriculum design. According to Pareek and Rao (1980), "functional equivalence of a behaviour exists when the behaviour in question has developed in response to a problem shared by two or more social/cultural groups, even though the behaviour in one society may be superficially quite different from the behavior in another society" (p.131). For example, in the introductory course, material on therapy is typically limited to major mental-health treatment approaches that have been, or are currently, in use in North America and Europe. An alternative strategy focuses on therapy's *function* as a process that reduces psychological difficulty and facilitates adjustment. This latter strategy moves us toward the global perspective of Phase 5 in which such treatments as *Curanderismo* or Shamanism are included along with discussions of cognitive therapy or systematic desensitization. By examining our courses through McIntosh's framework, we can begin to reduce marginalization and more fully address the diversity of human behavior.

IDENTIFYING BIAS WITHIN CROSS-CULTURAL LITERATURE

In many respects, cross-cultural psychology is an ideal resource for curriculum transformation. The field is full of publications that advocate and provide guidance on fostering intercultural competence. Furthermore, intercultural competence is a requirement for conducting cross-cultural research, in that the main focus of its methodology is to achieve equivalence between cultures studied in terms of the functions of phenomena of interest, instrumentation and procedures employed, and the interpretation of data. Yet, as Triandis (1994) observed, cross-cultural psychology has not escaped the ethnocentric and androcentric biases that have shaped psychology as a whole. Persons of European ancestry generally determine the standard from which cross-cultural comparisons are made, and North Americans of color are virtually invisible in cross-cultural psychology. In addition, cross-cultural research on women has tended to focus on traditionally female domains and is often excluded from key cross-cultural publications. For example, the vast majority of cross-cultural research on parenting investigates only mothers' behavior. Other forms of bias, such as heterosexism, ageism, classism, and ableism also characterize the cross-cultural literature, often taking the form of omissions or invalid assumptions about the characteristics of research participants. Ironically, ethnocentrism is a significant concern in the cross-cultural literature and is manifested in a variety of ways, including *emics* (culture-specific constructs) imposed as though they are *etics* (universal), ethnocentric standards of comparison, and failure to recognize within-group diversity.

Emics Imposed as Etic

The emic-etic distinction is a useful framework for exploring ethnocentrism in course content. Pike (1954) first used these words to describe approaches to the study of language and culture. The term *emic* is derived from phonemics (the study of phonemes, sound distinctions meaningful in a particular language) and is used to describe culture-specific constructs. The term *etic* is derived from phonetics (a general system that can be used to classify any body of language behavior) and is used to describe phenomena that are universal across cultures. In cross-cultural psychology, and psychology in general, we often find emic concepts imposed as if they are etic (Berry, 1969). Although cross-cultural research has challenged the universality of many imposed etics, including the concepts of *self* (Markus & Kitayama, 1991) and *intelligence* (e.g., Azuma & Kashiwagi, 1987; Romero, 1994), this tendency to treat the culture-specific as universal remains. It is not unusual to find studies originating in North America or Europe that are replicated outside of these regions without modifying the concepts studied or research instruments to make them cross-culturally applicable. It is useful to discuss explicitly the emic-etic distinction with students and provide them with opportunities to practice identifying emic phenomena (such as *secure attachment, fundamental attribution error*, and *social loafing*) that have been imposed as etic.[3]

Ethnocentric Standards of Comparison

Besides being able to identify emics imposed as etic, teachers striving for a more culturally inclusive curriculum must also be able to identify and avoid ethnocentric standards of comparison. For example, when cultural differences are viewed through a *Western/Nonwestern* lens, the message conveyed is that what is Western is central — and thus the standard of comparison — and that all other cultures are less significant and less distinctive. A similar bias is produced by the *White/Nonwhite* dichotomy. To avoid ethnocentric standards of comparison,

---

[3] In fact, it has been suggested (Triandis, 1997) that psychology as it is taught in most English speaking nations might be more accurately termed "Western Indigenous Psychology" so as to recognize its emic nature.

cross-cultural phenomena may be discussed in terms of the specific cultural groups involved (e.g., European American, and Japanese) or the relevant variables underlying the comparison (e.g., individualism and collectivism).

Ethnocentric standards of comparison are also implied when unnecessary distinctions are drawn between functionally equivalent objects or phenomena. For example, Moore (1988) pointed out that the homes of African people are often needlessly referred to as *huts,* and that the word *tribe*, although frequently used to identify diverse peoples within African nations, is rarely used to refer to diverse peoples within European nations. Students and teachers can work together to determine whether such language contributes to describing relevant cross-cultural differences, or if it only serves to promote ethnocentrism.

Failure to Acknowledge Within-Group Diversity

As research on the out-group homogeneity effect (Judd & Park, 1988) would predict, the focus on between-group differences in cross-cultural psychology is associated with a tendency to underestimate the similarities between groups (Brouwers, van Hemert, Breugelmans, & van de Vijver, 2004) and to ignore the variability within groups. One way that cross-cultural research has ignored or minimized within-group diversity is the tendency to equate nationality with culture in selecting research participants. Data gathered from small, typically more highly educated, samples from a specific country are often presented as representing the culture as a whole. In addition, findings about these research participants may then be generalized to discussions of entire ethnic groups or geographical regions. Studies of Taiwanese or Malaysian participants, for example, should not be presented as describing "Asian behavior." Similarly, data collected from predominantly white, North American college populations do not provide an appropriate basis for conclusions about "Western values" or "American behavior."

A more extreme failure to acknowledge within-group diversity occurs when findings from one country are generalized to an entire region or group of regions based on presumed cultural similarities. For example, Matsumoto (1999) found that information on self-construal from small samples in a few countries (primarily in East Asia) was generalized to the regions of Asia, Africa, and South America. Once teachers and students develop the ability to identify emics imposed as etics, ethnocentric standards of comparison, and the tendency to minimize within-group diversity, they can more effectively work together as agents of curriculum transformation.

CREATING A CLASSROOM ENVIRONMENT CONDUCIVE TO EXPLORING ISSUES OF DIVERSITY

As teachers work toward greater cultural inclusivity in their courses, they may find that modifying course content is but one component of the curriculum-transformation process. Creating a classroom environment conducive to exploring issues of diversity involves attending to a wide range of factors, including the nature of readings and examples used, the requirements of outside activities, the cost of books and materials, as well as the instructor's pedagogical style.

A significant challenge in teaching multicultural course material is discussing cultural differences without creating or reinforcing stereotypes. Bronstein and

Quina (1988) stated that the risk of creating stereotypes is particularly high when people are labeled on the basis of a single dimension and placed in opposition to other labeled groups for the purpose of comparison. This is precisely the format in which cross-cultural findings are typically presented. Tatum (1992) recommended establishing clear guidelines for discussion in order to create a classroom in which students feel comfortable acting as full participants. These include maintaining confidentiality, refraining from blatant or subtle put-downs, and speaking in terms of personal experiences rather than generalizations. Students may more readily comply with such guidelines if they play a role in their formulation.

In addition to setting clear ground rules for discussion, stereotypes may be inhibited by specifying the characteristics of research participants in cross-cultural comparisons. Betancourt and Lopez (1993), for example, noted the frequency with which culture, race, and ethnicity are confounded with socioeconomic variables. By focusing on demographic characteristics (e.g., social class and gender) of comparison groups, within-group diversity is emphasized and the likelihood that stereotyped conclusions will be drawn about an entire culture decreases.

An additional strategy for minimizing the tendency to stereotype is to familiarize students with the cognitive processes involved in the formation and maintenance of stereotypes (see, for example, Macrae, Stangor, & Hewstone, 1996; Schneider, 2003). Once students view stereotyping as a result of errors in information processing, they are better able to discuss stereotypic comments without making personal attacks. It is sometimes useful to have students practice analyzing stereotypes that are expressed in films, published narratives, or Web pages by identifying the errors involved in attention, categorization, memory, and attributional processes that may be the source of a stereotype, and discuss the types of information that would be required to disconfirm these stereotypes. Stewart's (2001) classroom activity, for example, required students to examine the psychological bases for a series of commonly stated beliefs about prejudice and stereotyping (e.g., "I am colorblind to race."). By initially obtaining views about cultural differences from outside the class, teachers also can minimize the likelihood that students will be placed in the uncomfortable and unjust position of representing an entire cultural or ethnic group.

Creating a classroom environment conducive to exploring issues of diversity involves consideration of not only the subject matter and classroom dynamics, but student characteristics as well. Students' cultural background has a significant impact on classroom-related behavior and, thus, participation. For example, a classroom environment in which students need to be aggressive or interrupt the instructor or other students in order to participate may systematically disadvantage those students whose cultures do not encourage such behavior. Other culturally patterned behaviors relevant to the classroom setting include ease with expressing personal feelings (Lynch, 1997), comfort in group activities (Chan, 2003), and language-related behaviors such as dialect, conversation pace, and turn taking (Lynch, 1997). Allowing students a range of participation options may result in greater inclusion of diverse student voices.

Diversity can also be valued by acknowledging that the campus and classroom are themselves characterized by a specific culture with which many students may be unfamiliar. Successful cross-cultural adjustment is facilitated by enlisting the aid of cultural insiders who can explain the implicit rules for behavior in that culture (Ward, Bochner, & Furnham, 2001). In working with those college students for whom the campus and classroom environments represent unfamiliar cultures, teachers may serve as cultural insiders. Rather than misattribute difficulties in this setting to personal deficiencies, teachers can help students gain specific cultural knowledge such as how to read a syllabus, lead a discussion, or use library databases. Although this focus on "cross-cultural training" of students does not do away with the need to make the curriculum more inclusive, it may help to bring previously silenced voices into the psychology classroom.

With recent efforts to transform curricula has come a need to systematically evaluate these efforts and their effect on students and faculty (Beaudry & Davis, 1997; Ocampo et al., 2003). One component of such evaluations might be the use of nonpublic mechanisms for reacting to course materials and discussions (e.g., written comments, journal entries, anonymous surveys) to monitor the degree to which students feel that the classroom environment is conducive to exploring issues of diversity.

IMPLICATIONS FOR TEACHERS AND STUDENTS

The experience of curriculum transformation and the accompanying search for interdisciplinary resources provides teachers of psychology with a unique opportunity to reexamine their own perspectives and biases (Kitano, 1997). Teachers may emerge from this process with a more innovative pedagogical style, as they find that interactive teaching strategies help students engage with ambiguous or emotionally charged issues (Gloria, Rieckmann, & Rush, 2000). Teachers also may incorporate innovative pedagogy out of the need to find time in their courses to address diverse perspectives. Although cross-cultural perspectives should not be relegated to the margins, these perspectives can enter our courses in a variety of ways besides core lecture or text — such as lecture examples, outside assignments, student research papers, journals, interviews, films, community involvement, jigsaw readings (a cooperative learning strategy in which each student learns about a specific section of the assigned readings and then shares this knowledge with other students who have become experts on different sections; Aronson, Blaney, Stephan, Sikes, & Snapp, 1978), and electronic discussion boards. Ultimately, faculty should be reassured that, as Matsumoto (interviewed in Hill, 2000, p.72) suggested, "it is more important that the instructor teach students how to think critically about cultural differences and cultural influences on human behavior in general, rather than to learn as much as you can about any specific cultural group."

For students, involvement in curriculum transformation may at first cause some anxiety and perhaps resistance as they realize that these new perspectives challenge the universality of material in other courses they are taking or have taken. But if teachers give students the skills and resources to become partners in the curriculum transformation process, they may soon embrace the role of change agent and have an impact on other psychology courses and courses across the curriculum. One method of explicitly training students in curriculum transformation is to familiarize them with the concepts of imposed etics and functional equivalence and then have them rewrite a portion of a text to make it more inclusive of diverse perspectives (Goldstein, 2000).

Curriculum transformation is an ongoing process based on the evolving perspectives of both the individual teacher and the discipline. By becoming familiar with the content and methods of cross-cultural research and incorporating these perspectives into their curricula and pedagogy, teachers of psychology can work toward a discipline that speaks to and from the diversity of human experience.

REFERENCES

Aronson, E., Blaney, N., Stephan, C., Sikes, J., & Snapp, M. (1978). *The jigsaw classroom*. Beverly Hills, CA: Sage.

Azuma, H., & Kashiwagi, K. (1987). Descriptors for an intelligent person: A Japanese study. *Japanese Psychological Research, 29*, 17-26.

Beaudry, J. S., & Davis, J. E. (1997). Evaluating the results of multicultural education: Taking the long way home. In A. I. Morey & M. K. Kitano (Eds.), *Multicultural course transformation in higher education: A broader truth* (pp. 242-257). Boston: Allyn & Bacon.

Berry, J. (1969). On cross-cultural comparability. *International Journal of Psychology, 4*, 119-128.

Betancourt, H., & Lopez, S.R. (1993). The study of culture, ethnicity, and race in American psychology. *American Psychologist, 48*, 629-637.

Bock, P. K. (1995). *Rethinking psychological anthropology: Continuity and change in the study of human action*. Prospect Heights, IL: Waveland Press.

Bohan, J. S. (Ed.). (1992). *Seldom seen, rarely heard: Women's place in psychology*. Boulder, CO: Westview.

Bowleg, L., Craig, M. L., & Burkholder, G. (2004). Rising and surviving: A conceptual model of active coping among Black lesbians. *Cultural Diversity & Ethnic Minority Psychology, 10,* 229-240.

Bronstein, P., & Quina, K. (Eds.). (1988; 2003). *Teaching a psychology of people: Resources for gender and sociocultural awareness*. Washington, DC: American Psychological Association.

Brouwers, S. A., van Hemert, D. A., Breugelmans, S. M., & van de Vijver, F. J. R . (2004). A historical analysis of empirical studies published in the *Journal of Cross-cultural Psychology*: 1970-2004. *Journal of Cross-cultural Psychology, 35*, 251-262.

Chan, C. S. (2003). Psychological issues of Asian Americans. In P. Bronstein & K. Quina (Eds.), *Teaching a psychology of people: Resources for gender and sociocultural awareness* (pp. 179-193). Washington, DC: American Psychological Association.

Clark, K. B., & Clark, M. P. (1939). The development of consciousness of self and the emergence of racial identification in Negro preschool children. *Journal of Social Psychology, 10*, 591-599.

Clark, K. B., & Clark, M. P. (1947). Racial identification and preference in Negro children. In T.M. Newcomb & E.L. Hartley (Eds.), *Readings in social psychology* (pp. 169-178). New York: Holt.

Clark, K. B., & Clark, M. P. (1950). Emotional factors in racial identification and preference in Negro children. *Journal of Negro Education, 19*, 341-350.

Cole, M. (1996). *Cultural psychology: A once and future discipline*. Cambridge, MA: Harvard University Press.

Cush, D. T., & Buskist, W. (1997). Future of the introductory psychology textbook: A survey of college publishers. *Teaching of Psychology, 24*, 119-122.

Davis-Russell, E. (Ed.). (2002). *California School of Professional Psychology handbook of multicultural education, research, intervention, and training*. San Francisco: Jossey-Bass.

Dunn, D. S. (2004). Teaching about the origins of behavior: A course on evolutionary and cultural psychology. *Teaching of Psychology, 31*, 126-127.

Enns, C. Z. (1994). On teaching about the cultural relativism of psychological constructs. *Teaching of Psychology, 21*, 205-211.

Enns, C., & Sinacore, A. (2004). *Teaching and social justice: Integrating multicultural and feminist theories in the classroom*. Boston: Allyn & Bacon.

Enriquez, V. (1997). Filipino psychology: Concepts and methods. In H. S. R. Kao & D. Sinha (Eds.), *Asian perspectives on psychology* (pp. 40-53). Thousand Oaks, CA: Sage.

Gloria, S. M., Rieckmann, T. R., & Rush, J. D. (2000). Issues and recommendations for teaching an ethnic/culture-based course. *Teaching of Psychology, 27*, 102-107.

Goldstein, S. B. (1995). Cross-cultural psychology as a curriculum transformation resource. *Teaching of Psychology, 22*, 228-232.

Goldstein, S. B. (2000). *Cross-cultural explorations: Activities in culture and psychology*. Boston: Allyn & Bacon.

González, Y. S., Moreno, D. S., & Schneider, B. (2004). Friendship expectations of early adolescents in Cuba and Canada. *Journal of Cross-cultural Psychology, 35,* 436-445.

Guzman, L. P., Schiavo, R. S., & Puente, A. E. (1992). In A. E. Puente, J. R. Matthews, & C. L. Brewer (Eds.), *Teaching psychology in America: A history* (pp. 189-217). Washington, DC: American Psychological Association.

Hall, C. C. I. (1997). Cultural malpractice: The growing obsolescence of psychology with the changing U.S. population. *American Psychologist, 52,* 642-651.

Hill, G. W., IV. (2000). Incorporating a cross-cultural perspective in the undergraduate psychology curriculum: An interview with David Matsumoto. *Teaching of Psychology, 27,* 71-75.

Hilliard, A. G. (1991/1992). Why we must pluralize the curriculum. *Educational Leadership, 49,* 12-15.

Hull, D. B. (2001). Teaching students about international psychology. *Teaching of Psychology, 28,* 29-32.

Judd, C. M., & Park, B. (1988). Out-group homogeneity: Judgments of variability at the individual and group levels. *Journal of Personality and Social Psychology, 54,* 778-788.

Kim, U., & Berry, J. W. (Eds.). (1993). *Indigenous psychologies: Research and experience in cultural context.* Newbury Park, CA: Sage.

Kitano, M. K. (1997). A rationale and framework for course change. In A. I. Morey & M. K. Kitano (Eds.), *Multicultural course transformation in higher education: A broader truth* (pp. 1-17). Boston: Allyn & Bacon.

Kowalski, R. M. (2000). Including gender, race, and ethnicity in psychology content courses. *Teaching of Psychology, 27,* 18-24.

Lehman, D. R., Chiu, C., & Schaller, M. (2004). Psychology and culture. *Annual Review of Psychology, 55,* 689-714.

Levine, A., & Cureton, J. S. (1998). *When hope and fear collide: A portrait of today's college student.* San Francisco: Jossey-Bass.

Lonner, W. J. (2003). Teaching cross-cultural psychology. In P. Bronstein & K. Quina (Eds.), *Teaching gender and multicultural awareness: Resources for the psychology classroom* (2nd ed., pp. 169-177). Washington, DC: American Psychological Association.

Lynch, E. W. (1997). Instructional Strategies. In A. I. Morey & M. K. Kitano (Eds.), *Multicultural course transformation in higher education: A broader truth* (pp. 56-70). Boston: Allyn & Bacon.

Macrae, N. C., Stangor, C., & Hewstone, M. (1996). *Stereotypes and stereotyping.* New York: Guilford.

Markus, H. R., & Kitayama, S. (1991). Culture and the self: Implications for cognition, emotion, and motivation. *Psychological Review, 98,* 224-253.

Matsumoto, D. (1999). Culture and self: An empirical assessment of Markus and Kitayama's theory of independent and interdependent self-construal. *Asian Journal of Social Psychology, 2,* 289-310.

Mays, V. M., Rubin, J., Sabourin, M., & Walker, L. (1996). Moving toward a global psychology: Changing theories and practice to meet the needs of a changing world. *American Psychologist, 51,* 485-487.

McIntosh, P. (1983). *Interactive phases of curricular re-vision: A feminist perspective* (Working Paper No. 124). Wellesley, MA: Wellesley College, Center for Research on Women.

Moore, R. S. (1988). Racist stereotyping in the English language. In P. S. Rothenberg (Ed.), *Racism and sexism: An integrated study* (3rd ed., pp. 376-386). New York: St. Martin's.

Ocampo, C., Prieto, L. R., Whittlesey, V., Connor, J., Janco-Gidley, J., Mannix, S., et al. (2003). Diversity research in *Teaching of Psychology*: Summary and recommendations. *Teaching of Psychology, 30,* 5-18.

Pareek, U., & Rao, T. V. (1980). Cross-cultural surveys and interviewing. In H. C. Triandis & J. W. Berry (Eds.), *Handbook of cross-cultural psychology: Vol. 2. Methodology* (pp. 127-179). Boston: Allyn & Bacon.

Pike, K. L. (1954). *Language in relation to a unified theory of the structure of human behavior.* Glendale, CA: Summer Institute of Linguistics.

Puente, A. E., Blanch, E., Candland, D. K., Denmark, F. L., Laman, C., Lutsky, N., et al. (1993). Toward a psychology of variance: Increasing the presence and understanding of ethnic minorities in psychology. In T. V. McGovern (Ed.), *Handbook for enhancing undergraduate education in psychology* (pp. 71-92). Washington, DC: American Psychological Association.

Quina, K., & Bronstein, P. (2003). Gender and multiculturalism in psychology: Transformations and new directions. In P. Bronstein & K. Quina (Eds.), *Teaching gender and multicultural awareness: Resources for the psychology classroom* (pp. 3-11). Washington, DC: American Psychological Association.

Rabain-Jamin, J., Maynard, A. E., Greenfield, P. (2003). Implications of sibling caregiving for sibling relations and teaching interactions in two cultures. *Ethos, 31,* 204-231.

Romero, M. E. (1994). Identifying giftedness among Keresan Pueblo Indians: The Keres Study. *Journal of American Indian Education, 34,* 35-58.

Schneider, D. J. (Ed.), (2003). *The psychology of stereotyping.* New York: Guilford.

Sexton, V. S., & Hogan, J. D. (Eds.). (1992) *International psychology: Views from around the world.* Lincoln, NE: University of Nebraska Press.

Simoni, J. M., Sexton-Radek, K., Yescavage, K., Richard, H., & Lundquist, A. (1999). Teaching diversity: Experiences and recommendations of American Psychological Association Division 2 Members. *Teaching of Psychology, 26*, 89-95.

Stewart, T. L. (2001). The "Small Talk" activity: An interactive, applied learning technique. *Teaching of Psychology, 28*, 52-54.

Tatum, B. D. (1992). Talking about race, learning about racism: The application of racial identity development theory in the classroom. *Harvard Educational Review, 62*, 1-24.

Torney-Purta, J. (1984). Annotated bibliography of materials for adding an international dimension to undergraduate courses in developmental and social psychology. *American Psychologist, 9*, 1032-1042.

Triandis, H. C. (1994). *Culture and social behavior.* New York: McGraw-Hill.

Triandis, H. C. (1997). Cross-cultural perspectives on personality. In R. Hogan, J. Johnson & S. Briggs (Eds.), *Handbook of personality psychology* (pp. 439-464). San Diego: Academic Press.

Triandis, H. C., & Brislin, R. W. (1984). Cross-cultural psychology. *American Psychologist, 9*, 1006-1016.

Ward, C., Bochner, S., & Furnham, A. (2001). *The psychology of culture shock* (2nd ed.). Sussex: Routledge.

Yang, K. S. (2000). Monocultural and cross-cultural indigenous approaches: The royal road to the development of a balanced global psychology. *Asian Journal of Social Psychology, 3*, 241-263.

Ye, Z. (2004). The Chinese folk model of facial expressions: A linguistic perspective. *Culture & Psychology, 10*, 195-222.

APPENDIX A: CROSS-CULTURAL PSYCHOLOGY RESOURCES

Journals

Arab Journal of Psychiatry
Asian Journal of Social Psychology
Cross Cultural Management
Cross-Cultural Research
Cultural Diversity and Ethnic Minority Psychology
Cultural Diversity and Mental Health
Culture and Psychology
Culture, Health & Sexuality
Culture, Medicine & Psychiatry
Ethnic & Racial Studies
Ethnicity and Health
Hispanic Journal of Behavioral Sciences
International Journal of Cross Cultural Management
International Journal of Intercultural Relations
International Journal of Psychology
Journal of Asian Pacific Communication
Journal of Black Psychology
Journal of Cross-Cultural Psychology
Journal of Ethnic & Cultural Diversity in Social Work
Journal of Ethnicity in Substance Abuse
Psychologia: An International Journal of Psychology in the Orient
Social Identities: Journal for the Study of Race, Nation & Culture

Texts

Brislin, R. (2000). *Understanding culture's influence on behavior* (2nd ed.). Fort Worth, TX: Harcourt Brace.

Gardiner, H., & Kosmitzki, C. (2002). *Lives across cultures: Cross-cultural human development* (2nd. ed.). Boston: Allyn & Bacon.

Goldberger, N., & Veroff, J. (1995). *Culture and psychology reader.* New York: NYU Press.

Lonner, W. J., Dinnel, D. L., Hayes, S. A., & Sattler, D. N. (Eds.). (2002-2004). *Online readings in psychology and culture.* http://www.ac.wwu.edu/~culture/readings.htm

Matsumoto, D. R. (2004*). Culture and psychology* (3rd ed.). Pacific Grove, CA: Brooks/Cole.

Price, W. F., & Crapo, R. H. (2002). *Cross-cultural perspectives in introductory psychology* (4th ed.). Belmont, CA: Wadsworth.

Segall, M. H., Dasen, P. R., Berry, J. W., & Poortinga, Y. H. (1999). *Human behavior in global perspective* (2nd ed.). Boston: Allyn & Bacon.

Shiraev, E., & Levy, D. (2004). *Cross-cultural psychology: Critical thinking and contemporary applications* (2nd ed.). Boston: Allyn & Bacon.

Smith, P., & Bond, M. H. (1999). *Social psychology across cultures* (2nd ed.). Boston: Allyn & Bacon.

Reference Materials

Bernal, G., Trimble, J. E., Burlew, A. K., & Leong, F. T. (Eds.). (2002). *Handbook of racial and ethnic minority psychology*, Thousand Oaks: Sage.

Berry, J. W., Poortinga, Y. H., Segall, M. H., & Dasen, P. R. (2002). *Cross-cultural psychology: Research and applications*. (2nd Ed.). Cambridge, UK: Cambridge University Press.

Berry, J. W., Poortinga, Y. H., Pandey, J., Dasen, P. R., Saraswathi, T. S., Segall, M. H., & Kagicibasi, C. (Eds.). (1997). *Handbook of cross-cultural psychology* (2nd ed., Vols. 1-3). Needham Heights, MA: Allyn & Bacon.

Matsumoto, D. (1994). *Cultural influences on research methods and statistics*. Prospect Heights, IL: Waveland.

Matsumoto, D. R. (Ed.). (2001). *Handbook of culture and psychology*. New York: Oxford University Press.

Activities and Simulations

Goldstein, S. B. (2000). *Cross-cultural explorations: Activities in culture and psychology*. Boston: Allyn & Bacon.

Hofstede, G. J., Pedersen, P. B., & Hofstede, G. (2002). *Exploring culture: Exercises, stories, and synthetic cultures*. Yarmouth, ME: Intercultural Press.

Seelye, H. N. (1996). *Experiential activities for intercultural learning*. Yarmouth, ME: Intercultural Press.

Singelis, T. M. (Ed.). (1998). *Teaching about culture, ethnicity and diversity: Exercises and planned activities*. Thousand Oaks, CA: Sage.

Web Sites

Center for World Indigenous Studies: http://www.cwis.org/
Diversity Web — curriculum transformation resources: http://www.diversityweb.org
International Association for Cross-Cultural Psychology: http://www.iaccp.org
Office of Teaching Resources in Psychology: http://www.lemoyne.edu/OTRP/index.html
Society for Cross-Cultural Research: http://www.fit.edu/CampusLife/clubs-org/sccr/
Society for Intercultural Education, Training and Research: http://www.sietar.org

CHAPTER FIVE

USING EVOLUTIONARY THEORY TO PROMOTE CRITICAL THINKING IN PSYCHOLOGY COURSES

Peter Gray
Boston College

PSYCHOLOGY IS A vast and diverse subject. Those of us who teach introductory psychology are acutely aware of this fact. All aspects of behavior and thought, from the elements of sensory perception to the dynamics of social groups, lie within our purview. How can we teach this vast subject in an intellectually coherent manner?

Perhaps we should begin by asking: What is the common denominator of psychology? What cuts across the whole range of the discipline? The answer, of course, is that all of the things that psychologists study are products of the brain. The brain is a biological organ that was built gradually over countless generations through the process of evolution by natural selection. That fact gives us a starting point in developing and evaluating theories in every realm of psychology, and it provides a logical foundation for integrating the entire field.

Nearly all psychologists accept the basic premise of evolutionary theory, whether or not they use it explicitly in their thinking and teaching. It can be stated, somewhat oversimply, as follows: All living species, including humans, acquired their present forms and mechanisms through natural selection, by which those randomly occurring genetic changes that helped individuals to survive and reproduce were passed along from generation to generation and those that hindered survival and reproduction were lost.

The evolutionary theme can help us to integrate the various realms of psychology and can provide a foundation for thinking critically about theories and ideas within each realm. More specifically, it can provide a foundation for (a) thinking about the functions of all of our psychological capacities and tendencies; (b) thinking critically about the use of cross-species comparisons in psychology; and (c) evaluating classic theories in psychology. These benefits of integrating evolutionary theory into our teaching apply to all courses in psychology, not just the introductory course. In what follows, I discuss these values one at a time. In the process, I hope also to clear away some misperceptions that seem to have inhibited many teachers of psychology from using the evolutionary theme.

A Foundation for Thinking About Functions

Concerning any universal human ability or tendency we can ask the question: Why would this capacity or tendency have come about in the course of our evolution? That is, how might it have promoted the survival of our ancestors and the reproduction of their genes? We can ask this functionalist question about basic processes within each realm of our discipline. We can ask it about basic learning processes, about basic mechanisms of sensation and perception, about each category of drives and emotions that make up the human psyche, and about the processes that make us social animals and give us unique personalities. Asking the question and attempting to answer it can promote critical thinking about each topic we teach or study. Let me illustrate this with three examples, drawn from three different realms of psychology.

Example 1: What Is the Function of Guilt?

Emotions that are universal to human beings must have evolved to serve some function or functions. Consider guilt, which people everywhere have the capacity to experience. Psychologists often think of guilt as something negative. There are, certainly, people who suffer needlessly from too much guilt, and there are harmful, guilt-inducing parenting styles. However, if we are to begin at ground level in understanding guilt we must begin by asking about its adaptive value. Why would natural selection have endowed us with the capacity for this particular type of painful experience?

The first idea that comes to many people's minds when they think about the value of guilt is that it is good for the species. It tends to keep people from cheating or hurting others, so we can live relatively peaceably together. It is good for me that you have the capacity for guilt, because that capacity helps keep you from hurting me, and vice versa. Evolutionists today, though, generally do not accept good-for-the-species arguments. For guilt to have evolved, it must have served some function for the individual who experiences guilt. My guilt must benefit me; your guilt must benefit you.

According to a modern evolutionary theory of guilt, my guilt benefits me because it motivates me to behave in ways that help me retain long-term cooperative relationships with other people. We depend on cooperative relationships for our survival and reproduction — relationships with our friends, with our colleagues, and with our spouse. We may be tempted from time to time to cheat on our partners in those relationships. The downside of such cheating is that it may lead our partners to abandon us — to stop cooperating. My guilt reduces the chance that I will cheat on people with whom I am in valuable long-term relationships and increases the chance that if I do cheat I will somehow make amends that will help restore the relationship.

Evolution-based theories of behavior are, like any other theories, useful only to the degree to which they make predictions that can be tested empirically. A prediction of this theory of guilt is that guilt is a function not just of the amount of hurt we have caused to someone else but also of the degree to which that person is valuable to us as a partner. This prediction is consistent with research findings. For example, Baumeister, Stillwell, and Heatherton (1995) asked university students to recall and write out two episodes in which they caused someone else to become angry at them, one in which they experienced guilt and one in which they didn't. The researchers found that the guilt stories were far more likely to involve a victim who was respected by and had a mutually giving relationship with the transgressor than were the nonguilt stories. The stories also revealed that guilt motivated the transgressors to apologize and in other ways make amends.

Example 2: What Is the Function of Sleep?

Human beings everywhere sleep about 8 hours out of every 24, mostly at night. Why? Behavioral researchers have developed two, not-incompatible theories concerning the functions of sleep, the *restoration theory* and the *preservation-and-protection theory*.

According to the restoration theory, our tissues tend to wear out during the day and we need to restore them with a period of rest. Sleep indeed is a time of rest: muscles are relaxed, metabolic rate is down, and growth hormone, which promotes body repair, is secreted at a higher-than-normal rate (Douglas, 2002; Siegel, 2003). Laboratory rats that are completely deprived of sleep for many days develop lesions in various bodily tissues and eventually die (Everson, 1993). This theory, however, does not explain the large differences across species in sleep time. At one extreme, large grazing animals like bison and horses average only 2 or 3 hours of sleep per 24 hours. At the other extreme, some animals, such as opossums and bats, sleep for an average of 20 or more hours each 24 hours. The restoration theory also fails to explain why certain rare human beings, who lack a normal sleep drive and who sleep far less than the usual 8 hours, don't suffer physically from lack of sleep (Meddis, 1977).

According to the preservation-and-protection theory, sleep evolved to preserve energy and protect the individual during that portion of each 24-hour day when there is relatively little value and considerable danger in moving around. We humans are designed to function well in daylight. We depend on vision. At night, when it is dark, we are better off tucked away someplace, hidden, asleep. Support for the preservation-and-protection theory comes primarily from cross-species comparisons (Allison & Cicchetti, 1976; Webb, 1982). Large grazing animals have to spend lots of time eating and can't hide very well while asleep, so they sleep little. Bats and opossums are well adapted for hiding in out-of-the-way places and need relatively little time to obtain food (in such forms as high-calorie insects and grubs), so they spend most of their time asleep. The theory also explains differences in the timing of sleep. Animals that rely heavily on vision generally forage during the day and sleep at night. Conversely, animals like mice and rats that rely more on other senses, and are preyed upon by animals that use vision, generally sleep during the day and forage at night.

Both theories appear to have some validity. Some degree of sleep seems to be essential for body repair, and this may explain why all vertebrates spend at least a small portion of each 24 hours asleep. However, variation across species in sleep time and timing seems to be best explained in terms of optimal strategies for preservation and protection, which depend on the animal's ecology.

An understanding of function is valuable even for researchers whose main focus is on mechanism. Hypotheses about mechanisms follow from ideas about functions. This point is nicely illustrated in the case of sleep. If you believe that sleep serves primarily restorative functions, you might look for sleep-inducing chemicals in the body that are products of tissue wear-and-tear. On the other hand, if you believe that the preservation-and-protection theory is most valid, you might look for sleep-inducing mechanisms that are responsive to the day-night, light-dark cycle. Researchers indeed have found mechanisms that link sleepiness with the day-night cycle (Lavie, 2002), but have failed to find mechanisms that link it with a correlate of tissue wear-and-tear, and this adds further support to the preservation-and-protection theory.

Example 3: What Is the Function of Bitter Taste?

Evolutionary theory provides a useful foundation for examining the properties of all sensory systems. Sensory systems evolved not to provide full, true accounts of the physical world but rather to provide the kind of information that an individual needs to survive and reproduce. This point is nicely illustrated with the example of bitter taste.

Bitterness is not, as some students suppose, a property of the chemical that finds itself on our tongue. Bitterness is purely a psychological experience, a perception that we impose upon the chemical. When scientists examine the various chemicals that taste bitter to us they find that many of them are very different from one another chemically. The one factor that unites most bitter-tasting chemicals is that they are either toxic to humans and other mammals or chemically closely related to something that is toxic. When scientists examine the receptor cells for bitter taste, they find on them roughly 50 to 80 different receptor proteins, each capable of binding a different set of chemicals (Dulac, 2000).

In the course of evolution, an animal that sensed as bitter, and therefore rejected, a particular poisonous substance would have a survival advantage. In the course of further evolution, new mutations would add new receptor sites to the bitter receptor cells, expanding the bitter taste to other toxic substances. This analysis also helps us make sense of certain variations in sensitivity to bitter taste. Among humans, women are generally more sensitive to bitter taste than are men, and women become still more sensitive to that taste during the first 3 months of pregnancy (Duffy & Bartoshuk, 1996). A possible reason is found in evidence that the human fetus is highly subject to damage by poisons during the first 3 months of its development (Profet, 1992). Young children are also generally more sensitive to bitter taste than are adults, and this may help protect them from poisons during the years before they have learned to distinguish well between what is or is not safe to eat (Cashdan, 1994).

Overcoming the Tendency to Pathologize in Psychology

An evolutionary perspective can help to counter students' and many psychologists' bias to overemphasize pathology and ignore adaptive functions. Concern for evolutionary function is useful even in the realm of clinical psychology. For example, nearly all people have the capacity to become depressed in response to certain conditions and anxious in response to other conditions, and these tendencies suggest that such states may have adaptive functions. Moderate depression seems to promote realistic self-appraisal and life change following repeated failure (Nesse, 1990). Various anxiety disorders seem to be linked to normal anxiety states that evolved because they enhance vigilance in dangerous situations (Marks & Nesse, 1994). Today, when even mild forms of depression and anxiety are often treated with drugs, as if they were diseases, questions about the value of such states are of considerable practical importance.

A FOUNDATION FOR THINKING CRITICALLY ABOUT CROSS-SPECIES COMPARISONS

Students are often puzzled about why psychologists think they can learn anything useful about human beings by studying other animals. Without a foundation in evolutionary theory, students are unequipped to appreciate such research or think critically about it. In particular, without such a foundation, they cannot recognize that two fundamentally different kinds of similarities exist across species — *homologies* and *analogies* (Lorenz, 1974).

Homologies are similarities that result from common ancestry. We are similar to other animals in many ways because we are genetically related to them. We have similar sets of genes, which create similar structures (including brain structures), which predispose us to similar behaviors. All animals originated from a common ancestor, so it is not surprising that some homologies — such as those in the basic structure of DNA molecules and in the structure of certain enzymes — can be found between any two species. However, the more closely related two species are, the more homologies they show.

Analogies, in contrast, are similarities that result from convergent evolution. Convergent evolution occurs when different species, because of some similarity in their habitats or lifestyles, independently evolve a common characteristic. An example is the convergent evolution of wings and flight in bats, birds, and butterflies. The study of analogies and the study of homologies serve different purposes, as discussed below.

The Value of Studying Analogies

Analogies give us clues about the functions of behavioral characteristics. If a similar characteristic evolved in more than one, relatively unrelated species, we can look at those species to see what is similar about other aspects of their habitats and styles of life that might have led to natural selection for that characteristic. The cross-species comparisons of sleep that support the preservation-and-protection theory provide good examples of the value of analogies. Researchers looked at animals that sleep a lot, or a little, or at night, or during the day, and asked: What does each group have in common that would have led them to evolve this similarity in sleep habits?

Consider also the attempt to understand the functions of various species-typical mating patterns. Human beings are, worldwide, at least somewhat monogamous. Unlike our close cousins the chimpanzees and bonobos, which are not at all monogamous, we tend to form relatively exclusive, long-term bonds with our mating partners. Animals that approach or exceed us in degree of monogamy can be found among species that are much more distantly related to us than are chimpanzees and bonobos. Among the most fully monogamous species are gibbons, foxes, and geese. Analysis of such species suggests that monogamy — and all of the psychological equipment that supports it (including romantic attachment and sexual jealousy) — evolves in conditions in which offspring can be raised much more successfully by two parents working together than by one parent alone (Dewsbury, 1988).

The Value of Studying Homologies

Homologies are useful for studying the mechanisms of behavior. Convergent evolution can produce analogous behaviors that operate through different mechanisms. Therefore, researchers who seek to understand the physiological mechanism of some form of human behavior through experiments on another species must choose a species in which the relevant behavior is homologous, not analogous, to that in humans. Many basic mechanisms of learning, motivation, emotion, and sensation are homologous across all or at least most mammalian species, and researchers have learned much about these by studying them in such animals as rats and mice.

Homologies also are useful for tracing the evolutionary origins of particular human behaviors. Darwin (1872/1965) pioneered the use of homologies for this purpose in his comparisons of the facial expressions of emotions in humans with those of various species of monkeys and apes. Modern extension of this work has led to the hypothesis that the human happy smile and human greeting smile have distinct evolutionary origins (Hooff, 1972; Redican, 1982). According to this hypothesis, the happy smile evolved from the relaxed open-mouth display, which accompanies rough-and-tumble play in most primates, and the greeting smile evolved from the silent bared-teeth display, which is a sign of submission and nonaggression in most primates. This theory differs from the more commonly accepted hypothesis proposed by Ekman (1992), which supposes that the happy smile is the only true smile and that other smiles are "false smiles," put on when one wishes to appear happy.

A FOUNDATION FOR THINKING CRITICALLY ABOUT CLASSIC THEORIES IN PSYCHOLOGY

All of the grand, classic theories of psychology, which we still teach in our courses, are theories of human nature. All of them attempt to account for vast sweeps of human behavior through the application of a relatively small number of general principles, which are assumed to apply to people everywhere. Any theory of human nature is, implicitly or explicitly, a theory about products of natural selection. For the most part, the architects of psychology's grand theories did not use evolutionary thinking when developing their theories, but teachers and students can bring it to bear in critiquing those theories: How plausible is it that natural selection would have produced the underlying behavioral mechanisms posited by a given theory? How would each mechanism promote the survival and reproduction of our ancestors? Attempting to answer such questions requires identifying the general principles associated with each theory. What follows are some hints about the lines that such thinking might take when applied to three of psychology's broadest and most influential theories.

Application to Freud's Psychoanalytic Theory of Personality

Superficially, Freud's focus on unconscious motivation and instincts, particularly on sex and aggression, seems quite compatible with a Darwinian view of the person. On closer inspection, however, we discover that Freud's way of thinking about these topics was almost the opposite of Darwin's. In Freud's theory, pathology appears as primary and adaptation secondary: According to Freud, primary process thought, which fails to distinguish fantasy from reality, is the most fundamental form of human reasoning; incestuous wishes constitute the most primitive form of the sex drive; and a death instinct is the foundation of human aggression (Hall, 1979). It is hard to imagine any way of squaring these ideas with the Darwinian mandate that the earliest and most basic form of any behavior-controlling mechanism must have imparted some adaptive advantage.

Perhaps the most accepted of Freud's ideas today is his concept of defense mechanisms, his view that people often deny or distort reality to create a more positive view of themselves and their situation. If defense mechanisms are part of human nature, then they must in some way promote survival and reproduction, or at least must have done so in our evolutionary past. In Freud's theory, defense mechanisms serve the function of reducing anxiety. But why would natural selection create a mechanism to reduce anxiety? Anxiety itself evolved for a purpose: to make us vigilant in the face of dangers and to avoid unnecessary risks. In what conditions might a reduction in anxiety promote survival and reproduction? This question, which Freud did not consider, can lead to refinements in the theory of defenses and new behavioral predictions.

One possible way to reconcile Freud's idea of defense mechanisms with natural selection is to suppose that such mechanisms operate primarily in situations where we are better off ignoring anxiety. From this perspective, defense mechanisms may serve for anxiety a function similar to that which endorphins serve for pain (Goleman, 1985; Nesse & Lloyd, 1992). Pain serves obvious evolutionary functions: It motivates us to protect our bodily tissues from damage. Sometimes, however — such as when we must escape from a predator — we are better off ignoring pain. Endorphins are secreted as part of the body's response to such threats, and they function to inhibit pain and permit vigorous action. By analogy, there may be times when it is best for us to ignore anxiety. When the source of anxiety is something that we cannot control in any realistic way, we might benefit from denying its existence or minimizing its seriousness. Such denial or distortion reduces our worry about things we cannot control and allows us to focus on what we can control. This explanation makes a testable prediction that goes beyond Freud's theory. It predicts that defense mechanisms should be triggered by situations or characteristics that we cannot control more than by those that we can control. I should defend myself against anxiety about the inevitability of death but not against anxiety about standing too close to the edges of cliffs.

Another possible Darwinian explanation of defense mechanisms is that their ultimate function is not anxiety reduction but impression management (Alexander, 1979; Nesse & Lloyd, 1992; Trivers, 1985). People who project an image of being beneficent, competent, and confident are better at securing the cooperation of other people than are people who project the opposite image. It may be easier for us to project positive images of ourselves if we believe those images to be true than if we believe them to be false. From this view, defensive self-deception serves the ultimate purpose of deceiving others. This theory makes different predictions about the situations that should activate defense mechanisms than does the anxiety-reduction theory. It suggests that defenses should be triggered more by threats to the esteem that others accord us than by other types of events. The distorted picture that we create in ourselves should be a picture that would cause others to view us as valuable to them and worth helping.

Application to Rogers's and Maslow's Humanistic Theories

Carl Rogers and Abraham Maslow are often accused, quite justly, of presenting an overly optimistic, unscientific account of human nature. Had these theorists brought an evolutionary perspective to bear, they might have developed the fundamental concepts of their theories in ways that are more plausible and testable.

Consider, for example, Rogers's (1959) view of the *real self* as a phenomenological entity distinct from *conditions of worth* imposed by others. From an evolutionary view, such a distinction may well make sense. Human beings, for good evolutionary reasons, have a strong drive to secure and maintain the acceptance and approval of other human beings. For equally good evolutionary reasons, humans exploit that drive in others by making their acceptance and approval contingent upon conditions of worth — conditions that benefit the approving party. Given these facts, it makes some sense that humans would acquire, through natural selection or learning or both, a sense of their real selves, something that would help them keep their own self-interests distinct from the interests of others. The two sets of interests sometimes overlap and sometimes do not. We must not become so wrapped up in pleasing others as to neglect our own survival and reproductive needs.

Thus, Rogers's theory that people have two separate self-concepts — one of their real self and one of a self that is imposed on them by others — is evolutionarily plausible. However, his view that the real self is the source of all that is good in us, and that the imposed self is the source of all that is bad, does not seem plausible. Greed, aggression, and other antisocial motives are as much a product of natural selection, and hence part of our real selves, as are cooperation and other prosocial motives. A Darwinian analysis of the real versus imposed self would examine the ways in which evolutionary self-interest coincides with, or runs counter to, the interests of others with whom we interact.

Another basic concept of humanistic theory, for both Rogers and Maslow, is that of *self-actualization*. To Rogers, the self-actualizing drive is the drive "to be all that you can be," a definition that most psychologists regard as too vague to use as a foundation for research. In Maslow's (1970) theory of a hierarchy of human drives, the self-actualizing drive occupies the top rung. Maslow's hierarchy as a whole — with physiological needs at the base, social needs in the middle, and actualizing needs at the top — makes some evolutionary sense. Survival requires that physiological needs take first priority. Social needs, although not quite as immediately demanding, are also of constant concern; we need to keep others' approval in order to secure their cooperation in meeting our physiological needs. However, what exactly are the actualizing needs and how are they adaptive?

For both Rogers and Maslow, people are self-actualizing when they engage in playful, creative, and explorative ventures that are not triggered by immediate survival demands. People do indeed play and explore, and so do other animals. The humanistic concept of an actualizing drive would make evolutionary sense if it were reframed as an *educative drive*. In the course of human evolution, those individuals who spent their free time playing, exploring, and creating may have acquired skills and knowledge that made them more flexible in adapting to future crises, more attractive to potential mates, and more valued by the community than those who spent their free time simply waiting to meet the next immediate survival demand (for research and ideas concerning the evolutionary value of play, see Power, 2000).

Application to Piaget's Theory of Cognitive Development

Piaget contended that people everywhere undergo a series of metamorphoses in their thinking over the course of childhood (Inhelder & Piaget, 1958). The final stage, reached at about age 13, is that of formal-operational reasoning, characterized by the ability to manipulate mental symbols in mathematically logical ways regardless of the symbols' references.

A Darwinian analysis of Piaget's theory immediately raises questions that were not raised by Piaget. How is the form of reasoning at each stage of development adapted to the child's needs at that stage? Does formal-operational reasoning characterize adult thinking worldwide, and, in particular, does it characterize adult thinking in hunter-gatherers, who live in ways most comparable to those in which our species evolved? How is such reasoning linked to finding food, warding off predators, negotiating social agreements, attracting mates, or raising children? When adults in any culture reason about survival-related issues, do they really manipulate abstract symbols in certain mathematically defined ways or do they manipulate concrete symbols in ways that accord with their acquired means-ends knowledge concerning the specific type of problem that they are thinking about?

An evolutionary perspective forces us to transcend our parochial view of the world when we develop or critique theories of human nature. Formal-operational reasoning, whether or not it is ever achieved, is a developmental goal of the kinds of schools and colleges with which Piaget was always associated, and preoperational and concrete-operational reasoning seem to match reasonably well with the curriculum demands of the early school grades. Piaget minimized the influence of schooling in his theory and focused on the child's self-discoveries, but he seems to have posited that the Euro-American school curriculum represents a universal developmental sequence that is inherent to the human mind. Research on human reasoning actually suggests that, even in our highly schooled society, and even when they are solving the kinds of "abstract" problems that are taught in schools, adults think concretely, not abstractly (Ceci, 1993; Johnson-Laird, 2002).

IMPLICATIONS FOR TEACHERS AND STUDENTS

The primary goal of education in psychology should not be to acquire bits and pieces of psychological information or to memorize various theories. Rather, the primary goal should be to learn to think critically about such information and theories. In this essay, I have illustrated, with many examples, how an evolutionary perspective can contribute to such thinking. Such a perspective provides a foundation for thinking about the functions of universal human drives, abilities, and tendencies; for understanding what can or cannot be learned about human beings through cross-species comparisons; and for critiquing classic theories in psychology.

Overcoming Mistaken Beliefs That Have Led Some to Avoid Evolutionary Theory

I hope that this essay has also helped to dissolve some of mistaken beliefs that inhibit some teachers and students of psychology from paying much attention to evolutionary theory. One such belief is that evolutionary theory applies only to certain "biological" topics in psychology — most notably aggression, cooperation, and mating. But all basic behavioral mechanisms are products of evolution by natural selection, and therefore evolutionary thinking can be applied meaningfully across the whole range of our discipline.

The most frequently voiced objection to the use of evolutionary theory in psychology, in my experience, is that evolutionary accounts amount to "mere speculation" and cannot be tested empirically. Of course, all theorizing involves speculation. Speculation is fundamental to theory-building in psychology and in all other sciences. The evolutionary perspective does not promote wildness of speculation, but rather provides guidance and restraint. Every theory must be compatible not just with the data but also with the idea that, over the course of evolution, the psychological mechanism under consideration has tended to promote individuals' survival and reproduction. Theories that have developed from an evolutionary perspective, like all theories in psychology, are testable to the degree that they make predictions about observable phenomena. Each of the specific evolution-based theories mentioned in this essay can be elaborated into a reasonable set of predictions about the contexts and the specific forms in which the behaviors are most likely to occur. Alternative theories of the evolutionary function of a human tendency can be pitted against one another if the theories make different predictions.

Specific Ways to Bring an Evolutionary Perspective to the Classroom

To integrate an evolutionary perspective meaningfully into a psychology course, I suggest the following specific steps (for more elaboration, see Gray, 1999):

♦ Explain clearly the concept of evolution by natural selection and its relevance to psychology. Some students mistakenly think of evolution as having foresight, able to prepare organisms for future needs. Some overgeneralize the concept of evolutionary fitness to include qualities other than those that increase the survival and reproduction of genes. To use evolutionary theory meaningfully, students must first understand the theory.

♦ Ask about the possible evolutionary function of each basic human characteristic discussed in the course. Such questions lead students to think deeply about the characteristic. Make it clear, however, that a theory about function is not necessarily correct simply because it seems evolutionarily plausible. Each proposal about function should be followed up by a question about how to test that functional theory. What predictions does the theory make about observable behavior?

♦ Use evolutionary theory to help students overcome the pathology bias. Many students equate psychology with the study of psychopathology. They are drawn to the harmful consequences of universal human tendencies and fail to think about the adaptive qualities of those tendencies. An evolutionary perspective can help students appreciate and want to learn more about normal, adaptive behavior.

♦ When humans are compared with other species, discuss the evolutionary rationale for each comparison. Ask students whether the cross-species similarity under discussion is likely to be an analogy or a homology. Describe how the answer to that question affects the kinds of conclusions that might be drawn from studies of that similarity.

♦ Ask students to critique classic theories from an evolutionary perspective. Such critiques require that students identify the basic premises of each theory and think about the implications of those premises for survival and reproduction. In some cases, such critiques lead to proposals for modifying the theory and for testing its modified form empirically.

♦ Use the evolutionary perspective to foster critical thinking. All of the preceding steps are ways to involve students in critical thinking. Your use of the evolutionary perspective should make it clear that this perspective is not a royal road to truth in psychology. It does not shortcut the need for empirical research, but helps guide our thinking about the plausibility of alternative theories and about reasonable ways of testing them.

I hope these ideas are helpful to you as you plan your own courses and that ultimately they will help to foster your students' understanding and critical thinking.

REFERENCES

Alexander, R. D. (1979). *Darwinism and human affairs*. Seattle: University of Washington Press.

Allison, T., & Cicchetti, D. V. (1976). Sleep in mammals: Ecological and constitutional correlates. *Science*, *194*, 732-734.

Baumeister, R. F., Stillwell, A.M., & Heatherton, T.F. (1995). Personal narratives about guilt: Role of action control and interpersonal relationships. *Basic and Applied Social Psychology*, *17*, 173-198.

Cashdan, E. (1994). A sensitive period for learning about food. *Human Nature*, *5*, 279-291.

Ceci, S. J. (1993). Contextual trends in intellectual development. *Developmental Review*, *13*, 403-435.

Darwin, C. (1965). *The expression of the emotions in man and animals*. Chicago: University of Chicago Press. (Original work published 1872)

Dewsbury, D. A. (1988). The comparative psychology of monogamy. In D. W. Leger (Ed.), *Comparative perspectives in modern psychology. Nebraska Symposium on Motivation, 1987* (pp. 1-50). Lincoln: University of Nebraska Press.

Douglas, N. J. (2002). *Clinician's guide to sleep medicine*. London: Arnold.

Duffy, V. B., & Bartoshuk, L. M. (1996). Sensory factors in feeding. In E. D. Capaldi (Ed.), *Why we eat what we eat: The psychology of eating* (pp. 145-171). Washington, DC: American Psychological Association.

Dulac, C. (2000). The physiology of taste: Vintage 2000. *Cell, 100,* 607-610.

Ekman, P. (1992). Facial expressions of emotion: New findings, new questions. *Psychological Science*, *3*, 34-38.

Everson, C. A. (1993). Sustained sleep deprivation impairs host defense. *American Journal of Physiology*, *265*, R1148-R1154.

Goleman, D. (1985). *Vital lies, simple truths*. New York: Simon & Schuster.

Gray, P. (1999). Using evolution by natural selection as an integrative theme in psychology courses. In B. Perlman, L. I. McCann, & S. H. McFadden (Eds.), *Lessons learned: Practical advice for the teaching of psychology* (Vol. 1, pp. 153-158). Washington, DC: Association for Psychological Science.

Hall, C. S. (1979). *A primer of Freudian psychology: 25th anniversary edition*. New York: Mentor.

Hooff, J. A. van (1972). A comparative approach to the phylogeny of laughter and smiling. In R. A. Hinde (Ed.), *Non-verbal communication* (pp. 209-241). Cambridge: Cambridge University Press.

Inhelder, B., & Piaget, J. (1958). *The growth of logical thinking from childhood to adolescence*. New York: Basic Books.

Johnson-Laird, P. N. (2002). Peirce, logic diagrams, and the elementary operations of reasoning. *Thinking and Reasoning, 8*, 69-95.

Lavie, P. (2002). Sleep-wake as a biological rhythm. *Annual Review of Psychology, 52*, 277-303.

Lorenz, K. Z. (1974). Analogy as the source of knowledge. *Science, 185*, 229-234.

Marks, I. M., & Nesse, R. M. (1994). Fear and fitness: An evolutionary analysis of anxiety disorders. *Ethology and Sociobiology, 15*, 247-261.

Maslow, A. H. (1970). *Motivation and personality*. (2nd ed.). New York: Harper & Row.

Meddis, R. (1977). *The sleep instinct*. London: Routledge & Kegan Paul.

Nesse, R. M. (1990). Evolutionary explanations of emotions. *Human Nature, 1*, 261-289.

Nesse, R. M., & Lloyd, A. T. (1992). The evolution of psychodynamic mechanisms. In J. H. Barkow, L. Cosmides, & J. Tooby (Eds.), *The adapted mind: Evolutionary psychology and the generation of culture* (pp. 601-624). Oxford: Oxford University Press.

Power, T. G. (2000). *Play and exploration in children and animals*. Mahwah, NJ: Erlbaum.

Profet, M. (1992). Pregnancy sickness as adaptation: A deterrent to maternal ingestion of teratogens. In J. H. Barkow, L. Cosmides, & J. Tooby (Eds.), *The adapted mind: Evolutionary psychology and the generation of culture* (pp. 327-365). Oxford: Oxford University Press.

Redican, W. K. (1982). An evolutionary perspective on human facial displays. In P. Ekman (Ed.), *Emotion in the human face* (pp. 212-280). Cambridge: Cambridge University Press.

Rogers, C. R. (1959). A theory of therapy, personality, and interpersonal relationships, as developed in the client-centered framework. In S. Koch (Ed.), *Psychology: A study of a science* (Vol. 3, pp. 184-256). New York: McGraw-Hill.

Siegel, J. M. (October, 2003). Why we sleep. *Scientific American, 289*, 92-97.

Trivers, R. L. (1985). *Social evolution*. Menlo Park, CA: Benjamin/Cummings.

Webb, W. B. (1982). Some theories about sleep and their clinical implications. *Psychiatric Annals, 11*, 415-422.

This chapter is an updated and much-revised version of an article by Peter Gray entitled "Incorporating Evolutionary theory into the teaching of psychology," published in *Teaching of Psychology, Volume 23* (1996), pp. 207-214. That paper itself was based on a talk presented by the author at the Seventeenth Annual National Institute on the Teaching of Psychology, St. Petersburg Beach, Florida in January, 1995.

CHAPTER SIX

THE BRAIN AND YOUR STUDENTS

How to Explain Why Neuroscience Is
Relevant to Psychology

Stephen M. Kosslyn
Harvard University

Robin S. Rosenberg
Lesley University

BARELY A WEEK goes by without an announcement of some new advance in neuroscience research. Often the new research findings arise from neuroimaging studies, which may use techniques like positron emission tomography (PET) or functional magnetic resonance imaging (fMRI) to show that certain brain areas are activated when people perform specific tasks. Many of these advances directly bear on the nature of psychological phenomena, but it is often not clear how to teach this information in a way that is meaningful and interesting to psychology students. Not being neuroscientists, many students do not feel motivated to learn the results of brain studies because, from their point of view, associations between a particular task and where the brain happens to be activated when that task is performed seem arbitrary and irrelevant.

To counter this attitude, teachers of psychology need to show students how understanding the brain is relevant to psychology. The brain, after all, is the seat of cognition, affect, and consciousness — and thus its characteristics surely affect the nature of our thoughts, feelings, and behavior.

We have developed two related approaches to integrating neuroscience into psychology, which we illustrate in this chapter. First, we show how discoveries about the brain can help us to establish the reality of psychological phenomena and distinguish among them, and help us understand mental processes more deeply. Second, we take a step back and exploit an important general principle: Any psychological phenomenon can be addressed from multiple levels of analysis. The brain does not exist in a vacuum, and putting it in context — seeing its role in our thoughts, feelings, and behavior, alone and in groups — allows students to see how the brain affects everyday phenomena.

FACTS ABOUT THE BRAIN INFORM PSYCHOLOGY

In this section we discuss how findings about the brain illuminate three general types of psychological questions: (a) whether a psychological phenomenon actually exists; (b) whether two phenomena are distinct or instead are different facets of the same thing; and (c) why people think, feel, or behave in specific ways in specific circumstances.

Psychological Reality?

Facts about the brain can tell us whether a phenomenon is "psychologically real." Introspection, or even behavioral data, may not prove sufficient to implicate a specific mental phenomenon; such data can often be explained in many different ways (e.g., Anderson, 1978). Facts about the brain can play a decisive role in documenting that a mental phenomenon actually exists.

Do mental images exist? Consider this quote from John B. Watson, the founder of behaviorism:

> What does a person mean when he closes his eyes or ears (figuratively speaking) and says, "I see the house where I was born, the trundle bed in my mother's room where I used to sleep — I can even see my mother as she comes to tuck me in and I can even hear her voice as she softly says good night"? Touching, of course, but sheer bunk. We are merely dramatizing. The behaviorist finds no proof of imagery in all this. *We have put all these things in words long, long ago* ... (Watson, 1928, pp. 76-77)

Pylyshyn (1973, 1981, 2003) and others echoed this view years later, conceptualizing cognition as analogous to programs running on a computer. In their view, such programs use language-like internal representations (lists of facts, tables of information, and so on), and do not involve images in any sense. According to this view, the "picture-like" aspects of mental imagery are purely epiphenomenal. Like the heat from a light bulb when one is reading, these characteristics do not play a role in information processing. Are reports of using images in reasoning and recall to be taken as simply figures of speech, or do they reflect fundamental facts about how the mind works?

Visual mental images have been shown to exhibit three kinds of properties (for reviews, see Kosslyn, 1980, 1994). Try this (or have your students try it): Count, from memory, how many windows are in your living room. Most people report that they visualize the room and mentally scan along the walls, counting the windows. Did you notice the locks on the windows? Go back and try to "see" what they look like in your image. If you watch someone else doing this, you will probably see their eyes move to the side, and often jerk as they "fixate" on successive windows. This demonstration suggests that visual mental images have three properties: (a) spatial extent (objects in images appear to embody distance, like the walls in your image of your living room); (b) limits on spatial extent (objects in images do not extend indefinitely; just as you cannot see behind your head during perception, you "see" only a limited slice of the room in imagery); and, (c) grain (if objects are too small, they are hard to "see," as the window locks probably were the first time you counted the windows). These introspections were initially supported by behavioral findings (for distance, see Kosslyn, 1973; Kosslyn, Ball, & Reiser, 1978; for limited extent, see Kosslyn, 1978; for grain, see Kosslyn, 1975, 1976). However, these results proved controversial, and did little to convince skeptics of the psychological reality of imagery (e.g., see Kosslyn, 1980, 1994; Pylyshyn, 1981, 2003; Tye, 1991).

Enter the brain. In the monkey brain, 32 cortical areas have now been shown to play a role in visual perception (Felleman & Van Essen, 1991). Fifteen of these areas are *topographically organized* — that is, they preserve the spatial structure of the retina. When a monkey is shown a pattern, the pattern falling on the retina is literally preserved by the pattern of neurons firing in these cortical areas (e.g., see Tootell et al., 1982). These topographically mapped areas have three relevant properties: They have spatial extent; they evolved only to process the input from the eyes and hence have *limited* spatial extent; and they have grain (conferred by *spatial summation* — the fact that stimuli that are close enough together will be averaged by a given visual neuron, which blurs the distinction between the stimuli).

Thus, it is of great interest that visual mental imagery typically activates some of these areas in the human brain. The majority of both PET and fMRI studies have documented such activation (for reviews, see Kosslyn & Thompson, 2003; Mellet, Petit, Mazoyer, Denis, & Tzourio, 1998; Thompson & Kosslyn, 2000). In addition, the spatial properties of visualized objects affect the specific pattern of activation in these areas, and do so in much the same ways in perception (when people see the objects). In perception, objects that stimulate the fovea activate the very back parts of primary visual cortex, and increasingly larger objects stimulate increasingly anterior parts of this structure (Fox et al., 1986). The same is true in visual mental imagery, even when people have their eyes closed (Kosslyn, Thompson, Kim, & Alpert, 1995).

But these findings — like all neuroimaging findings — are purely correlational; they only show that activation in a brain area accompanies a particular kind of mental processing. In order to establish that the brain areas play a causal role in such processing, a different method is required. For example, magnetic stimulation can temporarily impair the functioning of part of the cortex. If that part of the cortex plays a causal role in a performing a particular kind of task, then participants should perform the task more poorly following such magnetic stimulation. Relying on this logic, researchers first asked participants to memorize sets of stripes, and later asked them to close their eyes and visualize pairs of stripes in order to compare them (e.g., in terms of their relative length or width). This task not only activated the primary visual cortex, but also was impaired when magnetic stimulation had temporarily disrupted this cortex. Moreover, the magnetic stimulation had much the same effects in the corresponding perceptual task, when the participants viewed the stripes instead of visualizing them (Kosslyn et al., 1999). Thus, neuroscience research has been able to help answer the question of whether mental images exist: They do.

Is hypnosis just playacting? Some researchers and theorists have claimed that hypnosis is a distinct psychological state that allows one to focus attention very precisely (e.g., Hilgard, 1965; Hilgard & Hilgard, 1975; Kihlstrom, 1987; Spiegel & Spiegel, 1987), whereas others have claimed that hypnosis is nothing more than a role in which people cooperate with the wishes of the hypnotist (e.g., Barber, 1961; Spanos, 1986).

One way to judge the merits of these two claims is to study the neural correlates of hypnosis. The key idea is that people cannot voluntarily alter the neural mechanisms that signal a particular mental state. Thus, if hypnosis is accompanied by distinct brain states, it cannot be ascribed simply to play-acting. To test this, Kosslyn, Thompson, Costantini-Ferrando, Alpert, and Spiegel (2000) selected a group of highly hypnotizable people (as measured by standard scales) and showed them colored and grayscale patterns while scanning their brains with PET. In brief, researchers presented the pattern in color or grayscale, and asked the participants to alter their perception (if needed) in order to see each version either in color (even if it was actually gray) or in grayscale (even if it was actually in color). Finally, the participants performed these tasks while being hypnotized or while not being hypnotized.

Kosslyn et al. (2000) first located the classic "color area" of the brain (in the fusiform/lingual region (in the back, underside of the brain) by examining the results when participants were told to perceive the colored display as being in color versus when they were told to perceive the grayscale display as gray. Two regions within the color area (as identified earlier by other laboratories, e.g., Lueck et al., 1989) were activated, one in the left cerebral hemisphere and one in the right. Kosslyn et al. (2000) then examined how hypnosis affected activation in these areas. Both the left- and right-hemisphere color areas were activated when the participants were hypnotized and were asked to perceive color — whether or not they were actually shown the color or the grayscale stimulus. In fact, these areas were activated to comparable degrees when hypnotized participants mentally added color to grayscale stimuli as when they were presented with actual color stimuli. Similarly, these areas were "turned down" when hypnotized participants were asked to see gray — whether or not they were actually shown the color or grayscale stimulus. All that mattered to hypnotized participants is what they experienced seeing, not the actual nature of the stimulus.

For the left-hemisphere color area, these results were obtained only when the participants were hypnotized. When they were not hypnotized, the actual nature of the stimulus determined how the area responded. In contrast, for the right hemisphere color area, activation was always determined by what the participants were told to perceive. If they were asked to perceive color, the area was activated — both when the participants had been hypnotized and when they were not hypnotized but were asked to visualize the appropriate colors or grayscale.

In short, hypnosis can alter the state of brain areas. What the participants *experienced* seeing overrode the actual stimulus input when they were hypnotized. The right-hemisphere color area apparently is more sensitive than the left to the effects of mental imagery per se, but the left required hypnosis in order to be modulated by experience.

Thus, results from neuroscience research are helping supply answers to questions about whether certain psychological phenomena exist. At least with regard to mental imagery and hypnosis, the answer appears to be yes.

Same or Different?

Relatively recent research in neuroscience has also enabled behavioral scientists to resolve old questions about whether two different psychological phenomena are in fact distinct from each other, or whether they simply reflect different facets of the same underlying mechanism. For example, we consider whether classical conditioning and operant conditioning are really different forms of learning, and whether behavior therapy works the same as medication in the treatment of a disorder.

Classical versus operant conditioning. Classical and operant conditioning both establish an association — the former between a stimulus and a response, the latter often between a discriminative stimulus and a response, which rests on an additional association between the response and a consequence. Moreover they both have several elements in common: extinction and spontaneous recovery; generalization and discrimination; moderating factors that affect response acquisition, such as time (e.g., the length of time between the conditioned stimulus and the unconditioned stimulus, or immediate versus delayed reinforcement); and both are subject to constraints on what can be learned easily. However, with classical conditioning, the response must be elicited, and thus the types of behaviors amenable to classical conditioning are generally limited to involuntary behaviors. In contrast, with operant conditioning the learner gives responses that are not necessary elicited, which are then followed by a reinforcer that increases the probability that the learner will make that response in that setting in the future.

Given the similarities between the two types of conditioning, some researchers (e.g., Kosslyn, Ganis, & Thompson, 2003; Pylyshyn, 2003) have debated whether they really are different, or are just different procedures that produce a similar end. Researchers have shown that voluntary movements can be shaped via classical conditioning (Brown & Jenkins, 1968), and "involuntary" responses can be operantly conditioned (such as learning to control tense jaw muscles to decrease facial pain, Dohrmann & Laskin, 1978). However, the fact that the same ends can be reached does not imply that the means to those ends are the same; by analogy, bats, birds and helicopters fly, but in different ways.

Perhaps the best evidence that the two kinds of conditioning are distinct is the fact that they rely on different neural systems. Indeed, when we looked at the brain systems underlying learning, we realized that posing the question in terms of classical versus operant condition was misleading. Not only do classical and operant conditioning clearly draw on different mechanisms, but different types of classical conditioning themselves rely on different systems. For example, whereas classical conditioning of fear draws on the amygdala (e.g., LeDoux, 1996), classical conditioning of eye blinks relies heavily on the cerebellum (Thompson & Krupa, 1994). In contrast, operant conditioning does not rely on either structure, but does make use of the dopamine-based "reward system" that relies on a part of the brain called the nucleus accumbens (e.g., see Robbins & Everitt, 1998). Neuroscience is able to show that different systems are used in the different types of learning.

Behavior therapy versus medication. Another example in which neuroscience research helps sort out whether two phenomena are the same or different can be found in the success of two treatments for obsessive-compulsive disorder (OCD): medication (fluoxetine, better known as Prozac) and behavior therapy. Both treatments can be helpful in reducing symptoms, but do they accomplish this end in the same way? To address this question, Baxter et al. (1992) used PET to examine the brain function of OCD patients in two conditions, either before and after behavior therapy or before and after receiving fluoxetine. The scans revealed that behavior therapy and fluoxetine both resulted in decreased activity in a part of the brain called the right caudate (part of the basal ganglia, which is involved in producing "automatic behaviors"). Schwartz, Stossel, Baxter, Martin, and Phelps (1996) replicated the effects of behavior therapy on the brain. Thus, evidence shows that behavior therapy and the drug alter the function of one area in common.

However, the drug also affected two other areas, the anterior cingulate and thalamus, both of which are involved in attention. The effects of the two treatments on the brain are not identical. When we come to understand better what different parts of the brain do, we can understand why drugs and behavior therapy have some similar effects but also have different effects. Moreover, simply because the drug affected more areas does not necessarily imply that it is better. The activation of these additional brain areas may reflect side effects. Depending on what these additional areas do, behavior therapy might turn out to be the more focused, appropriate intervention. Neuroscience research sheds light on the nonidentical effects of the two treatments.

Explanations of Phenomena

Perhaps the most general use of data about the brain is to help us understand how a particular psychological event occurs. Students are more likely to become interested in neuroscience research when the research explains psychological experiences of which they have firsthand knowledge. To illustrate this approach, we focus on common events: emotion-modulated startle and "hunches."

Emotion-modulated startle. If you are like most people, you have experienced walking down a street alone late at night and suddenly hearing a noise behind you. The realization that it was probably just a cat knocking over a trashcan probably came well after you were startled by the sound and your heart started racing. When in a state of nervousness, fear, or in some other intense emotional state, people are prone to being startled (e.g., see Le Doux, 1996). A large body of research has shown that the amygdala plays a crucial role in this sort of emotion-modulated startle; the structure is activated in startling situations, and patients who have impaired amygdalae do not show this startle reaction (see Damasio, 1994; Le Doux, 1996).

Emotion-modulated startle can be induced if one hears a scary story (e.g., a campfire ghost story late at night) followed by a loud sound. Students often get a lot more out of a discussion about emotion-modulated startle when they themselves experience such a response. To try this with your students, invite students to close their eyes while you read aloud a short scary story in a soft theatrical voice; at some point near the end of the story, create a loud noise by slamming a book on the table. (Note that we suggest you let students know in advance that the goal of the demonstration is to startle them, and that students who don't want to be startled should keep their eyes open.) This sort of demonstration is interesting to students (and teachers) because it shows that the amygdala can be modulated by the cognitive systems based in the cortex. Listening to a scary story can make us become anxious — which in turn makes us prone to being startled. This phenomenon clearly highlights the close link between emotion and cognition, which is interesting because our teaching experience suggests that many students intuitively feel that emotion and cognition have nothing to do with one another.

Hunches. A hunch is a belief, not based on explicit reasoning, that a problem can be solved in a certain way or that a situation will develop in a certain way. Hunches arise prior to conscious reasoning and usually cannot be justified rationally. To study the development of hunches, Bechara, Damasio, Tranel, and Damasio (1997) asked people to play a gambling game that involved taking cards from different decks. Participants were given a sum of play money at the outset, and drew cards that either awarded them additional money or penalized them. Cards were arranged into four decks, and some decks were "riskier" than others. Cards from the riskier decks could result in large losses. Participants were not warned that the decks differed in how risky they were, but after drawing many cards they typically figured this out. However, before they were consciously aware of the differences among the decks, they usually had a hunch. This hunch was not only a subjective feeling but also was the source of a skin-conductance response (SCR), which occurred right before the participants drew a card from a risky deck. Such responses occurred when the brain sent signals to the body that certain choices were risky, even before the participants consciously realized it.

Perhaps the most interesting results concern the contrast between the normal participants and patients who had damage to the ventral medial frontal lobes, part of the brain known to play a crucial role in using emotional information to guide behavior (see Damasio, 1994). These patients never showed skin-conductance responses prior to making a choice, and never expressed having a hunch. Moreover, by the end of the game, even the normal people who never consciously figured out the situation still chose properly, but the patients never did. In fact, the three patients who did figure out how the decks were set up still chose incorrectly! These patients never produced skin conductance responses, and continued to choose poorly even though they understood the situation.

According to Damasio, hunches are based on covert signals that arise before a person has thought through a situation, and these signals are based on a kind of "implicit memory." Without such emotional nudges, people do not choose wisely. In daily life, patients with damage to the ventral medial frontal lobes squander their money, have erratic personal lives, and may fight with coworkers.

Whether or not Damasio's views are correct, the exciting aspect of this finding is that once we know that a certain brain area is crucial to the phenomenon, we have a lever to understand the phenomenon in greater detail. The vague problem, "what is a hunch?" now can be recast as, "how does this brain area function so that we have hunches?"

NEUROSCIENCE AND LEVELS OF ANALYSIS

As we hope we have just shown, neuroscience can become more interesting when it illuminates psychological phenomena. A single principle underlies this approach, which rests on exploiting the concept of *levels of analysis*. The idea is simply to put the brain in a broader context, allowing facts about the brain to illuminate facets of phenomena at other levels of analysis. We can focus on three levels: First, the *level of the brain* is concerned with biological mechanisms, such as neural circuits, functions of lobes, and the effects of hormones. It is also concerned with the effects of genes on those mechanisms. Second, the *level of the person* is concerned with the content of people's mental processes. The content of mental processes includes beliefs (e.g., ideas, knowledge, expectations), desires (e.g., hopes, goals, needs), and feelings (e.g., fears, guilt, love). Whereas the level of the brain focuses on mechanisms for their own sake, independent of any particular content, the level of the person focuses on the content per se. Third, we focus on the *level of the group*. This includes the physical and social world. The physical world is our material environment, both natural and manmade. The social world is our interactions with other people, ranging from our relationships to our culture. Moreover, groups — like individuals — have their own behavior and mental processes (shared identity, beliefs, normative behaviors). Thus, the level of the group refers to the influence that other people and the physical environment have on us and that we have on other people.

A key part of the levels approach is an emphasis on the fact that *events at each of the levels affect events at the other levels*. Events at the different levels are constantly interacting. For example, right this minute your brain is processing these swiggly black lines in front of you, interpreting them as conveying meaning (level of the brain). These lines were created by others (specifically, we authors — level of the group) in order to convey specific ideas (level of the person). If we have successfully conveyed that information, your beliefs will change (level of the person), which in turn will affect not only how your brain organizes and stores information in the future, but possibly even how you interact with other people. By emphasizing the key role of the brain in such interactions, students can immediately see why the brain can speak to important issues in psychology.

When we ask whether mental images exist, for example, we use events in the brain to help us understand events at the level of the person, in this case the contents of conscious experience and beliefs about properties of objects. Facts about the brain inform us why we have particular experiences (level of the person), why we are aware of some aspects of objects with some kinds of images (e.g., tiny ones) and other aspects with other kinds of images (e.g., large ones). Thus, this example can be used to illustrate how events at the different levels are constantly interacting, and why understanding events at the level of the brain is relevant to understanding events at the other levels — such as the nature of conscious experience. Indeed, if we ask you to visualize a particular object, that social interaction can lead your brain to produce a specific experience (which involves interactions among events at all three levels) — and depending on the nature of the image, you will report different things to us.

When asking about hypnosis, we not only use events in the brain to explain aspects of experience and knowledge (level of the person), but we can also see how the very act of being hypnotized — which is a social encounter — affects the brain (and in turn affects one's experiences). Thus, all three levels of analysis are involved in this example.

In our example of classical versus operant conditioning, we saw how facts about brain mechanisms allow us to distinguish among different kinds of learning. Because they are different systems, a given person might be good at one kind of learning but not another, and vice versa for another person. Thus, knowledge that the systems are distinct can tell us something about how people differ in their abilities to acquire certain knowledge — allowing us, again, to draw a link between the level of the brain and the level of the person. People who have acquired different knowledge behave differently, including when interacting with other people. For instance, some people are more prone to experiencing conditioned fear responses than are other people. Such people are likely to have more fears and phobias, and interact differently with people and their environment than individuals whose brains are less likely to acquire such conditioned emotional responses.

In the example of treatments for OCD, the social interactions underlying behavior therapy were found to change the metabolism of a certain part of the brain, and to do so in the same way that a drug does. It suggests that whatever the two types of therapy have in common may be mediated by that part of the brain. Events in the brain not only affect beliefs (helping the patient to overcome his or her disruptive beliefs), but also affect how these patients interact with others (at the level of the group) because they are less restricted in their daily activities.

Our example of emotion-modulated startle also involves all three levels of analysis. Consider again a campfire ghost story, which leads everyone to jerk when a loud noise is produced at the end. The state of the amygdala is affected by one's comprehension of the story, which involves tapping into stored knowledge and beliefs at the level of the person. One aspect of being a skillful storyteller is being able to tap into that knowledge, thus knowing how to make the listener tense and ripe for the coup de grace at the end of the story. Thus, to understand emotion-modulated startle, one must understand the dynamics of the social situation — and to understand those dynamics (i.e., why someone is telling a particular story in a particular way), one must understand the mechanisms that underlie the phenomenon.

Hunches are another example: They clearly play a key role in gambling, for instance, and gambling is a social activity. The discoveries about the brain-bases of hunches allow us to understand how the roulette player may sense a "winning streak" — and a detailed understanding of how this brain area works (effectively or not so effectively) perhaps someday can help to explain why some people seem to gamble foolishly, not learning from experience. Such behavior can have a devastating effect on the gambler's life, and the lives of members of the gambler's family.

IMPLICATIONS FOR STUDENTS AND TEACHERS

Students can be fascinated by facts about the brain when they are brought to bear on topics in which they are interested, and are used in a way that illustrates how events in the brain affect the person and the group — and vice versa. The illustrations presented here are merely examples of ways in which facts about the brain can come alive for students. The general principle at work is that putting findings about the brain in a broader context helps students better understand and appreciate the material. Our experience has been that students become interested in findings about the brain when a controversy or question about a psychological phenomenon is illuminated. In addition, simply showing how the brain is not isolated from the person, the group, or the rest of the world can be eye-opening for students; they come to understand that understanding the brain can help them understand the nature of their feelings, thoughts, goals, relationships with others, and interactions with the environment — topics about which students typically are very curious. To draw facts about the brain clearly into the domain of psychology *as the student conceives of it*, teachers need to consider how specific brain events inform events at other levels of analysis. By integrating the brain into a larger context, it should become clear why learning about the brain informs us about key characteristics of psychology.

Here are some guidelines for providing such a context for findings and theories about the brain:

♦ Do the findings and theories about the brain help determine whether a psychological phenomenon exists? If so, explain both the phenomenon and the debate, providing demonstrations, video clips, or other material to illustrate the phenomenon or aspects of a key study.

♦ Do the findings and theories help make distinctions among similar phenomena or provide evidence that similar phenomena are facets of the same things? If so, explain the phenomena and why it matters whether or not they are distinct. If possible, provide demonstrations, video clips, or other material to demonstrate the phenomena.

♦ Explain to students how researchers progressed from general questions about a psychological phenomenon or process to the particulars of the specific task they used in their neuroimaging study. Explain how the task relates to the phenomenon under investigation.

♦ Explain to students how the findings about the brain provide insight into the origins or operation of a phenomenon. Generalize from the tasks used in specific studies to real-world situations or phenomena of interest to students.

♦ Using a levels-of-analysis framework, point out specific ways that findings about the brain do not exist in a vacuum: Neural processing affects, and can be affected by, an individual's beliefs, thoughts, feelings, goals (level of the person) and his or her interactions with other people and the environment (level of the group). Always bring the brain back to the world, and back to phenomena that grab the students' interest.

REFERENCES

Anderson, J. R. (1978). Arguments concerning representations for mental imagery. *Psychological Review, 85*, 249-277.

Barber, T. X. (1961). Physiological effects of "hypnosis." *Psychological Bulletin, 58*, 390-419.

Baxter, L. R., Schwartz, J. M., Bergman, K. S., Szuba, M. P., Guze, B. H., Mazziotta, et al. (1992). Caudate glucose metabolic rate changes with both drug and behavioral therapy for obsessive-compulsive disorder. *Archives of General Psychiatry, 49*, 681-689.

Bechara, A., Damasio, H., Tranel, D., and Damasio, A. R. (1997). Deciding advantageously before knowing the advantageous strategy. *Science, 275*, 1293-1295.

Brown, P. L., & Jenkins, H. M. (1968). Auto-shaping of the pigeon's key peck. *Journal of the Experimental Analysis of Behavior, 68*, 503-507.

Damasio, A. R. (1994). *Descartes' error: Emotion, reason, and the human brain*. New York: Grosset/Putnam.

Dohrman, R. S., & Laskin, D. M. (1978). An evaluation of electromyographic biofeedback in the treatment of myofacial pain-dysfunction syndrome. *Journal of the American Dental Association, 96*, 656-662.

Fellemen, D. J., & Van Essen, D. C. (1991). Distributed hierarchical processing in primate cerebral cortex. *Cerebral Cortex, 1*, 1-47.

Fox, P. T., Mintun, M. A., Raichle, M. E., Miezin, F. M., Allman, J. M., & Van Essen, D. C. (1986). Mapping human visual cortex with positron emission tomography. *Nature, 323*, 806-809.

Hilgard E. R. (1965). *Hypnotic susceptibility*. New York: Harcourt, Brace & World.

Hilgard, E. R., & Hilgard, J. R. (1975). *Hypnosis in the relief of pain*. Los Altos, CA: Kaufman.

Kihlstrom, J. F. (1987). The cognitive unconscious. *Science, 237*, 1445-1452.

Kosslyn, S. M. (1973). Scanning visual images: Some structural implications. *Perception and Psychophysics, 14*, 90-94.

Kosslyn, S. M. (1975). Information representation in visual images. *Cognitive Psychology, 7*, 341-370.

Kosslyn, S. M. (1976). Can imagery be distinguished from other forms of internal representation?: Evidence from studies of information retrieval times. *Memory and Cognition, 4*, 291-297.

Kosslyn, S. M. (1978). Measuring the visual angle of the mind's eye. *Cognitive Psychology, 10*, 356-389.

Kosslyn, S. M. (1980). *Image and mind*. Cambridge, MA: Harvard University Press.

Kosslyn, S. M. (1994). *Image and brain*. Cambridge, MA: MIT Press.

Kosslyn, S. M., Ball, T. M., & Reiser, B. J. (1978). Visual images preserve metric spatial information: Evidence from studies of image scanning. *Journal of Experimental Psychology: Human Perception and Performance, 4*, 47-60.

Kosslyn, S. M., Ganis, G., & Thompson, W. L. (2003). Mental imagery: Against the nihilistic hypothesis. *Trends in Cognitive Science, 7*, 109-111.

Kosslyn, S. M., Pascual-Leone, A., Felician, O., Camposano, S., Keenan, J. P., Thompson, W. L., et al. (1999). The role of area 17 in visual imagery: Convergent evidence from PET and rTMS. *Science, 284*, 167-170.

Kosslyn, S. M., & Thompson, W. L. (2003). When is early visual cortex activated during visual mental imagery? *Psychological Bulletin, 129*, 723-746.

Kosslyn, S. M., Thompson, W. L., Costantini-Ferrando, M. F., Alpert, N. M., & Spiegel, D. (2000). Hypnotic visual illusion alters color processing in the brain. *American Journal of Psychiatry, 157*, 1279-1284 .

Kosslyn, S. M., Thompson, W. L., Kim, I. J., & Alpert, N. M. (1995). Topographical representations of mental images in primary visual cortex. *Nature, 378*, 496-498.

LeDoux, J. (1996). *The emotional brain*. New York: Simon and Schuster.

Lueck, C. J., Zeki, S., Friston, K .J., Deiber, M .P., Cope, P., Cunningham, V. J., et al. (1989). The colour centre of the cerebral cortex in man. *Nature, 340*, 386-389.

Mellet, E., Petit, L., Mazoyer, B., Denis, M., & Tzourio, N. (1998). Reopening the mental imagery debate: Lessons from functional neuroanatomy. *NeuroImage, 8*, 129-139.

Pylyshyn, Z. W. (1973). What the mind's eye tells the mind's brain: A critique of mental imagery. *Psychological Bulletin, 80*, 1-24.

Pylyshyn, Z. W. (1981). The imagery debate: Analogue media versus tacit knowledge. *Psychological Review, 87*, 16-45.

Pylyshyn, Z. (2003). Return of the mental image: Are there pictures in the brain? *Trends in Cognitive Sciences, 7*, 113-118.

Robbins, T. W., & Everitt, B. J. (1998). Motivation and reward. In M. J. Zigmond, F. E. Bloom, S. C. Landis, J. L. Roberts, & L. R. Squire (Eds.), *Fundamental neuroscience* (pp. 1245-1260). New York: Academic Press.

Schwartz, J. M., Stoessel, P. W., Baxter, L. R., Martin, K. M., & Phelps, M. E. (1996). Systematic changes in cerebral glucose metabolic rate after successful behavior modification treatment of obsessive-compulsive disorder. *Archives of General Psychiatry, 53*, 109-113.

Spanos, N. P. (1986). Hypnotic behavior: A social-psychological interpretation of amnesia, analgesia, and "trance logic." *Behavioral and Brain Sciences, 9*, 449-502.

Spiegel, H. & Spiegel, D. (1987). *Trance and treatment: Clinical uses of hypnosis*. Washington, DC: American Psychiatric Press.

Thompson, R. F., & Krupa, D. J. (1994). Organization of memory traces in the mammalian brain. *Annual Review of Neuroscience, 17*, 519-549.

Thompson, W. L., & Kosslyn, S. M. (2000). Neural systems activated during visual mental imagery: A review and meta-analyses. In A. Toga & J. Mazziotta (Eds.), *Brain mapping II: The applications* (pp. 535-560). New York: Academic Press.

Tootell, R. B. H., Silverman, M. S., Switkes, E., & De Valois, R. L. (1982). Deoxyglucose analysis of retinotopic organization in primate striate cortex. *Science, 218,* 902-904.

Tye, M. (1991). *The imagery debate*. Cambridge: The MIT Press.

Watson, J. B. (1928). *The ways of behaviorism*. New York: Harper.

We thank Christine Souter for valuable comments on an earlier draft, and generations of Sophomore Tutors at Harvard University for trying out these ideas and for providing valuable feedback. Preparation of this chapter was supported by National Science Foundation under grant REC-0106760 and NIH Grant 5 R01 MH60734-03.

CHAPTER SEVEN

STORYTELLING AS A TEACHING STRATEGY

Laura E. Berk

Illinois State University

WHILE TEACHING ABOUT the many facets of human behavior in our introductory classes, my colleagues and I frequently bemoan the fragmentation of knowledge that our undergraduate courses convey. We move through a host of theories, research studies, and topics as the semester flies by and then find ourselves fielding a barrage of questions as exam time nears: "Do I need to know that?" "What's important and what's trivial?" How does all this relate to me?" These perennial queries about the importance and relevance of our knowledge base compel us to consider whether we are truly reaching our students — helping them discern, comprehend, and retain essential information and improve their understanding of themselves and other people.

There is a movement in psychology devoted to life-story narrative as a legitimate way of investigating the richness of subjective experience that drives human behavior. That movement is, in large measure, a reaction to the piecemeal approach our students bemoan — an approach that, too often, seems to overwhelm them with volleys of weakly integrated information, handicapping their learning. This bit-by-bit view of human functioning, narrative psychologists claim, stems from our field's strong adherence to quantitative measurement. For all the strengths of quantitative inquiry, relying on it as the sole basis for teaching runs the risk of leaving the learner — especially, the naïve learner — mired in information that they must somehow assimilate, without a discernable path to the higher-level goal of making it all meaningful.

When, in describing a theory and related research, we stop to tell our students an illustrative story, slumped bodies straighten, eyes perk up, hands shoot into the air, and we say to ourselves, "Now, they're with me!" This change in demeanor is much more than a reaction to novelty in the midst of classroom routine.

Storytelling is one of the oldest teaching strategies known to humankind, and it remains among the most effective.

Nearly three-quarters of a century ago, educational philosopher John Dewey (1934) made an important distinction between inner and outer attention. Long before the college years, students become expert in outer attention, in which they take in information but fail to comprehend fully their teacher's purpose. Inner attention, in contrast, refers to a deeper understanding, one in which the teacher's and the student's perspectives interconnect and the student truly grasps the insights of the field. In psychology, more than in other disciplines, experience is a vital foundation for students' inner attention and meaningful learning (Deniston-Trochta, 2003). In this chapter, I show how integrating life-story narratives into the teaching of psychology greatly eases students' task of making sense of psychological knowledge, as they place that knowledge in the context of their own lives and the lives of others.

TEACHING WITH A LIFE STORY: AN EXAMPLE

Stories that can potentially imbue the subject matter of psychology with living meaning are wide ranging. Among them are tales about friends or acquaintances, stories from the news media, segments of published biographies and autobiographies, and stories about ourselves. Before telling a story in my classes, I often ask a question about an important issue in the field and get students to state their opinions on the topic. Posing a provocative problem often induces dissonance that students want to resolve, and therefore helps ensure that the story will engage them.

For example, to open a unit on language development in my child-development course, I ask students for their thoughts on the following issue: "Are language and communication essential for the development of complex, reflective thought? Or can we acquire uniquely human, higher cognitive processes (such as planning, problem solving, and imagination) without language, our primary means of social contact with others? To shed light on this age-old question about the role of language in mental life, I tell students the story of Helen Keller, who from age 19 months — when illness robbed her of both sight and hearing — was deprived of the visual and aural stimulation on which children typically depend for rapid language learning. The following excerpts about Keller's life are derived from her autobiography, *The Story of My Life* (Keller, 1902/1988), and some of her letters and speeches.

Born in 1880 in Tuscumbia, Alabama, Keller, so her parents later told her, had an eager, self-assertive, and sociable disposition, and she was an imitator and early talker, saying her first words quite plainly before her first birthday. When in the middle of her second year — the period during which toddlers' vocabulary advances rapidly — Keller suddenly lost the ability to see and hear. What language she had acquired also vanished, and her lively disposition transformed into a vacant gaze. Still, the girl seemed driven to make contact with others. At times, she would stand between two people who were conversing and touch their lips. Then she moved her own lips and gestured frantically. When her efforts proved fruitless and no one responded, Keller's frustration mounted to such a peak that she kicked and screamed until she fell into a state of exhaustion. These rages invariably followed her failures to make herself understood. As she grew older, the eruptions occurred daily, and sometimes hourly.

Like deaf children whose parents communicate only verbally and do not sign (Goldin-Meadow & Mylander, 1998), Keller tried to invent her own form of communication in the face of sensory barriers to acquiring language from others. During her 6 years without a teacher, she invented just over 60 gestures. Among these limited signs were a pulling motion to mean *come*, a pushing motion to mean *go*, a slicing-and-buttering motion to mean *bread*, and pretending to shiver and turn on the freezer to mean *ice cream*. I ask my students to consider Keller's slow rate of gestural progress compared with the rapidity of the typical child's language acquisition during the preschool years: 10,000 words mastered by age 6, amounting to an average of five words per day (Anglin, 1993).

Without the language skills to converse with others, Keller remained locked, as she later described, "in an inhuman silence that severs and estranges" (Keller, 1902/1988, p. 35). Letters from family members and friends described her as "a wild, destructive animal." They tell how she broke dishes and lamps and grabbed from others' plates at mealtime. Following an incident in which Keller pinched and attacked her grandmother, a letter from her uncle admonished her mother "never to bring Helen to Grandmother's house again" (Lash, 1980).

Recounting her early childhood, Keller emphasized the disorientation and desperation that resulted from being deprived of the ability to communicate and therefore to think — qualities, she stated, that make a person human (Keller, 1902/1988, p. 22). I point out to my students that young Keller's impulsivity and explosiveness bear a strong resemblance to findings on deaf children of hearing parents, who do not have access to sign language as a rich basis for communicating with others. Compared to hearing children and to deaf children of deaf parents (for whom sign language is their native tongue), such children are far more likely to have frequent tantrums and be easily distracted and angered (Arnold, 1999; Marschark, 1993). The combination of impoverished parent–child communication and weak or absent self-control predicts serious delays in cognitive and social development (Bornstein, Selmi, Haynes, Painter, & Marx, 1999; Spencer & Lederberg, 1997).

Just before Keller's seventh birthday, her desperate parents hired her famous teacher, Anne Sullivan. Recognizing the importance of teaching Keller language, Anne quickly capitalized on the girl's intact sense of touch, spelling words into her hand. That famous moment, when Keller stood by a water pump and realized that *w-a-t-e-r* meant the cool liquid flowing over her hand, launched her access to a shared system of communication. The rest of that day, Keller touched numerous objects, eager to learn their names. During succeeding weeks, she added modifiers and verbs to her vocabulary and mastered the rules for expressing thoughts in sentences. Within a year, she began to master sign language, to read in Braille, to hand-write letters and daily entries in her journal, and to display an impressive quickness of thinking. Before long, she resolved to learn to speak by lightly touching another person's face to feel the position of the lips and tongue and then imitating the sounds. Although the process was slow and tedious and her articulation remained imperfect, Keller eventually became an accomplished orator, author, and crusader for the oppressed.

Language, then, enabled Keller to undergo a transformation from a mimicking animal to a conversing, thinking human being who, in her lifetime, made outstanding intellectual and social contributions. She commented:

> Before my teacher came to me, I did not know that I am. I lived in a world that was a no-world … I did not know that I knew [nothing], or that I lived or acted or desired. … I never contracted my forehead in the act of thinking … My inner life, then, was a blank without past, present, or future, without hope or anticipation, without wonder or joy or faith. (Keller, 1920, pp. 113–114)

The central role of language in the formation of mind and self is conspicuously evident in Keller's story. Her life offers unique insights into the consequences of profound early curtailment of language and the dawning of awareness that followed its acquisition. With language, a recent biographer summed up, Keller's "blind eyes saw, her deaf ears heard, and her muted voice spoke" (Einhorn, 1998, p. xxiii).

How Stories Foster Understanding of Human Behavior

My students, almost without exception, are moved by Helen Keller's story. Telling it, in fact, is among the few times during the semester when I can hear a pin drop — when I know, "I have them." It is also true of other stories I have used in my classes, too. I use stories as an organizing framework for class sessions, not for the explicit purpose of capturing my students emotionally and cognitively. But the fact that stories readily do capture their attention is profound confirmation of storytelling's power as a teaching tool. What happens when students are so moved? Scholars of storytelling as pedagogy claim that students cross the dividing line from *absorbing information* to *constructing meaning* (Bruner, 1986; Deniston-Trochta, 2003; Nagle, 2002).

Bruner (1990) pointed out that understanding human behavior depends on appreciating how people's actions are influenced by their beliefs and intentions. This understanding is achieved by participating in the way people naturally represent their experiences: through narrative discourse. As Bruner noted, "The very shape of our lives — the rough and perpetually changing draft of our autobiography that we carry in our minds — is made understandable to ourselves and to others through this narrative system of communication" (p. 33). In essence, Bruner argued, constructing stories is the major means through which we make sense of our lives and practices.

To illustrate this, think about what you would do if you were asked to tell the story of your life, or to recount a particular period in that story. In forming a spontaneous autobiography, you would link together smaller stories about incidents and occasions, with yourself at the center and other people in supporting roles. You would also arrange the stories sequentially, to conform to a culturally accepted organization of time. You would not only recount what happened but also *justify* the stories — that is, make them comprehensible to your listener and yourself by explaining, in the language of everyday discourse, why the events happened as they did.

Investigators of both child and adult development have, in the past two decades, become increasingly concerned with studying narrative. Emerging from this research literature is convincing evidence that narrative is a basic means for interpreting experience. For example, when toddlers first begin to speak, their main interest is talking about what people do and the consequences of their behavior, as in "Tommy hit" (Tommy hit me) and "Mommy car" (Mommy left in the car; Brown, 1973). Around age 2, children add descriptions of their own and others' internal states, using such words as *want*, *happy*, *mad*, and *think* (Bloom, 1998). Their early assertions about human action, desire, emotion, and perspective are the stuff of which narratives are made.

This armament of narrative tools enables children, as early as their preschool years, to comprehend the narratives of expert members of their culture and to begin to construct their own narratives. Across cultures, in families in which parents and children spend much time together, there is an abundant flow of stories recreating personal experiences. Through those stories, children construct increasingly elaborate images of themselves and acquire culturally accepted ways of organizing and interpreting their experiences. As a byproduct of participation, they gain a rich understanding of their own and others' mental lives, which aids them greatly in the explanation of their own and others' behavior (Fivush & Reese, 2002).

Because narratives are basic to our everyday interpretation of experience, they facilitate students' grasp of research and theoretical abstractions in a number of ways, which I will now describe.

Easing Information Processing

When teachers describe a story incident to illustrate a principle, they reduce processing demands on students. Thinking with relatively unfamiliar generalizations (e.g., "Is language essential for developing higher cognitive processes?") and drawing conclusions is cognitively demanding. Using illustrative stories eases information processing because it couches the abstractions in familiar terms that are close to the way people typically think about their own experiences. As a result, information becomes more understandable and memorable.

Making Sense of Psychological Processes

Stories contain a rich, naturalistic database for attributing meaning to behavior and communicating that meaning to others. Consequently, the phenomena represented in stories are relevant to a wide array of psychological theories. As people engage in narrative, they clarify their goals, values, and efforts to achieve positive outcomes in their world. They also confirm their self-worth by justifying their viewpoints and behavior to themselves and others (Baumeister & Newman, 1994).

Furthermore, in sharing stories, people often explore and try to reconcile widely differing perspectives. As a result, their narratives often bring into bold relief the mistaken assumptions that people make about one another. For example, a clinical psychologist related to her students several stories that highlighted the prejudice and discriminatory treatment that poverty-stricken families encounter — sometimes at the hands of the very professionals entrusted with helping them (Schnitzer, 1996). One story, called "They Don't Come In," tells of a mother and her children who waited 4 hours in a public health clinic for an appointment. The mother finally acceded to the cries of her restless, hungry youngest child for a snack and temporarily left the waiting room. In the meantime, the doctor appeared, inferred that the mother had failed to keep her appointment, and construed her absence as an irresponsible failure to provide her child with needed health care. A charge of child neglect was filed.

Enriching Understanding

Any single life story has multiple implications and potential interpretations. Consequently, we usually can return to a previously used story, extending its meaning for students. For example, in my child-development classes, I revisit Helen Keller's story to clarify a concept that is currently receiving much attention: *resilience*, the capacity to adapt effectively in the face of threats to well-being. Helen clearly displayed several of the personal and contextual ingredients of resilience that have recently been identified in a host of empirical investigations, including high intelligence; a determined, sociable disposition; and a warm, supportive relationship with a special adult (Masten & Reed, 2002; Masten et al., 1999).

I also draw on Keller's story to demonstrate the power of the human mind, when vitalized by communication with others, to compensate for profound sensory deprivation. From an early age, Keller could neither see nor hear; yet her speeches, essays, and books are richly laced with visual and aural imagery. Consider this highly visual description of a mimosa tree in the garden of her home: "Yes, there it was near the fence at the turn of the path, all quivering in the warm sunshine, its blossom-laden branches almost touching the long grass. Was there anything so exquisitely beautiful in the world before?" (Keller, 1902/1988, p. 21).

As Helen explained, this appreciation of the visual — of light, color, form, pattern, and depth — is not exactly the same as the sighted person's. But by using the same sensory language as all people, the mind of the person with a sensory deficit is influenced by the absent sense and can construct a representational world sufficiently similar to that of others that she can understand their experiences and be understood by them. Helen clarified:

> Perhaps my sun shines not as yours. The colors that glorify my world … may not correspond exactly with those you delight in; but they are nonetheless color to me. The sun does not shine for my physical eyes … nor do the trees turn green in the spring; but they have not therefore ceased to exist, any more than the landscape is annihilated when you turn your back on it. (Keller, 1902/1988, p. 23)

In these comments about her mental construction of a visual world, Keller offers students a noteworthy lesson in human perception and cognition: Can the brain engage in visual imagery centrally, in the secondary (or higher) visual areas of the cerebral cortex, without receiving sensory information directly from the eyes?

Keller's story suggests an affirmative answer, one that agrees with research on blind individuals, including those who from birth were unable to see. Like Keller, they use information gathered through touch, body movements, and language to form mental representations that are remarkably similar to the visual images of sighted people. With those images, they depict objects, orient in space, and generate cognitive maps (Chatterjee & Southwood, 1995; Loomis et al., 1993). Still, primary visual information processing enhances visual imagery, even though it is not necessary for it. People who are blind often perform poorly on active imagery tasks, such as following a path using a cognitive map (Stuart, 1995; Vecchi, 1998). Keller displayed this difficulty to an extreme degree. Friends and relatives reported that she had trouble finding her way even in highly familiar environments. She would often get up from a chair in her living room to go to the kitchen or bedroom and head the wrong way.

Stories Highlight the Significance of Culture

Narratives, with their emphasis on the storyteller's goals, values, and perspectives, vary widely across cultures. One of the most dramatic ways to impress upon students the profound impact culture has on our self-definitions and interpretations of experience is through an examination of the narratives of individuals from other cultures. In an investigation from which I often draw examples for my classes, researchers compared family storytelling in six Irish-American homes in Chicago and six Chinese homes in Taiwan (Miller, Fung, & Mintz, 1996; Miller, Wiley, Fung, & Liang, 1997). Parents in both cultures engaged their preschool children in narratives about pleasurable holidays and leisure excursions (such as a recent trip to the zoo) about as often and in similar ways. Chinese parents, however, more often told lengthy stories about the child's past misdeeds such as using impolite language, writing on the wall, or playing in an overly rowdy way. These narratives stressed the impact of the child's misbehavior on others ("You made Mama lose face!"), and often ended with directing teaching of proper behavior ("Saying dirty words is not good").

Influenced by Confucian traditions of strict discipline and social obligations, the Chinese parents integrated those values into the stories they told their young children, affirming the importance of not disgracing the family and, in the conclusion to their stories, explicitly conveying expectations for proper social behavior. In contrast, the Irish-American parents rarely dwelt on misdeeds in storytelling. Instead, they downplayed the child's shortcomings ("She must be tired today") or cast them in a positive light ("He's a spunky, assertive little fellow, isn't he?"), perhaps to promote positive self-esteem, which is highly valued in Western, and especially American, culture (Baumeister, Campbell, Krueger, & Vohs, 2003). The Chinese parents, then, used storytelling to foster collectivistic values of obligations to others, whereas the American parents used it to cultivate children's individuality (Miller, Wang, Sandel, & Cho, 2002).

Culture influences not just the content of narratives but their structure, thereby demonstrating profound variation in people's basic organization of experience and thinking. Because Western personal stories follow a culturally specified script in which experiences are ordered in time, build to a high point, describe a critical event, and resolve it, we often have great difficulty processing stories that proceed according to alternative organizations.

A case in point that I present to my students is the life story of Jessie Lennon (1996), an Australian Aborigine who took an epic honeymoon journey, on foot and jumping "the fast goods trains" (mail delivery trains). Jessie related her story orally, and later it was recorded and published. Unlike the linear stories we tell, Jessie's life events are undated, and they are not labeled with our familiar marker of time: age. Jessie never says, "When I was 4, this happened, when I was 10, this happened, and when I was 20, this happened." Instead, her narrative blends several related experiences, some of which stimulate others, producing a story with rapid shifts in times and settings. Here is an excerpt from her honeymoon expedition:

> We get married and we went to this one place, Finniss Springs. We get worried then — too far away. And one young fella … he said, "Come on! Let's go back!"
>
> "Yes," we said, we can go back. *Kulpanyi tjina* — walk back home … Then early morning I was sleeping, and my old man [husband] been telling his cousin … "Cook a damper *kangkuru* [kangaroo] — sister-cousin. *Kulpanyi ngura-kutu* — We're going home!"
>
> … We did walk back. Dad (husband) didn't know the country coming back from Finniss Springs …
>
> Later on … I was sittin' down and he was digging hole. I wanted him to dig all those *tjunkul tjunkuls*, water root plants . . . And he been digging them, you know. I could see him worrying too . . .
>
> Then when it get a bit darker, we see the lights coming — long way … It's the fast goods train. It's our train going through there . . . And he [husband] jumped on! And … I been *ngalya kalpanyi,* climbing up towards him … He just grabbed me … So we lay along then hanging on to one another to Kingoonya …
>
> And that train just come in … Jumped down, quick way again. We ran into his father up there. … He grabbed us and loved us up and said, "I'm glad that you come back. I thought I lost you two!" (Lennon, 1996, pp. 37–38, 48, 50–52)

At first glance, many students judge Jessie's story to be jumbled and unsystematic. However, I insist that they take a closer look, pointing out that research shows that some American ethnic minorities tell similarly constructed stories (Kang, 2003; McCabe, 1998). Rather than creating a strictly time-marked and ordered narrative, these cultural groups use a *topic-associating style,* in which they link together an array of related, significant experiences. For example, in an investigation of children's show-and-tell narratives at school, one African American 9-year-old told of having a tooth pulled, then described seeing her sister's tooth being pulled, next indicated how she removed one of her own baby teeth, and concluded enthusiastically, "I'm a pullin'-teeth expert … call me, and I'll be over" (McCabe, 1997, p. 164). Used to a different story structure, many teachers of minority children criticize the topic-associating approach as disorganized. When they do so (I emphasize to my students) they devalue those children's worldview and culture.

USING STORIES TO HELP STUDENTS CRITICALLY EVALUATE PSYCHOLOGICAL RESEARCH

Precisely because it captures the way people mentally organize their inner selves and the experiences of their lives, eliciting narrative is increasingly being relied on as a research method. As with other qualitative procedures, investigators who choose to gather narratives enter more fully into the research process than they do when they apply more "objective" methods. Herein lie the strengths and pitfalls of narrative. Juxtaposing it against other, more standardized research procedures permits students to examine the merits and limitations of each approach.

In a unit on death and dying in my lifespan-development course, I show my students a videotaped interview that I conducted with Chuck, a 59-year-old man dying of prostate cancer. Chuck's story is especially well suited to discussions of personality, stress, and coping. A teacher and then high school principal, Chuck dealt with his impending death by using it as an opportunity to teach others about terminal illness. He not only spoke to my students on video but also permitted our local newspaper to write a series of articles chronicling his last year, in which he described the physical and emotional adjustments he faced and the social supports that contributed to his serenity. Chuck noted that, in childhood, he had had to deal with serious problems, including parental divorce, his mother's inability to rear him (an aunt and grandmother had brought him up), surgery to remove a baseball-sized tumor from his chest, being blinded in one eye as a result of a car accident, and overcoming a failing record as a student. "My past experiences have played a tremendous role in how I have looked at my current situation. I've been very fortunate that I've been able to work out life's problems, with the help of family members and friends" (Berk, 1997). Epitomizing the set of personality traits that make up hardiness (Maddi, 1999; Pollock & Duffy, 1990), Chuck related how he had informed teachers and students at his school of his illness in a way that "made them accept and feel comfortable with it;" gathered with his wife and children to discuss how to spend their limited time left together; and made decisions about medical interventions that emphasized quality, rather than length, of remaining life. He explained:

> From the very beginning, I've looked at this in as positive a way as possible … My advice to others [with life-threatening illnesses]: Don't sit around and wait for death to happen. Perhaps, in a sense, we're all terminally ill because we never know what's around the corner. So let's just live life to the fullest, in whatever way we can." (Berk, 1997)

After viewing the videotape of Chuck's story, I ask my students, "Suppose I had simply followed Chuck around and recorded his behavior periodically, or used a uniform survey or checklist to gather information about him? They readily articulate that eliciting Chuck's story comes closer than any other technique to representing Chuck's thoughts and emotions. One student drew a connection with her own childhood experience of divorce:

> In our text, it says that if you rate children's adjustment, kids are mostly looking OK by about two years after their parents split up. After my parents divorced when I was 10, as a 12-year-old I looked OK from the outside, too. I was happy at school and had lots of friends. But if you had looked at my insides, had asked me how I felt, I could have told you how much I longed for some semblance of family life. To this day, I still carry around that longing.

Her remarks illustrate variations in findings on the long-term impact of divorce, depending on the method of inquiry researchers select (Hetherington & Kelly, 2003; Wallerstein, Lewis, & Blakeslee, 2000).

At the same time, my students volunteer that Helen Keller, in her autobiography, and Chuck, in his videotaped reflections on dying, might not have been entirely forthright about their thoughts and feelings. Furthermore, even if they were forthright, they might not have recalled everything accurately. "Maybe," said one skeptical student, "Chuck had a strong need to sum up his life as good and gratifying, After all, there wasn't much time left to refine it."

When invited to do so, my students engage in lively debate about the usefulness of narrative, much like disagreements between researchers over the validity of qualitative versus quantitative research procedures. Most students, however, are defenders of the unique insights that life stories offer. Some note that to engage in storytelling about highly personal and sensitive topics, it is difficult for most people to *not be themselves* for long. "If Chuck weren't telling it how he felt, it would eventually show," said one student proponent of the power of narrative. "You can tell by Chuck's demeanor that he's not playacting. He's being himself." Remarks like these open the door to a consideration of how one discerns whether Chuck is reflecting his real inner self and whether most people can agree with such an assessment. These are routes to discussing the ideas of reliability and validity — concepts that are highly challenging for beginning students but made easier to understand, so I have found, in the context of powerful examples like Chuck's story.

From gathering stories themselves, some students encounter conditions that awaken them to the realization that narrative is a more effective tool for gaining insight into the inner selves of some people than it is for others. A lifespan development student reported,

> I asked my grandmother, who had just celebrated her fiftieth wedding anniversary, what she thought made her marriage last so long. She had little to say. She isn't college educated, she isn't very verbal, and she might not be accustomed to reflecting on her marriage.

Besides verbal ability, culture makes a difference in the elaborateness of narrative. For example, Western children and adults produce more free-flowing, complex conversations about personal experiences than do their East Asian counterparts, whose collectivist cultural values cause them to feel embarrassed about engaging in talk that focuses on themselves (Han, Leichtman, & Wang, 1998; Pillemer, 1998; Weintraub, 1978).

IMPLICATIONS FOR TEACHERS AND STUDENTS: INTEGRATING LIFE-STORY NARRATIVES INTO THE CLASSROOM

By using life stories as an illustrative teaching tool, we can enhance students' understanding of human behavior in many ways. Stories link theory and research to real lives, thereby contextualizing the knowledge base of our field. Stories provide unique, clarifying insights into motivations that drive human behavior. In the course of exploring narrative examples, students often engage intensely with the subject matter. As stories capture their attention, students gain a deeper grasp of theoretical generalizations, which become more memorable. In addition, life-story narratives enhance students' capacity to see examples of psychological principles in their own lives. When I tell stories in class, I find that students spontaneously offer many more examples from their own experiences. Finally, integrating life stories into the teaching of psychology provides a satisfying response to student demands for relevance and usefulness in their courses.

I conclude with some suggestions, derived from my own efforts to teach with storytelling. First, compelling stories are easy to find because they are every-where. Almost any life has something to teach, and our capacity to use life-story narratives in the classroom is greatly aided by their omnipresence. Effective sto-ries can concern such profound and significant issues as Helen Keller's resolve to surmount deafness and blindness or Chuck's adaptation to terminal illness. They can also be narrower: an adolescent's transition from elementary to junior high school; a young adult's adaptation to a first job; a member of a minority group encountering painful incidents of prejudice and discrimination; or a middle-aged individual recounting what it was like to turn 40 years old. We can elicit stories from people we know and then retell their tales, or the storyteller can be invited to class or be recorded on videotape, speaking for him- or herself. We can also tap the plethora of fascinating stories within biographies and autobiographies at our local libraries and in the human-interest sections of our newspapers (see, for example, Benjamin, 2005; Sdorow, 2005).

Second, when telling compelling stories in the classroom it helps to have en-ergy, expressiveness, and enthusiasm. Fortunately, as we have seen, stories are an early developing, common form of discourse; before we entered school, most of us began to acquire skills for good storytelling through everyday conversation. Consequently, finding the storyteller in each of us is not difficult. Nevertheless, rehearsing a dramatic narration in front of a mirror with animated gestures and variations in voice and facial expressions can help make a story come alive for students when the story is told in class. We also can capitalize on today's "smart classrooms" to create seamless, highly involving multimedia tales — for exam-ple, by using PowerPoint to highlight major story events and their significance, display accompanying photos of story characters, and (if available) show video clips of important happenings. Whether we create a simply told tale or an elabo-rate, theatrical presentation, the keys to effective classroom storytelling are the same as the keys to good teaching: careful planning and practice.

Third, having students tell stories, orally in class or in written assignments, can expand their learning. After I tell students a story, I frequently ask them for a short narrative or two on the same theme. Often their responses confirm and ex-pand on the topic at hand. However, sometimes their tales offer counterexamples and, as a result, spark critical thinking about theory and research. Moreover, I find that during in-class sharing of narratives, even the most reticent students — ones who have never contributed to class discussion — find a voice through storytell-ing. Because exchanging stories is such a familiar form of everyday discourse, it eases shy students' anxiety about joining in class discussion, helps connect them to their classmates, and fosters their active participation in the classroom.

Yet another approach I use to enhance subject-matter mastery through storytelling is the *portraits assignment*, in which students select a topic, write a three-page narrative about their own significant experiences or those of someone they know related to that topic, and then explain how those experiences illustrate important principles and findings — or, alternatively, offer exceptions and, thereby, illustrate individual and cultural variations. Students respond enthusiastically to the portraits assignment. Some titles of recent papers they prepared in my child- and lifespan-development courses include "Jim and Henry Adopt Luke, a Drug-Addicted Newborn," "Ten-Year-Old Amy Copes with Her Parents' Divorce," "Anselmo is Forced to Retire," "Sasha, a Russian High School Exchange Student, Spends a Year in the United States," "Helen Learns She Has Breast Cancer," and "Stereotypes of Aging: 86-Year-Old Esther Has Dinner at a Chicago Restaurant."[1]

Although storytelling as a teaching strategy has seldom been investigated systematically, one case study of a distinguished professor, widely recognized at a large university for his teaching excellence, found that a major factor in his popularity was his frequent, effective storytelling (Cooper, Orban, Henry, & Townsend, 1983). The professor explained, "The lecture is not in little segments. I don't rush through to cover X amount. I think, 'What do they need to know and how best can I get it to them?'... I like to tell a story" (p. 176). At the end of the semester, his students consistently expressed confirming reactions, such as these:

"He holds your interest; he uses relevant stories, which break up the routine. He seems more human, down to earth. I see him as another individual rather than someone inaccessible up on a platform."

"One reason he's so good is the way he communicates . . . He motivates me to try harder. He tells stories and backs them up with facts and examples. They click in my head. I remember his stories." (p. 177)

Research has yet to address gains in student involvement and learning that accrue from thoughtful storytelling. Yet remarks like these suggest that the benefits of teacher–student sharing and interpretation of stories are far-reaching.

REFERENCES

Anglin, J. M. (1993). Vocabulary development: A morphological analysis. *Monographs of the Society for Research in Child Development, 58*(10, Serial No. 238).

Arnold, P. (1999). Emotional disorders in deaf children. In V. L. Schwean & D. H. Saklofske (Eds.), *Handbook of psychosocial characteristics of exceptional children* (pp. 493–522). New York: Kluwer.

Baumeister, R. F., & Newman, L. S. (1994). How stories make sense of personal experiences: Motives that shape autobiographical narratives. *Personality and Social Psychology Bulletin, 20*, 676–690.

Baumeister, R. F., Campbell, J. D., Krueger, J. I., & Vohs, K. D. (2003). Does high self-esteem cause better performance, interpersonal success, happiness, or healthier lifestyles? *Psychological Science in the Public Interest, 4*, 1–44.

Benjamin, L. T. Jr. (2005). Archival adventures: History lessons from reading other people's mail. In B. Perlman, L. I. McCann, & W. Buskist (Eds.), *Voices of experience: Memorable talks from the National Institute on the Teaching of Psychology* (Vol. 1, pp. 17-32). Washington, DC: Association for Psychological Science.

Berk, L. E. (1997). *Videotaped interview with Chuck Snook.* Normal, IL: Illinois State University Television Production Studio.

Bloom, L. (1998). Language acquisition in its developmental context. In D. Kuhn & R. S. Siegler Eds.), *Handbook of child psychology, Volume 2: Cognition, perception, and language* (5th ed., pp. 309–370). New York: Wiley.

---

[1] To obtain a copy of the portraits assignment, contact the author at leberk@ilstu.edu.

Bornstein, M. H., Selmi, A. M., Haynes, O. M., Painter, K. M., & Marx, E. S. (1999). Representational abilities and the hearing status of child/mother dyads. *Child Development, 70*, 833–852.

Brown, R. (1973). *A first language: The early stages.* Cambridge, MA: Harvard University Press.

Bruner, J. (1986). *In search of mind: Essays in autobiography.* Cambridge, MA: Harvard University Press.

Bruner, J. (1990). *Acts of meaning.* Cambridge, MA: Harvard University Press.

Chatterjee, A., & Southwood, M. H. (1995). Cortical blindness and visual imagery. *Neurology, 45,* 2189–2195.

Cooper, C., Orban, D., Henry, R., & Townsend, J. (1983). Teaching and storytelling: An ethnographic study of the instructional process in the college classroom. *Instructional Science, 2,* 171–190.

Deniston-Trochta, G. M. (2003). The meaning of storytelling as pedagogy. *Visual Arts Research, 29,* 103–108.

Dewey, J. (1934). *Art as experience.* New York: Capricorn Books.

Einhorn, L. J. (1998). *Helen Keller, public speaker.* Westport, CT: Greenwood.

Fivush, R., & Reese, E. (2002). Reminiscing and relating: The development of parent–child talk about the past. In J. D. Webster & B. K. Haight (Eds.), *Critical advances in reminiscence work: From theory to applications* (pp. 109–122). New York: Springer.

Goldin-Meadow, S., & Mylander, C. (1998). Spontaneous sign systems created by deaf children in two cultures. *Nature, 391,* 279–281.

Han, J. J., Leichtman, M. D., & Wang, Q. (1998). Autobiographical memory in Korean, Chinese, and American children. *Developmental Psychology, 34, 701*–713.

Hetherington, E. M., & Kelly, J. (2003). *For better or for worse: Divorce reconsidered.* New York: Norton.

Kang, J. Y. (2003). On the ability to tell good stories in another language: Analysis of Korean EFL learners' oral "frog story" narratives. *Narrative Inquiry, 13,* 127-149.

Keller, H. (1920). *The world I live in.* New York: Century.

Keller, H. (1988). *The story of my life.* New York: Signet. (Original work published 1902)

Lash, J. P. (1980). *Helen and teacher.* New York: Delacorte.

Lennon, J. (1996). *And I always been moving!* Coober Pedy, South Australia: Australia Council for the Arts.

Loomis, J. M., Klatzky, R. L., Golledge, R. G., Cicinelli, J. G., Pellegrino. J. W., & Fry, P. A. (1993). Nonvisual navigation by blind and sighted: Assessment of path integration ability. *Journal of Experimental Psychology: General, 122,* 73–91.

Maddi, S. R. (1999). The personality construct of hardiness: 1. Effects on experiencing, coping, and strain. *Consulting Psychology Journal: Practice and Research, 51,* 83–94.

Marschark, M. (1993). *Psychological development of deaf children.* New York: Oxford University Press.

Masten, A. S., Hubbard, J. J., Gest, S. D., Tellegen, A., Garmezy, N., & Ramirez, M. (1999). Adaptation in the context of adversity: Pathways to resilience and maladaptation from childhood to late adolescence. *Development and Psychopathology, 11,* 143–169.

Masten, A. S., & Reed, M. J. (2002). Resilience in development. In C. R. Snyder & S. J. Lopez (Eds.), *Handbook of positive psychology* (pp. 74–88). New York: Oxford University Press.

McCabe, A. (1997). Developmental and cross-cultural aspects of children's narration. In M. Bamberg (Ed.), *Narrative development: Six approaches* (pp. 137–174). Mahwah, NJ: Erlbaum.

McCabe, A. E. (1998). *Chameleon readers: Teaching children to appreciate all kinds of good stories.* New York: McGraw-Hill.

Miller, P. J., Fung, H., & Mintz, J. (1996). Self-construction through narrative practices: A Chinese and American comparison of early socialization. *Ethos, 24,* 1–44.

Miller, P. J., Wang, S., Sandel, T., & Cho, G. E. (2002). Self-esteem as folk theory: A comparison of European American and Taiwanese mothers' beliefs. *Parenting: Science and Practice, 2,* 209–239.

Miller, P. J., Wiley, A. R., Fung, H., & Liang, C.-H. (1997). Personal storytelling as a medium of socialization in Chinese and American families. *Child Development, 68,* 557–568.

Nagle, R. (2002). Transforming the horde. In C. A. Stanley & M. E. Porter (Eds.), *Engaging large classes: Strategies and techniques for college faculty* (pp. 315–323). Bolton, MA: Anker.

Pillemer, D. B. (1998). *Momentous events, vivid memories.* Cambridge, MA: Harvard University Press.

Pollock, S. E., & Duffy, M. E. (1990). The Health-Related Hardiness Scale: Development and psychometric analysis. *Nursing Research, 39,* 218–222.

Schnitzer, P. K. (1996). "They don't come in!": Stories told, lessons taught about poor families in therapy. *American Journal of Orthopsychiatry, 66,* 572–582.

Sdorow, L. M. (2005). The people behind psychology: Enliven your lectures with biographical vignettes. In B. Perlman, L. I. McCann, & W. Buskist (Eds.). *Voices of Experience: Memorable talks from the National Institute on the Teaching of Psychology* (Vol. 1, pp. 1-16). Washington, DC: Association for Psychological Science.

Spencer, P. E., & Lederberg, A. (1997). Different modes, different models: Communication and language of young deaf children and their mothers. In L. B. Adamson & M. Romski (Eds.), *Communication and language acquisition: Discoveries from atypical development* (pp. 203–230). Baltimore, MD: Paul H. Brookes.

Stuart, I. (1995). Spatial orientation and congenital blindness: A neuropsychological approach. *Journal of Visual Impairment and Blindness, 89*, 129–141.

Vecchi, T. (1998). Visuo-spatial limitations in congenitally totally blind people. *Memory, 6*, 91–102.

Wallerstein, J. S., Lewis, J., & Blakeslee, S. (2000*). The unexpected legacy of divorce: The 25 year landmark study*. New York: Hyperion.

Weintraub, K. J. (1978). The value of the individual: Self and circumstance in autobiography. Chicago: University of Chicago Press.

VOICES OF EXPERIENCE

CHAPTER EIGHT

"WHAT'S YOUR PREDICTION?"

Introducing Psychology via Common Sense

Saul Kassin

Williams College

WHEN I WAS preparing to apply to graduate school, living in New York City, I was torn between the desire to attend the best possible program, wherever that might take me, and the impulse to stay close to my girlfriend of 3 years. Only 21 years old at the time, I wondered: How would long distance affect our relationship? Everyone I knew had an opinion. One view was that the bond would weaken: "Out of sight, out of mind." Another was that our relationship would be enhanced: "Distance makes the heart grow fonder." There were two opposing folk theories — both derived from common sense and both plausible. (To complete the story: I left the city, my girlfriend and I broke up a year later, and I met my wife in graduate school.)

One of the challenges in teaching psychology — compared to teaching chemistry, math, economics, history, creative writing, or a foreign language — is that our students do not enter the classroom as blank slates onto which we etch our imprint of the science of psychology. Quite to the contrary, college students and other laypeople are "implicit psychologists," armed with intuitive and often nonconscious theories of personality, social behavior, motivation, human development, abnormality, and other aspects of mind and behavior (Heider, 1958; Wegner & Vallacher, 1977). Interested in lay conceptions of intelligence, for example, Sternberg, Conway, Ketron, and Bernstein (1981) asked college students, commuters, and shoppers to write down the characteristics of an intelligent person and produced a long list of traits, including: *reasons logically, makes sound decisions, sizes up new situations well, reads widely, has good ideas, solves problems quickly, thinks before speaking, accepts others for what they are*, and *has an interest in world events*.

I open every class and almost every topic by touching base with commonsense theories of psychology that students bring to class. There are two reasons I like to do this. First, asking students to articulate their own commonsense theories as a preview to a topic forces them to think about that topic and commit themselves to a hypothesis. Commonsense theories of psychology can be self-contradictory and malleable. This exercise thus helps to preempt the "I knew it all along" feeling that students sometimes express in and after classes. That reaction springs from the *hindsight bias*, a tendency for people to think, after an outcome becomes known — like the result of a political election, the verdict in a high-profile trial, the winner of a sports championship, or the results of a program of research — that they knew in advance what that outcome would be (Fischhoff, 1975; Hawkins & Hastie, 1990). In fact, if students articulate their implicit theories early on in order to assess their baseline level of intuitive knowledge (i.e., the extent to which their beliefs are supported by the research), they could mark their progress over the course of a semester and experience a "Look at what I learned that I didn't already know" effect when it's over.

The second reason to check in on common sense is to get students into the habit of thinking like psychologists. Students should be aware of, and wary of, their own implicit theories, and should understand that implicit theories collectively held within a culture provide fertile ground for the development of myths. They also should be critical consumers of pop-psychology claims that they hear in the news, and should know that it is wise to seek out science-like proof to verify or debunk these claims — even when it comes to the commonsense beliefs of so-called experts. In *Escaping the Advice Trap*, Wendy Williams and Stephen Ceci (1998) gathered 59 real-life relationship problems from their own families and friends, and then sought solutions for each problem from two to five experts selected from a pool of 100 eminent psychologists and psychiatrists. When they compared the solutions proposed by the different experts they found that there was little agreement. In one case, for example, a young wife complained that her husband spent too much money on the family even when they were trying desperately to save for a house. One psychologist suggested that she control her husband's impulsive buying, another told her to loosen up and join in his spending, and a third advised her to seek a compromise of their values. "Just because a person is an expert," noted Williams and Ceci, "doesn't mean that his or her advice is right for you, or that a second expert wouldn't give you the opposite opinion" (p. xi).

How Common Sense Makes Psychology Relevant in Law

Before describing pedagogical methods of assessing students' intuitive theories, let me say more about why the common-sense issue is so important for psychologists — and for the discipline — to address. In recent years, researchers from many areas of psychology have systematically studied important issues in law, such as the factors that enhance or undermine the reliability of eyewitness identifications. As reported in Scheck, Neufeld, and Dwyer's (2000) *Actual Innocence*, recent DNA-exoneration cases have shaken the criminal justice system at its core, revealing that eyewitness errors are by far the single most common basis of wrongful convictions (http://www.innocenceproject.org/). The science of eyewitness memory is one of psychology's great success stories when it comes to application.

There are two ways that eyewitness researchers can help to prevent miscarriages of justice. The first is to use their research as a basis for procedural reforms that are designed to reduce eyewitness errors. This was successfully realized in a

1999 National Institute of Justice manual entitled *Eyewitness Evidence: A Guide for Law Enforcement* (see Wells et al., 2000). A second way for psychologists to assist is to serve as expert witnesses at trial when the sole evidence against a defendant is a problematic eyewitness identification. In cases of this nature, the purpose of a psychological expert is to educate the jury about factors that influence human perception and memory. Within the scientific community, there is general acceptance about a number of empirically based principles — for example, that witnesses are more accurate at same-race than other-race recognition, that memory can be corrupted by postevent information, and that self-reported confidence is malleable and not a reliable predictor of accuracy (Kassin, Tubb, Hosch, & Memon, 2001). In American courts, however, experts are sometimes excluded by trial judges, and not permitted to testify, on the ground that their testimony would not assist the jury. The rationale: Following common Bayesian logic (in which the impact of new information is measured against prior beliefs) and for subject matters that fall within the knowledge base of the average layperson, juries are presumed to be sufficiently equipped by common sense — and hence, do not need assistance from an expert.

The same dilemma presents itself when it comes to research on the psychology of interrogations and confessions. In criminal law, confession evidence is the government's most potent weapon — so much so, as one prominent legal scholar put it, that "the introduction of a confession makes the other aspects of a trial in court superfluous" (McCormick, 1972, p. 316). Yet confessions are also a recurring and disturbing source of controversy. As in the Salem witch trials of the 17th century, the pages of legal history reveal that certain social influence techniques of interrogation can lead people to confess to crimes they did not commit. As in the high-profile Central Park jogger case, it is estimated that roughly a quarter of all DNA-exoneration cases had contained false confessions in evidence and that innocent people are at risk inside the interrogation room (Kassin, 2005). One would think that the phenomenon of false confessions is highly counterintuitive, a flagrant breach of common sense. Yet even after I described for a Missouri judge significant psychological findings to the contrary — including Stanley Milgram's (1974) surprising and unpredictable research findings on obedience to authority, fundamental attribution error studies showing that people in general are undersensitive to the situational causes of human behavior, and forensic studies showing that mock jurors do not sufficiently discount confessions they see as coerced — he ruled to exclude my expert testimony on the ground that the jury is sufficiently equipped by common sense.

Bringing Commonsense Psychology Into the Classroom

There are plenty of ways to bring commonsense theories of psychology into the classroom. The simplest is what I call Putting Common Sense to the Test, an activity that involves creating a set of true/false questions to assess students' intuitive beliefs about substantive material to be discussed in class that day or week. For presentation purposes, it makes for good theater to put a handful of statements up, or distribute them before class, and then take a public show-of-hands survey of the results. You can then uncover the answers on the spot, one at a time, enabling students to score their own test. The discussion that is sure to follow can then be used to preview and heighten interest in the rest of the class — or the answers can be withheld until the topic is addressed, leading students to see and even to critique the research from which the answer was derived.

Commonsense psychology items are easy to write and present. Instruct students as follows: "Here are some statements that concern ____, a topic that we will address in today's class or in the coming week. Read each statement carefully and indicate whether you think it is generally true or false. When you have finished, try to estimate the number of answers you gave that were correct." (This last data point is interesting, as it can be used to show that students in general are more confident in their commonsense beliefs on some topics, such as close relationships, than on others, such as thinking and reasoning.) Box 1 presents a sample set of items that an instructor can use on the opening day of Introductory Psychology, to preview the syllabus, heighten student interest in the material, and generate lively discussion.

Asking students for their own beliefs about psychological phenomena is one way to check in on students' common sense. In fact, a particularly interesting variant of this exercise is to have students themselves administer a common-sense test to friends, which takes less than a minute, then tally the results and note the accuracies and misconceptions in their peers' beliefs. In this way, students get to approach the common-sense issue as researchers, not just as subjects. They also get to see firsthand the diversity of implicit psychology theories that people hold and the myths that characterize collective beliefs within a population.

BOX 1

PUTTING COMMON SENSE TO THE TEST

Answer True or False:*

_____ 1. Although 90 percent of Americans are right-handed, left-handedness is common in nonindustrialized cultures.

_____ 2. Some people dream; others do not.

_____ 3. Behaviorists often use punishment to eliminate unwanted behaviors.

_____ 4. Human memory capacity is limited and cannot truly be increased through the use of memory "tricks."

_____ 5. People are intuitively skilled at knowing when someone is lying or telling the truth.

_____ 6. Children's IQ scores are not predictive of their later grades in school.

_____ 7. A smile has different meanings in different cultures.

_____ 8. As the number of people in a group increases, so does their social impact on an individual.

_____ 9. A schizophrenic is someone with a multiple or split personality.

_____ 10. Stress can weaken the heart, but it cannot affect the immune system.

*All answers are False.

Many years ago, I stumbled onto and refined another activity that accomplishes even more in getting college students to think like psychologists. It all started when I was lecturing a class on Milgram's (1974) disturbing but classic obedience research. I described the whole experimental paradigm, including how subjects were recruited; the cover story they were told; the shock machine they were to use; the grunts, screams, and pleas of the learner; and the cold, bureaucratic prodding from the experimenter. Then I told students that an astonishing 65 percent of all subjects fully obeyed the experimenter's commands by delivering the maximum of 450 volts to the hapless and likeable confederate. Despite my widened eyes and the tone of disbelief in my voice, the students barely reacted. Some were too busy taking notes; most had not quite digested my words, much less the implications. I confronted the class with its nonresponsive reaction, but to no avail. One student, I recall, said he knew that most people were easy to push around so the result was not that surprising. I vowed that this would be the last time that I would allow students the opportunity to exhibit an "I knew it all along" effect about this research. The next time I taught Milgram, I described the situation but then stopped short of the results to elicit predictions from everyone in the class. I even called on willing students to explain the basis of their predictions. Almost to a person, the students underpredicted levels of full obedience. Then when I uncovered the results, the room filled with an audible gasp. Now *that's* the reaction I was hoping for.

From this experience, I went on to create a standardized activity I called What's Your Prediction? To orient students to a topic, and to get them thinking in concrete-operational terms, I try to provide them with a fully detailed account of an actual study. Some of the studies I have used are classics in the field, like Milgram's; others are new or hot off the presses. Some are highly controlled laboratory experiments; others are single case studies, field studies, archival or naturalistic observations, or self-report surveys. In some, I ask students to imagine being a participant in an experiment. In others, I cast them into the role of the researcher or an outside observer. In all cases, I have found that it is important to set the stage with a clear statement of the problem and a vivid description of the setting — including the procedures that were used and the dependent measures that were collected. Often I will "prime" the way students construe the problem and make a prediction by describing some alternative plausible theories. Once it is clear that students understand the problem and methods, I ask them all to predict the results. The actual findings are then revealed, and this inevitably is followed by a reaction and discussion of what they mean. The four steps of this activity are summarized in Box 2 (see Page 102).

I have now used this type of exercise for many years and found that it works like a charm. After students have thought about a problem and then publicly, typically by a show of hands, committed themselves to a specific prediction, they quite literally sit at the edge of their seats in anticipation of the actual results, eager to know what happened. When the results are revealed, there is an instant burst of emotion, a mixture of cheers, jeers, applause, and high-fives. Then when the initial outburst subsides, like clockwork, the hands go up — mostly from students who *mis*predicted the results. These students want to know more about the methods that were used, or how the participants were instructed, whether the experimenters and their cover stories were credible, or how the questions were worded. Often they suggest alternative methods of operationalizing variables or testing the same hypothesis. It's interesting to watch this process unfold. Just like scientists who are slow to revise or abandon their pet theories in the light of inconsistent data (Greenwald, Pratkanis, Leippe, & Baumgardner, 1986), undergraduates are reluctant to disbelieve the commonsense theories that underlay their predictions. As a result, they become engaged to think critically not only about their theory but about the methods that were used to test it. Yet an added "subliminal" benefit of this exercise is that it gets students accustomed to thinking about approaching questions about psychological phenomena in terms of introductions, methods, results, and discussions.

Let me illustrate this approach with three examples — all on different topics (intelligence, motivation, and psychotherapy), and each illustrating a different research methodology (archival analysis, field experiment, self-report survey). Although I have presented these specific examples elsewhere (Kassin, 2004), there is no limit to the numbers of such exercises that one can prepare.

WHAT'S YOUR PREDICTION:
ARE PEOPLE SMARTER TODAY THAN IN THE PAST?

The Situation

Just about everyone is curious about intelligence and the tests that are used to measure it. Most of the tests were created early in the 20th century, and since then, IQ-test scores have been used to determine children's academic potential

---

BOX 2

WHAT'S YOUR PREDICTION?

The Situation:
Students are asked to imagine being part of a study — as a participant, researcher, or observer. In all cases, they should be given a vivid account of the procedures used.

Make a Prediction:
Next, the students are told what measures were taken, perhaps sometimes provided with plausible hypotheses, and then asked to predict the results.

The Results:
The actual findings are then revealed in the same format in which the predictions were made. Often there is an audible gasp from the class, quickly followed by a combination of cheers and jeers.

What Does It All Mean?
Students become engaged in a discussion of the results, analyses of the methods used, proposals for follow-up studies, and what it all means — and doesn't mean — in theoretical and practical terms.

---

in schools throughout the world. The fact that people have been taking IQ tests for many years, and that you may have taken a test similar to one taken by your parents and grandparents, raises a fascinating question: Have scores changed over time? Are people today more or less smart than a few years ago, or is human intelligence too stable a trait to change in so short a time?

Being trained in psychology, you are accustomed to conducting experiments, often in the laboratory. To answer the question about IQ trends across generations, however, you will need to use different methods. You will need to gather old scores from tests that were taken at different times by comparable groups of people. So you contact researchers all over the world and ask if they would send you test scores that have been compiled over the years. In particular, you want scores from tests that were never altered over time and were given to large groups of adults of different generations. You receive the data you need from a number of developed countries — including Australia, Austria, Belgium, Brazil, Canada, China, France, Germany, Great Britain, Israel, Japan, the Netherlands, New Zealand, Norway, Switzerland, and the United States. Now it is time to analyze the results.

Make a Prediction

As we will see shortly, IQ tests are set so that the average score in the population is always 100. This means that if raw scores were to rise or fall over time, the scale would have to be readjusted like a thermostat in order to keep that average. The question is, what has happened to raw scores over the past 70 or so years? To make your prediction, look at Figure 1a and use the year 1920 as a starting point. Based on 1920 standards, which set the average IQ at 100, what do you think the raw, nonadjusted scores were in 1930, 1940, and other decades up to 1990? Has IQ steadily increased over time, decreased, fluctuated in response to historical events, or stayed essentially the same? Think carefully about the problem. Then, using Figure 1a, plot your predicted trend for each decade.

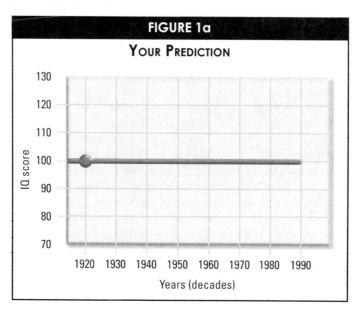

The Results

When James Flynn (1987) first compiled the IQ scores in 14 developed nations (he later added 6 more), the worldwide trend was unmistakable. If you look at Figure 1b you will see that from one generation to the next, without exception, there have been steady and massive gains in IQ scores — so much so that today's average adult scores 24 points higher than in 1920. Named after its discoverer, this phenomenon is now known as the Flynn effect.

What Does It All Mean?

For years, psychologists have hotly debated the nature of intelligence, the validity of the tests that are used to measure it, and the extent to which being smart is the product of nature or nurture. Flynn's discovery that IQ scores have risen sharply over the years has provoked discussion of these core issues. Are you really smarter than your ancestors, or is it possible that while IQ has risen, "intelligence" has not? What does the rise in IQ over such a short period of time imply about there being a genetic basis for intelligence? What environmental factors could have been responsible for the increase — could it be more time spent in school, parents with more education, better nutrition, or access to more information from radio, TV, and the Internet? What might we project through the 21st century? Researchers are now trying to answer these provocative questions (for updates, see Flynn, 1999; Neisser, 1998).

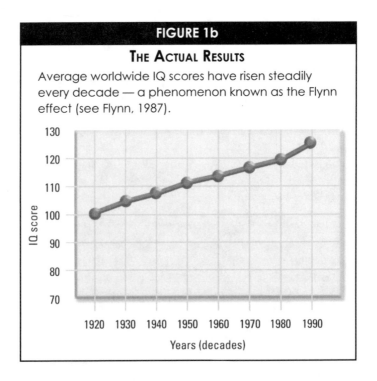

FIGURE 1b

THE ACTUAL RESULTS

Average worldwide IQ scores have risen steadily every decade — a phenomenon known as the Flynn effect (see Flynn, 1987).

VOICES OF EXPERIENCE

WHAT'S YOUR PREDICTION:
WHAT DOES IT TAKE TO MOTIVATE PEOPLE AT WORK?

The Situation

The year was 1927. Calvin Coolidge was president, Babe Ruth hit 60 home runs, Charles Lindbergh flew across the Atlantic Ocean for the first time, and the American economy seemed sound, though it would soon plummet into depression. Just outside Chicago, the Hawthorne plant of the Western Electric Company employed close to 30,000 men and women in the manufacture of telephones, wires, cables, and office equipment. As in other large companies, management wanted to boost the morale, motivation, and productivity of its employees. The bottom line was what mattered most.

At first, the Industrial Relations Branch of Western Electric thought that they could make workers at the plant more productive by altering the illumination levels in their factory. Proceeding in logical fashion, they increased the lighting for one group of workers in a special *test room*, kept the lighting unchanged in a *control room*, and then compared the effects on their productivity. Western Electric then brought in a team of experts to vary other conditions in the factory. For 5 years, groups of employees from various departments were selected to do their work in a test room where, at different times, they were given additional rest periods, coffee breaks, free midmorning lunches, shorter workdays, shorter weeks, a new location, overtime payments, personal financial incentives, dimmer lights, or just a different method of payment. At one point, the researchers even went back and merely reinstated the original prestudy conditions inside the test room.

Make a Prediction

The researchers involved in this project wanted to know how to increase the motivation and productivity of workers, as measured by their hourly output. Using existing performance levels at the plant as a basis for comparison, they asked what changes in the workplace would have a positive impact. Consider the conditions they varied listed below and check off those that, in your opinion, increased worker productivity.

Brighter lighting   _____
Dimmer lighting   _____
Two 5-minute rest periods   _____
1-hour-shorter workday   _____
1/2-day-shorter week   _____
15-minute rest + free lunch   _____
Financial incentives   _____
Back to original conditions   _____

The Results

If you thought that adding financial incentives would boost worker productivity, you were right. This change was followed by a 12.6 percent increase in hourly output. If you thought that a shorter workday or a shorter workweek or a free lunch had positive effects, you were right again. Brighter lighting? Yes. Dimmer light? Yes again. In fact, productivity rates increased no matter what the researchers did — even when they dimmed the lights so low that workers could hardly see and even when they merely reinstated the original prestudy conditions. So the correct prediction was to check off *all* conditions.

What Does It All Mean?

The Hawthorne project, which was described in a classic book, *Management and the Worker* (Roethlisberger & Dickson, 1939), has had a great influence on the study of human motivation in the workplace. At first, the researchers were puzzled and discouraged. With positive effects being observed in all test rooms (even when the original pretest conditions were in place), it seemed that the project had failed. Think for a moment about the results, however, and you will see why these studies have proved important. With striking consistency, workers became more motivated and more productive not because of any specific changes that were made but because they had been singled out for special assignment. Workers assigned to all test rooms knew that they were being studied, and they performed well with the added attention. This phenomenon, known as the Hawthorne effect, laid a foundation for the scientific study of behavior in the workplace and for the realization that people are motivated not only by money but also by their own needs and social relationships. The Hawthorne plant no longer exists, but the study conducted there has helped psychologists understand an important practical side of human motivation.

WHAT'S YOUR PREDICTION: DOES PSYCHOTHERAPY HELP?

The Situation

People who have personal problems — like being depressed or anxious, drinking too much, having marital trouble, or feeling generally unhappy without knowing why — wonder where they can turn for help. Sometimes people turn to friends, relatives, clergy, or family doctors; at other times, they seek help from psychologists, psychiatrists, and other mental-health specialists. Do the specialists really help? Do psychotherapy and other forms of mental-health intervention produce the kind of improvement we all hope for?

To answer these questions, *Consumer Reports* (*CR*) added a survey about psychotherapy to its annual questionnaire, in which readers are asked to rate laundry detergents, breakfast cereals, home appliances, automobiles, and other products and services. *CR* asked readers to fill out a special mental-health section "if at any time over the past three years you experienced stress or other emotional problems for which you sought help." The survey was mailed to 184,000 randomly selected subscribers, and 22,000 responded — a 13-percent response rate that is typical of *CR* surveys. Of those who returned it, 35 percent said they had a mental-health problem. Within this group, 40 percent sought some kind of professional help. Specifically, 2,900 sought help from a psychologist, psychiatrist, social worker, or marriage counselor; the others saw family doctors or self-help or support groups.

All respondents were asked to indicate the nature and severity of their distress and to provide background information about the cost, insurance, type of therapy, and other matters. Then they rated the extent to which their treatment helped with their specific problem (and, more generally, with their work and social lives and sense of personal fulfillment). They also indicated their overall level of satisfaction or dissatisfaction with the therapy.

Make a Prediction

On the question regarding improvement, survey respondents indicated whether the treatment made things a lot worse, somewhat worse, no different, somewhat better, or a lot better. So, how many do *you* think reported improvement? Specifically, what percentage of the respondents in this survey said they were somewhat better or a lot better after treatment? Was it 10 percent, 25 percent, 50 percent, or 90 percent? Next, consider the respondents' level of satisfaction with the therapy they received. What percentage do you think said they were highly satisfied? What percentage was fairly satisfied? Using the table below, make predictions for both sets of measures.

Measures	Overall responses
Improvement	___ % Somewhat better
	___ % A lot better
Satisfaction	___ % Fairly satisfied
	___ % Highly satisfied

The Results

In November 1995, *CR* published the results of this survey, the largest ever conducted on the topic, and concluded that patients in general derive substantial benefit from psychotherapy. Just how substantial was the overall level of improvement? Combining all the respondents — regardless of the type of problem they had, the type of therapist they saw, or the amount of time they spent in treatment — the percentages of those who said they were a lot better and satisfied were striking. As you can see in the table below, a total of 86 percent felt they were improved after therapy and 89 percent were satisfied with the experience.

Measures	Overall responses
Improvement	44% Somewhat better
	42% A lot better
Satisfaction	27% Fairly satisfied
	62% Highly satisfied

What Does It All Mean?

Over the years, the number of people seeking professional help for psychological problems has climbed. With soaring medical costs and the limits imposed by managed care and other health-insurance policies, those in need of help — the consumers of psychological treatments — need to know whether these treatments work. *Consumer Reports* has a reputation for being fair and objective in its evaluations of products and services. But are these particular survey results valid? Are *CR* subscribers representative of the population? Is it possible that people who were satisfied with their experience were more likely to take part in the survey than those not satisfied? Would they have felt better, eventually, without outside help? Is it possible that the self-reported improvements, which could not be externally verified, were exaggerated? Or is it possible that psychotherapy truly helps those in need?

When psychologist Martin Seligman (1995) presented the results to psychologists, he set off a wave of controversy. In 1996, the journal *American Psychologist* devoted an entire issue to commentary and debate about this study and what it meant. Some were critical of the study and its methods. Others, including Seligman, defended it and stood by the results. This controversy about whether psychotherapy is effective, for whom, and under what conditions, has a long history. In fact, controlled studies do show that psychological therapies (as well as many drug-based interventions) *are* generally effective, offering hope, social support, and an opportunity to open up for people in distress.

IMPLICATIONS FOR TEACHERS AND STUDENTS

The Merriam-Webster online dictionary defines the term *common sense* as "the unreflective opinions of ordinary people." When it comes to the subject matter of psychology, college students, like many laypeople, are highly opinionated. The problem with these commonsense beliefs is that they are often contradictory, elusive, and hard to pin down — which is why many of our most cherished and surprising discoveries, once they are revealed and explained, seem intuitive in hindsight (not only to college students, but to trial judges and others).

For psychology instructors, Putting-Common-Sense-to-the-Test and What's-Your-Prediction exercises are easy to write and to use in class. There are three good reasons to introduce psychology material in these ways.

First, these activities are engaging and just plain fun for students. There must be something about the competitive nature of the task that awakens and energizes the mind. I have not seen another method of presentation that quite motivates students to think and care about a phenomenon in this way. I should add, too, that opening a class with some type of common-sense quiz or prediction activity is a great way to "loosen the jar" and get students asking questions, speculating, and arguing. This technique helps to establish a classroom norm of interactivity that will outlast the exercise itself. A second benefit is to compel students to confront their own elusive, often-contradictory, implicit theories. Personally, I like to preempt the "I knew it all along" feeling students sometimes express and that can frustrate us as teachers. Allowing students to contemplate their own assumptions before they are exposed to psychology's theories and research has the added benefit of enabling them to see what they have learned — that they did not already know. Third, the prediction exercise gets students to think critically, like psychologists, about research methods. Because the activity is standardized in its structure, students become subtly acclimated to thinking about empirical psychology questions in terms of introductions, methods, results, and discussions of the implications; in a not-so-subtle way, they also come to realize that when it comes to designing a study to test a hypothesis, the devil is in the operational details. Now, if I could just get trial judges to think in these ways …

REFERENCES

Fischhoff, B. (1975). Hindsight/foresight: The effect of outcome knowledge on judgment under uncertainty. *Journal of Experimental Psychology: Human Perception and Performance, 1,* 288-299.

Flynn, J. R. (1987). Massive IQ gains in fourteen nations: What IQ tests really measure. *Psychological Bulletin, 101*, 171-191.

Flynn, J. R. (1999). Searching for justice: The discovery of IQ gains over time. *American Psychologist, 54*, 5-20.

Greenwald, A. G., Pratkanis, A. R., Leippe, M. R., & Baumgardner, M. H. (1986). Under what conditions does theory obstruct research progress? *Psychological Review, 93*, 216-229.

Hawkins, S. A., & Hastie, R. (1990). Hindsight: Biased judgments of past events after the outcomes are known. *Psychological Bulletin, 107*, 311-327.

Heider, F. (1958). *The psychology of interpersonal relations*. New York: Wiley.

Kassin, S. M. (2004). *Psychology* (4th ed.). Upper Saddle River, NJ: Prentice Hall.

Kassin, S. M. (2005). On the psychology of confessions: Does innocence put innocents at risk? *American Psychologist, 60*, 215-228.

Kassin, S. M., Tubb, V. A., Hosch, H. M., & Memon, A. (2001). On the "general acceptance" of eyewitness testimony research: A new survey of the experts. *American Psychologist, 56*, 405-416.

McCormick, C.T. (1972). *Handbook of the law of evidence* (2nd ed.). St. Paul, MN: West.

Milgram, S. (1974). *Obedience to authority: An experimental view*. New York: Harper & Row.

Neisser, U. (Ed.) (1998). *The rising curve: Long-term gains in IQ and related measures*. Washington, DC: American Psychological Association.

Roethlisberger, F. J., & Dickson, W. J. (1939). *Management and the worker*. Cambridge, MA: Harvard University Press.

Scheck, B., Neufeld, P., & Dwyer, J. (2000). *Actual innocence*. Garden City, New York: Doubleday.

Seligman, M. E. P. (1995). The effectiveness of psychotherapy: The *Consumer Reports* study. *American Psychologist, 50*, 965-974.

Sternberg, R. J., Conway, B. E., Ketron, J. L., & Bernstein, M. (1981). People's conceptions of intelligence. *Journal of Personality and Social Psychology, 41*, 37-55.

Wegner, D. M., & Vallacher, R. R. (1977). *Implicit Psychology: An introduction to social cognition*. New York: Oxford University Press.

Wells, G. L., Malpass, R. S., Lindsay, R. C. L., Fisher, R. P., Turtle, J. W., & Fulero, S. M. (2000). From the lab to the police station: A successful application of eyewitness research. *American Psychologist, 55*, 581-598.

Williams, W. M., & Ceci, S. J. (1998). *Escaping the advice trap*. New York: Andrews McMeel.

CHAPTER NINE

WAS IT GOOD FOR YOU, TOO?

Keeping Teaching Exciting for Us and for Them

Douglas A. Bernstein

University of South Florida

BEGAN TEACHING undergraduate courses in abnormal, clinical, and introductory psychology in 1967. This is plenty long enough to get fed up and bored with teaching and with students who ask me if I'm going to say anything important on the day they will be out of town, or whose excuses for missing a test include such things as "my mother had a vasectomy" or "a flaming squirrel set my yard on fire."

Still, I never fail to get nervous before I walk into the classroom. In other words, I'm still excited about teaching, and I would bet that you are, too. Yet, I sometimes wonder what we have to be so excited about. After all, we have to work hard at teaching, many of us have overly heavy teaching loads, we have committee and other responsibilities, we don't get paid that much, we don't always get a lot of support from administrators, and the status of teachers is not all that high in the public mind. (How much does your state legislature spend on education compared to professional athletics or highways or prisons?). Let's not forget the need to deal with student and parent complaints, and even lawsuits, arising from low grades and the like.

Perhaps most potentially depressing is anecdotal and other evidence showing that our students forget most of what we teach them within a few months, a few weeks, a few days, even a few minutes after we teach it. To me, when students ask if the final exam is going to be cumulative, they are really asking "Is it OK to start forgetting this stuff now, or should I wait until the end of the semester?"

Humorist Robert Benchley (1927) recognized the pervasiveness of this forgetting process in an article entitled "What College Did to Me." He listed all 39 things he could remember from his college days. Twelve were from his freshman year and just eight from his senior year, and included the following:

- Charlemagne either died or was born or did something with the Holy Roman Empire in 800.
- There is a law in economics called the law of diminishing returns.
- Queen Elizabeth was not above suspicion.
- The ancient Phoenicians were really Jews, and got as far north as England where they operated tin mines.
- Emerson left his pastorate because he had some argument about communion.
- Almost everything you need to know about a subject is in the encyclopedia.
- You can sleep undetected in a lecture course by resting the head on the hand as if shading the eyes.

In the same vein, comedian Don Novello (as Father Guido Sarducci) used to suggest that there be a Five Minute University that would teach in 5 minutes everything that a person will have remembered 5 years after completing a college degree. So the content of a course in Economics would consist entirely of the phrase "supply and demand," while the philosophy course would include only "I think therefore I am," and the psychology class would teach only the words "stimulus and response."

The situation isn't that bad, of course. It may be worse. Consider a study in which students took a test of basic psychological knowledge four months after completing an introductory psychology course. Their average score was 70 percent correct. Not bad, but the impressiveness of this performance was undermined by the 62-percent average score earned by a comparison group who had never taken a psychology course (Rickard, Rogers, Ellis, & Beidleman, 1988). In some cases, then, our students may not forget what we teach them; they might not have learned it to begin with, or they might have learned what they know before they ever took our classes.

I am obviously exaggerating the down side of teaching psychology, but only to make the point that there are things about the enterprise that can dampen anyone's enthusiasm for arising at dawn on a cold winter morning to go to class one more time and see how many students have decided to do the same. Yet, keeping ourselves fresh and enthusiastic as teachers is important for both educational and personal reasons. In terms of our educational impact, when we are having some fun as teachers we are likely to be more enthusiastic in the classroom, and this is likely to improve our teaching, our students' attentiveness, and our teaching evaluations. Students do not enjoy listening to teachers who are bored or depressed, so it is no wonder that student ratings of teacher effectiveness are strongly related to students' perceptions of teacher enthusiasm, caring, interest, and the like. Interestingly, these ratings are less strongly related to teachers' actual characteristics as measured by objective personality tests (Freeman, 1988). I guess it is important to remember that sincerity is the most important thing in life; once you can fake that, you've got it made.

Maintaining Enthusiasm for Teaching

How can we keep our excitement about teaching alive year after year? Here are some suggestions that I hope will serve as reminders to expert teachers and as new information for teachers who are just entering our field.

Be Selfish

First, I think we have to be a little bit selfish. By this I mean that, in addition to working at keeping our courses current and accurate for our students' sake, we should work just as hard at making teaching enjoyable for our own sake. After all, we're in our courses for the long haul; our students are gone after one term.

If you haven't already done so, give yourself permission to have a good time while you are teaching, and let your students know that, within limits, it's okay for them to have a good time while learning. This isn't always easy to do because of the archetypal image of dull teachers and dull teaching that lies somewhere in the minds of almost anyone who has ever been in school. For anyone who can break through these implicit expectations of what teaching and learning should be, being selfish enough to have fun in class should be no problem. Specifically, I suggest that, no matter what teaching format you prefer — lecture, discussion, seminar, collaborative learning, or whatever — you plan at least one major highlight for each and every class, a highlight that you will enjoy and can look forward to.

Classroom Demonstrations

Classroom demonstrations provide excellent examples of what I mean by highlights. Students love them, they learn from them, and they remember them. I suggest that you use them whenever possible and that you choose demonstrations that are fun for you as well as educational for your students. I like active demonstrations that prompt students to process course material more deeply than if I had just talked about it or used passive methods.

For example, you can lecture about the phenomenon of compliance, but it is so much more memorable for students, and so much more fun for you, to first demonstrate the power of an authority figure (you) to produce compliance. This quick demonstration involves nothing more than asking the class to do silly or pointless things, the sillier and more pointless the better. In my classes, I just say that I would like to conduct a simple demonstration that requires class participation. I then ask the students to think of a number from one to ten, to stand on one foot (the right if they are left-handed, and the left if they are right-handed) and then to hop the same number of times as the number they chose. If I feel like creating a little more fun, I also ask them to turn a complete circle (to the left if they are right-handed, to the right if they are left-handed) and then sit down. (Colleagues have suggested other tasks, such as having students exchange seats, glasses, or even articles of clothing with one another.) In some cases, I ask the class to give me a standing ovation, complete with whistles and cheers (it takes several tries before the desired level of enthusiasm is reached, but with encouragement, the results are rather gratifying).

When these ridiculous tasks are completed, I explain that the purpose of the demonstration was to illustrate compliance, and I ask the class why they did what I asked them to do. The ensuing discussion highlights the point that people routinely do what they are asked to do when the request comes from a legitimate authority, and provides a nice entree into consideration of other social phenomena such as conformity and obedience. Doing the demonstration with the entire class is much better than doing it with a single volunteer, first because the group format makes it impossible for any student to dismiss the power of compliance effects;

no one can claim, "I wouldn't have done that." In addition, including the entire class avoids the possibility of embarrassing a single volunteer.

I don't ever worry that such demonstrations might take up too much class time. I believe that college students of any age are, or should be, responsible adults, so I try to offer a course that provides them with both the opportunity and the encouragement to read and learn from the textbook, whether I have time to lecture on it or not. This approach is not a radical one, really. Even if it were possible to cover an entire textbook in class, students would still have a lot of learning to do outside of class. I simply try to structure my classes in a way that makes it more likely that they will do some of that independent learning. A wide range of ideas for classroom demonstrations is available in several handbooks (e.g. Benjamin, Nodine, Ernst, & Blair-Broeker, 1999; Ware & Johnson, 2000a, 2000b, 2000c), as well as in the instructor's manuals that accompany many psychology textbooks.

Remember to plan and even rehearse demonstrations before trying them out in class. The consequences of not doing so were dramatically demonstrated some years ago by a colleague who wanted to show his introductory psychology students how the principles of learning are applied to training dogs in the local police department's canine corps. He arranged to have an officer come to class with his police dog, but because of schedule conflicts there was no time to work out the details of the demonstration. The first time the professor laid eyes on the officer and the dog was when the former was punishing the latter just outside the classroom building. When asked what was going on, the officer said, "The first thing he has to learn is to fear you." This would have been a good time to cancel the demonstration, especially since the professor also noticed that the dog was blind in one eye (there had been an accident during an exercise designed to train him not to startle at the sound of gunshots). Undaunted, the professor brought the officer and the dog onto one side of the stage of his theater-size classroom, where the first event was to display the dog's instantaneous response to spoken commands. With a student volunteer standing on the other side of the stage wearing a full-length protective cuff on his arm, the officer told the dog to attack, and the animal immediately charged toward the student. Before he reached his target, the officer gave the "stop" command, and the dog tried to stop, but slid the rest of the way across the polished surface of the stage and began to chew on the padded arm of the now-frightened student. Needless to say, the students will long remember this demonstration — but they probably won't remember the learning principles it was designed to illustrate!

Active-Learning Opportunities

Opportunities for students to engage in active learning can also provide highlights for your teaching. For example, we can teach experimental research methods by lecturing on concepts such as independent and dependent variables, control groups, random sampling, and replication, but I find that students are more likely to focus on the material if they are first put in the position of a scientist. To heighten their involvement, and my enjoyment, I begin my first research-methods lecture by presenting students with a phenomenon that they would like to explain, but for which there is no obvious or easy explanation.

I accomplish this task by doing one or two simple but impressive magic tricks disguised as illustrations of my "psychic abilities," then I admit the ruse and invite the class to figure out how I could have fooled them. The beauty of this active-learning exercise is that skeptical students will have started trying to debunk my claim of special powers even before I admitted the truth, and those who had been convinced of the reality of my "paranormal" skills are now motivated to understand how they could have been so easily fooled. In other words, both groups will be challenged to use their critical-thinking skills, and to apply research methods in the service of those skills. By the way, these tricks are available in numerous sources, including magic books and the instructor's manual that accompany psychology textbooks, but if you prefer to use other, nonpsychic targets for critical thinking, consider displaying television commercials, print ads, newspaper stories, pseudoscientific web sites, or even psychology journal articles for your students to analyze.

As long as you present inherently interesting and provocative material (on, say, the value of dietary supplements, the dangers of cell phones, the effects of low-carb diets, the impact of day care, or the like) students are usually eager to begin their scientific analysis. To guide them, I like to offer a five-step outline for thinking critically — about psychology or anything else:

1. What am I being asked to believe?
2. What evidence is available to support the assertion?
3. Are there alternative ways of interpreting the evidence?
4. What additional evidence would help me to evaluate the alternatives?
5. What conclusions are most reasonable given the evidence available?

As another example of an active learning opportunity, consider the diagnosis of psychological disorders. After lecturing about various disorders, you could go on to lecture about the reliability of the diagnostic system. But you could also give students a chance to "diagnose" clinical cases presented through audio- or videotaped interviews, and to compare notes to estimate the reliability of their diagnostic decisions.

There are dozens of other active-learning opportunities to look forward to, if you take the time to incorporate them into your courses. Once you decide to incorporate active-learning experiences into your classes — for the benefit of your students and yourself — you can do it. Take any concept you teach and ask yourself: "What can I do to get my students to do something while learning this concept in addition to reading about it or listening to me talk about it?"

Cartoons

Another of my favorite teaching highlights in almost every class session is to use cartoons to illustrate the points I am making. I like to think that cartoons help students remember course material, but I use them partly because they provide enjoyment for me. I sometimes even put cartoons on exams or quizzes and then ask content questions about them. *Dilbert*, *The Far Side*, *Close to Home*, and many other cartoon series offer a wonderful source of hilarious new material to illustrate psychological principles and, sometimes, the misapplication of those principles. To give just one example, the first panel of a drawing published in *The*

New Yorker magazine shows a boy struggling to stay above water in a pond and telling his dog, Lassie, to "get help." The second panel shows the dog lying on a psychiatrist's couch while the therapist takes notes. What better way to illustrate the difference between surface structure and deep structure in language! There are copyright laws to consider when using cartoons, of course, but if you do not publish the material or benefit financially from its use, you are unlikely to run into serious problems.[1]

Music

Playing music in class is yet another kind of highlight to look forward to in class. I sometimes play taped music as the students enter the classroom, just before beginning a lecture, just before moving on to a new topic, or to give an example of some process or phenomenon. My choice of music is almost never in synch with my students' musical tastes, but that is not the point of presenting it. I ignore the moans and groans and after playing a (usually short) segment of a particular song, I ask the student to consider what it has to say about parenting, or depression, or prejudice, or whatever. Sometimes I ask how the song exemplifies, or contradicts, psychological principles and research results. Here are some examples:

♦ "She's Leaving Home" (The Beatles): effects of authoritarian parenting on child development and family relations
♦ "I Know What I Know" (Paul Simon): the impact of top-down processing and expectation in perception of ambiguous stimuli (play song segment twice; after telling students what the words are, they will be able to hear the words clearly)
♦ "The Girls All Get Prettier at Closing Time" (Mickey Gilley): motivation's effects on perception (students know the phenomenon as "beer goggles")
♦ "Please, Mister, Please, Don't Play B-17" (Olivia Newton John): impact of conditioned stimuli on the activation of emotional memory
♦ "Why Do We Want What We Know We Can't Have?" (Reba McEntire): Maslow's concept of deficiency motivation
♦ "It's in His Kiss" (Betty Everett): lie detection
♦ "You've Got a Friend" (James Taylor): role of social support in stress coping
♦ "Life Turned Her That Way" (Ricky Van Shelton): inherited vs. learned aspects of personality
♦ "Cleopatra, Queen of Denial" (Pam Tillis): psychological defense mechanisms
♦ "When Something Is Wrong with My Baby, Something Is Wrong With Me" (Sam and Dave): interdependence in intimate relationships

If your own choice of songs doesn't sit well with your students, invite them (or even assign them) to choose, transcribe, and discuss the lyrics of songs that they think better illustrate or exemplify psychological principles. (This is also a good way to expand and update your musical "repertoire" for future classes.)

---

[1] This cartoon originally appeared in *The New Yorker* and was reprinted in the March 2005 issue of the Association for Psychological Science *Observer*.

Classroom Examples

A final category of classroom highlights for you is the use of vivid, humorous, offbeat, or otherwise memorable examples of psychological concepts, principles, and phenomena. I treat my collection of examples like my collection of cartoons or music — that is, as a resource that I look forward to using and to which I am always adding. Now I am sure there are psychology teachers who can, on the spur of the moment, come up with clear, interesting, funny examples to illustrate perfectly almost any aspect of their lectures, but I am not one of them. I fill my lecture notes with several good examples of course content so that I will always remember the right one when I need it. Having several examples available also allows me to offer a second or third illustration if the first one does not do the job.

Sometimes, the best examples will occur to you in the shower, while you are driving, or maybe at the supermarket, so be sure to write them down as soon as possible and add them to your lecture notes, or just jot them in the margins of your lecture notes as highlights that you know will be fun to use.

Don't be afraid to use incidents from your personal life as classroom examples. Personal experiences that illustrate psychological material can humanize you in your students' eyes, and make you more likeable, even if — or especially if — the story makes you look foolish. When I lecture on psychodiagnosis, I never fail to describe the day when some friends and I were aboard a Washington-state ferryboat in the San Juan Islands. We noticed a man standing motionless at the stern with his arms spread wide above his head. As the only psychologist in the group, I concluded that the man was probably delusional, perhaps fancying himself a Christ figure. My friends were quite impressed with my instant diagnosis until some seagulls arrived to take from the man's outstretched hands the food he had been offering them. The moral of the story is not to jump to diagnostic conclusions until you have enough evidence to make an informed decision.

IMPLICATIONS FOR TEACHERS AND STUDENTS

So that is my sermon for today. I hope that those of you who are new to teaching will find my comments helpful for making teaching fun and that all you veterans will find at least some of these thoughts helpful in keeping teaching fun. Maintaining your enthusiasm has many side benefits. For one thing, you can turn a potential source of stress (teaching) into a source of enjoyment. In doing so, you can perhaps enjoy life a bit more and maybe even live longer. One psychology professor I know told me that the only time he wasn't upset about his impending divorce was when he was having a good time teaching his abnormal psychology course. Enjoying your teaching might also result in more interesting classes, more student learning, better teaching evaluations, and possibly larger pay raises. After all, as mentioned earlier, students do tend to give higher ratings to teachers whom they perceive as enthusiastic about their courses.

In short, if maintaining your enthusiasm as a teacher can bring a little better health and a little more wealth, why not make it one of your teaching goals? To help you remember to focus on this goal, build and rely on a social support network of other faculty who share this goal. Go to regional and national teaching conferences. Get together with other teachers on campus (not necessarily in psychology) to talk about teaching — perhaps at weekly or monthly lunches or coffee hours at which you can discuss syllabus construction, classroom management and discipline problems, student–faculty relations, gender issues, make-up policies, cheating, and the like. Visit other faculty's classrooms and invite them to visit yours. You'll probably find that you teach better than you ever thought you did, and you will also pick up valuable ideas for further improvement (Goss-Lucas & Bernstein, 2005). Don't forget to sign up for teaching-related Internet mail groups such as TIPS (Teaching in the Psychological Sciences; http://acsun.frostburg.edu/cgi-bin/lyris.pl?enter=tips&text_mode=0&lang=english), Psychteacher (http://teachpsych.lemoyne.edu/teachpsych/div/psychteacher.html), and CommColl (a discussion list especially for faculty teaching at two-year institutions (for information, send email to listserv@lsv.uky.edu). If you are not already a member, join the Society for the Teaching of Psychology, a group of the most enthusiastic teachers you will ever encounter (for more information, visit their Web site at http://teachpsych.lemoyne.edu/teachpsych/div/divindex.html). Finally, take advantage of books about the teaching of psychology, including volumes 1 and 2 of *Lessons Learned* (Perlman, McCann, & McFadden, 1999, 2004) and *The Teaching of Psychology* (Davis & Buskist, 2002).

I hope I have reminded you that, despite its potential for burnout and boredom, teaching psychology also offers the potential for endless stimulation and deep satisfaction. Teaching is, truly, what each of us makes of it. I hope that you make it not only a solid and research-based enterprise, but also one that is enjoyable for you as well as your students.

REFERENCES

Benchley, R. (1927). *The early worm*. Garden City, New York: Blue Ribbon Books.

Benjamin, L., Nodine, B., Ernst, R., & Blair-Broeker, C. (Eds.). (1999). *Activities handbook for the teaching of psychology* (Vol. 4). Washington, DC: The American Psychological Association.

Davis, S. F., & Buskist, W. (2002). *The teaching of psychology: Essays in honor of Wilbert J. McKeachie and Charles L. Brewer*. Mahwah, NJ: Erlbaum.

Freeman, H. R. (1988). Perceptions of teacher characteristics and student judgments of teacher effectiveness. *Teaching of Psychology, 15*, 158-160.

Goss-Lucas, S. & Bernstein, D. A. (2005). *Teaching psychology: A step by step guide*. Mahwah, NJ: Erlbaum.

Perlman, B., McCann, L. I., & McFadden, S. H. (1999). *Lessons learned: Practical advice for the teaching of psychology* (Vol. 1). Washington, DC: Association for Psychological Science.

Perlman, B., McCann, L. I., & McFadden, S. H. (2004). *Lessons learned: Practical advice for the teaching of psychology*. (Vol. 2). Washington, DC: Association for Psychological Science.

Rickard, H. C., Rogers, R., Ellis, N. R., & Beidleman, W. B. (1988). Some retention, but not enough. *Teaching of Psychology, 15*, 151-153.

Ware, M., & Johnson, R. (Eds.) (2000a). *Handbook of demonstrations and activities in the teaching of psychology, Volume 1: Introductory, statistics, research methods, and history* (2nd ed.). Mahwah, NJ: Erlbaum.

Ware, M., & Johnson, R. (Eds.). (2000b). *Handbook of demonstrations and activities in the teaching of psychology, Volume 2: Physiological-comparative, perception, learning, cognitive, and developmental* (2nd ed.). Mahwah, NJ: Erlbaum.

Ware, M., & Johnson, R. (Eds.). (2000c). *Handbook of demonstrations and activities in the teaching of psychology, Volume 3: Personality, abnormal, clinical-counseling, and social* (2nd ed.). Mahwah, NJ: Erlbaum.

CHAPTER TEN

HOW TO RUIN A PERFECTLY GOOD LECTURE

Presentation Software as a Teaching Tool

David B. Daniel
University of Maine at Farmington

I HAVE GIVEN the content of this chapter as a live presentation in many venues, to a variety of faculty, in a few different countries. Keeping true to the medium of presentation software — or "slideware" (Microsoft PowerPoint, Corel Presentation, Apple Keynote, etc.) — my presentation is highly visual, and, in keeping with my presentation style, it is fairly colloquial and informal. My goal, when I give this presentation, is to demonstrate to the audience what their students are put through when teachers use slideware and to question the universal use of this technology as a tool to promote learning. Provoking sometimes visceral reactions to common mistakes we make in our slideware presentations has been an effective method to prompt many members of my audience to reexamine their teaching methods. My goal in this chapter is not to provide a literature review or persuade anyone to change their teaching practices. I hope to encourage reflection on the place of slideware in your classroom in relation to your role as a teacher and to offer some suggestions about how best to use the technology.

Although the content of this chapter reflects my own personal experience and viewpoints, I am fortunate that the main points I make are broadly supported by a growing literature on the subject. However, I derived the content of this chapter firsthand, witnessing many teachers, both newer and more experienced, begin using slideware for the first time in their courses, General Psychology in particular. Often, I am fortunate to sit with the students as faculty make their presentations, listen to students' whispers, witness their reactions, and see what they are putting in their notes. As course coordinator, I also see the students' exam grades and work with particular students to improve their performance. Thus, I am privileged to view the use and outcomes of slideware from a variety of perspectives. I have found that there is a fairly typical set of mistakes that faculty seem to make at first. My hope is to encourage you to think about your options and select the most appropriate techniques and resources for your own personal learning objectives.

TIME MARCHES ON

I cannot tell you how many people come up to me after my presentations, proudly proclaiming that they are "old school," preferring overheads to slideware. I can relate. I remember when I was reluctant to move from the chalkboard to overheads. I recall watching otherwise competent instructors break into a cold sweat when the overhead bulb did not work or when they occasionally dropped their transparencies, fumbling around and putting them in the wrong order. I am sure there was a time when the chalkboard itself was considered an innovation and many people felt it to be the end of learning. It is amazing how soon we forget. Technology, it seems, is a relative term.

How does slideware compare to overheads in the classroom? In a recent study, DeBord, Aruguete, and Muhlig (2004) compared overhead use and slideware use on measures of student learning and preference. Both presentation modes had the same content. Not surprisingly, there was no difference in student learning. Students did, however, prefer the slideware format. Although I applaud these authors for offering data demonstrating that we do not lose anything in the transition, I believe that it is a mistake simply to view slideware as modern overheads. Just as overheads provided a wonderful opportunity to display graphs, pictures, and other visuals much more dynamically than on a chalkboard, slideware offers many powerful (and often distracting) new tools to enhance the visual display of information. In particular, slideware allows us to include a wider variety of pictures and graphs, in addition to motion, sound, video, and the ability to integrate all of these things into one smoothly running and comprehensive presentation. In this respect, simply putting the same content onto a new format is not a fair or, ultimately, useful comparison. In fact, there is a growing amount of evidence that multimedia components like slideware can increase learning and satisfaction in a variety of classroom settings (see Bagui, 1998; Erwin & Rieppi, 1999; Fletcher, 2003; Mayer, 2001). However, teachers' transitions to slideware should be done purposefully and with caution.

POWER CORRUPTS AND POWERPOINT CORRUPTS ABSOLUTELY

Try to imagine your favorite oration dissected and presented in a slideware format. (I like to use Martin Luther King's "I have a Dream" speech for this exercise.) As you imagine this, please note how the very act of using slideware changes the rhythm, presentation style, passion, and even content of the presentation. Such a change is seldom for the better. If we are to use slideware effectively, it must be viewed as a supplement to a learning experience. We must be ever mindful of the important ways we allow the format of slideware to alter, and often dilute, the power of our message.

In the hands of certain people — and we all know who they are — slideware can indeed be counterproductive. We have all sat through overly busy, text-laden presentations staring at someone's back while they read 3-foot-tall paragraphs to us. The fault lies in the execution more than the software itself. When I talk with many users of slideware about their perspective when they develop their presentations, they seldom report giving thought to the way slideware interacts with, and impacts, their lecture. However, this impact can be both subtle and substantive (Tufte, 2003). The linearity of the programs; the templates that encourage the user to break ideas into smaller, unintegrated bullets; and the many distracting options are all potential obstacles to teaching and learning.

Allowing the structure of these programs, rather than your own goals and methods, to become the primary guide for your presentations, creates a very real risk of obscuring rather than clarifying your point. In other words, if teachers do not assert themselves into the software, defining it as a teaching tool rather than a presentation template, the software may dominate the presentation, relegating the lecture to a note-taking ordeal instead of an opportunity for real learning. Slideware is not useful for every learning objective. Once you define your goals and learn the capabilities of slideware, you will most likely use it less often, and I view this as a sign of maturity. Simply put, slideware is good for some people, some of the time.

I believe that a large source of the strong feelings about slideware is confusion about its purpose. In many settings, slideware is used to present information. The goal is to share information and maybe to persuade. In teaching, however, the goal is not merely information dissemination. Rather, we are guiding students' thinking, and providing scaffolding and examples (e.g., Mayer, 2001). To many teachers, this distinction is very useful. I have found that simply viewing slideware as a tool for teaching as opposed to a presentation tool can lead to productive shifts in how teachers use it.

The primary difference associated with viewing slideware as a teaching tool, as opposed to a presentation tool, is with regard to the goals of the presentation. If your goal is to teach, your audience's reaction to the slides is much more important in the development of the presentation. The presentation becomes a cognitive guide. Rather than simply sharing information, your goal is to promote meaningful changes in memory, learning, and perspectives. Therefore, it is imperative that you develop your presentation with your students and their learning in mind. This task may be more of a challenge than you think. In the next few sections, I will demonstrate how the classroom setup and student habits can interfere with your role as a teacher when using slideware.

Classroom Characteristics

Many of our colleges and universities have begun retrofitting classrooms with digital projectors that allow teachers to hook up computers for multimedia presentations. On some campuses, like mine, these are called "smart classrooms." Ironic? As an example of how technology can take over the teaching process, I would like to offer my version of the evolution of the smart classroom and some of the consequences and challenges this evolution poses to good teaching.

Back in the old days, the teacher typically occupied the front of a classroom. From this vantage point, for good or ill, the teacher was at the center of attention. As films became available, a screen was placed in the teacher's position. There was no competition for prominence, as the film and teacher were seldom "on" at the same time. As overheads became available, the film screen was repurposed for the overhead projector. However, the teacher typically stood next to or near the projector, sharing the central space of the classroom. Digital projectors also project onto this same screen. Unlike overhead projectors, however, their placement is in direct competition with the teacher. The teacher is typically pushed off to the side of the classroom while the presentation has figuratively, and often quite literally, taken the teacher's place. To add insult to injury, the lights have to be dimmed substantially in order for the projected image to stand out. So, there you are, a teacher in the corner in the dark!

So "technology taking over the classroom" is more than just a metaphor, and it is not just a matter of the physical placement of the teacher. Just as slideware presentations can dominate the classroom and push the teacher to the side, the software also can substantially influence the structure of a lecture, shifting the prominence of the teacher–learner relationship toward a more passive, technology–transcriber relationship. In order for presentation software to be effective, teachers must reclaim their prominence in the classroom. When teaching in a classroom like the one described above, get a remote control (at the very least), and move out of the shadows.

Student Characteristics

If you ever get the opportunity, I encourage you to watch students during a slideware presentation. With every click onto a new slide, they look up at the screen, look down at their notebook, and furiously begin writing. The teacher talks, but the students are too busy writing down everything on the slide to listen. It is quite interesting to watch, and a great demonstration of conditioning (it kind of looks like pigeons pecking). This behavior is not limited to students, either. I was watching an audience of psychologists at a recent NITOP presentation as a wonderful speaker gave an interesting presentation. On either side of her was a screen where her slides could be seen. At each click the audience parted, looking to the right or left of the presenter, concentrating on the slide as opposed to the speaker. Later on, the presenter actually said that, from her vantage point, it looked like the parting of the Red Sea. In my experience, it is unreasonable to expect your audience to behave differently: It is simply what they do.

This observation is important and one that you need to consider. If your students define the slides as "notes," they will transcribe them. This perception seems only natural and students are remarkably resistant to suggestions to slow down or avoid copying slides verbatim. In my experience, making the slides available before or after class does little to curb this urge. Here is something I used to do with all of my classes. Early in the semester, and several times throughout, I used to place distracters on my slides. For example, I would write, "There are three main ingredients to a BLT." I would never mention the subject of bacon, lettuce, and tomato sandwiches, and the term "BLT" clearly had no relevance to the presentation. At the end of the lecture, I would ask my students to tell me what a BLT was and why it was important to our class. I used this demonstration to precipitate a lesson, explaining that they should avoid putting something in their notes until they knew what they were writing down and, even then, to use their own words. Each semester, we would all laugh at how stupid it was to write down everything, and each semester, the students would go back and do it again! So, I suggest that you simply accept that most students will feel an overwhelming compulsion to write down everything on a slide. The trick, then, is to use this tendency to your advantage. Or, at the very least, avoid having it become a distraction to learning.

The Role of the Teacher: Back to the Future

Few studies in the use of multimedia focus on, or even acknowledge, one of the most crucial elements in a classroom: the teacher. We are often the primary guide to the material and co-developer of the context. We facilitate learning in myriad ways. Pedagogical techniques and other tools of the trade are all filtered through us. The teacher sets the tone, manipulates context, and develops learning outcomes filtered through his or her skills, preferences, perspectives, and philosophy. We adapt, often in midstream, to the needs of the learner — for instance by altering our pace, changing our content, asking questions, and providing opportunities for discussion.

I believe that, in many cases, this new technology has taken the emphasis away from teaching and learning. Instead, we are being judged by how slick our presentations are, how many bells and whistles we integrate, and how cutting-edge we seem. Like everything else, though, technology has differential effects on learning depending upon how, when, and if, it is used (see Mayer, 2001). I want the reader to consider, at every point in the process, the crucial role of the teacher and the beauty of individual differences in teaching styles, goals, and students.

That said, it would be irresponsible for me to put forth hard-and-fast rules that all teachers should adhere to in every situation. There are few absolute universals and we should honor that fact. It is up to each teacher to develop the strategies, tools, and process that best help them achieve their teaching goals. When using slideware, you must ask yourself, before each presentation, whether its use will work well with your style, the content to be mastered that day, your audience, and that day's particular learning goals and objectives. If the answer is no, then be encouraged to leave the computer in the office.

PRIMUM NON NOCERE (FIRST DO NO HARM)

Use slideware because you believe it will enhance learning and the classroom experience for your students and for no other reason. Evaluate its effectiveness periodically to make sure that you are on the right track. If, after considering the pros and cons, you do decide to experiment with slideware, maybe I can save you some time. I have found that (in my opinion) there is a fairly typical set of mistakes that teachers seem to make at first, all revolving around one simple issue: *too much.* After some initial reluctance, many teachers quickly get fascinated with all of the bells and whistles. They see a program of empty slides and they want to fill them up — with too much text, backgrounds that interfere, fonts that are too small to read, noises that distract, and clip art that has no obvious relationship to the presentation. If there is one piece of general advice that I can offer someone interested in developing more effective slideware presentations, it is this: No matter how happy you are with your creation, keep attention focused on what is in front of you — the students and their learning.

We must be ever mindful that presentation software exists to provide an experience to the audience. Although certain aspects of these programs may be helpful to individual instructors as an organizational aid, I would argue that this aid is a side benefit. The vast majority of the evils of slideware in the classroom are perpetrated because the instructor does not take the perspective of the student or consider that the goal is teaching, as opposed to simply presenting. One of the great benefits of slideware is the potential to guide the attention of your audience. Alternatively, one of its great disservices is the tendency for it to become the central fixture in the classroom, trapping the attention of both presenter and student. *Less technology* and *more you* are usually better.

Below, I describe some fairly universal impediments to learning that I have consistently come across and offer several suggestions for improving the effectiveness of classroom presentations. I encourage you to view them skeptically and I strongly encourage you to experiment with various techniques and assess their usefulness in your own teaching context.

Too Much Text: More Means Less (Learning)

Just as students find it difficult to inhibit their impulse to write everything in their notes, many instructors have a difficult time not writing everything on their slides. One of the most common mistakes instructors make is to include everything that they want to say on their slides. If the text on the slides is that comprehensive, you need not be there and you will compromise your ability to teach. When the amount of text is great, what is a student's most likely response? Write it all down! Remember, the slides are for your students. Slideware is best used to depict those things that are best shown rather than said, as well as to emphasize certain points.

The inclusion of vast amounts of text is simply not an effective pedagogical technique. Too much text impedes processing by overloading learners and discouraging deeper levels of processing as they attempt to transcribe (Moreno & Mayer, 2002). In addition, there is ample evidence that oral narration is more effectively processed and retained than are written words on a slide in the context of the classroom (Goolkasian & Foos, 2002; Mayer, 2001; Mayer & Moreno, 1998; Moreno & Mayer, 1999). Comprehensive text in a multimedia presentation that is going to be read or summarized by the instructor is not as effective as direct and clear narration alone (Mayer, Heiser, & Lonn, 2001).

Even armed with this knowledge, this habit may be difficult to break. Recently, I gave some feedback to a colleague regarding his use of classroom slideware. After hearing many student complaints about how dense the text was on his slides ("We can't write it all down") and listening to his own frustration about student performance, I took an interest and visited one of his classes. His slides were so complete that virtually everything he said was written on the slide. I asked him why he put so much text on his slides. His reply: "If I don't put all that on there, I am tied to my notes or my memory." I pointed out that the students were not listening to him in their haste to transcribe the slides and shared with him some of the data suggesting that his technique was not as effective as it could be, especially with regard to learning. "That's OK, the most important information is on the slide anyway" he replied. Sounds like a self-esteem issue to me.

Your presence in the classroom should provide something beyond mere text and charts. In my opinion, the instructor described previously had admitted that he was not particularly important in that classroom. He had demoted himself from teacher to presenter — or more appropriately, to a reader, using a technique that was inefficient and not particularly conducive to learning. It is clear, in this case, that the slideware was interfering with learning, classroom culture, and the overall effectiveness of the course. Remember, my interest in the issue began from student complaints. If you are considering using slideware in your class, you should do so because you are convinced that it will make your class better for your students than it would be by not using it.

I am not advocating deleting all text from your presentations. Rather, I am suggesting that you use text strategically. Prioritize your information and create brief bullets that signal the theme, or main point, of your narration at critical transitions. It also is convenient to include definitions that you want students to transcribe verbatim (saves you from having to give the definition nine times until they write it all down). Decreasing the amount of text on the slide and augmenting it with your lecture allows you to provide an organizational framework for note-taking as well as provide cues to help students prioritize their processing, especially in introductory level courses. But, be careful. If you present, for example, three bullets simultaneously, you will find that students will be writing down the third bullet while you are just starting to discuss the first. I see this result all of the time and it is only a slight improvement over not using bullets at all. I strongly recommend that you present each bullet one at a time and not go on to the next until you are ready. Not only does this tactic now put you back in charge of the pace of your teaching, you will find that the bullets free the students to listen to your narration and think about what you are saying (see Mayer, Moreno, Boire, & Vagge, 1999). A change like this can have a dramatic and positive effect in your classroom.

Backgrounds and Fonts

Many instructors select bright and interesting backgrounds for their presentations. Some do so simply to make the visuals more attractive and others with the belief that these adornments will capture attention better. Although it is true that an attractive background may attract attention to the slide, your goal is to get students to pay attention to the content. If your background is competing with, or distracting from, your content, you may not be achieving your learning objectives. When selecting from the myriad patterns available for slide backgrounds, ask yourself if your selection increases readability. Backgrounds should optimize readability and reduce distraction. Select one that is plain, not distracting, and of high contrast to the font color. I tend to use a black background with white lettering in most rooms and switch to a white background with dark lettering when in a darker room (the white background reflects more light so my students can see me). Your primary objective is clarity and ease of processing. Keep it simple and keep it salient.

This same basic principle applies to font selection. In my experience, most instructors tend to choose fonts that are basic, clear, and easy to read. This choice may be due to the fact that most default fonts fit the bill. However, many teachers do not take into account the size and density of the text on the slide. How many times have you seen a presentation with lines and lines of small, densely packed text? Instructors tend to overload slides in an attempt to put everything on one slide. Such a self-imposed limitation is both unnecessary and counterproductive.

Limit the number of bullets or topics on each slide to no more than three to four and reserve the option to use multiple slides if needed. In general, if you can step back from your computer about 3 feet and read the words with ease, the font size is appropriate. This same strategy should work with the amount of space between lines of text and the separation bullets. If the separation makes it hard to read easily from a distance, increase it to draw your students' attention where you want it.

Sounds of Silence

Slideware programs have sounds available to accompany the entrance of text or transitions from slide to slide. In the vast majority of cases my advice is simple: Stay away from them. Irrelevant sounds and even background music are often annoying to the audience and they distract from learning (Moreno & Mayer, 2000). Ask yourself if the sounds help or distract from the message. If you keep them in your presentation, watch your students' faces. I have a colleague who loved to use these sounds. He would use a racecar sound for sentences to enter his slides, a laser-beam sound to accompany the letters in the titles, and a swishing sound for transitions from slide to slide. The first time he used these, the students were amused and would orient to these cute little sounds. His behavior was reinforced. With each click, he would look at the class like a comedian who had just delivered a punch line. As the lecture went on, the students became annoyed. By the end of the second class, the students were downright hostile. Abusing the sounds is counterproductive and distracting by most anyone's standards.

Seeing Is Believing? Clip Art and Pictures

One of the considerable strengths of slideware is the ability easily to add pictures, videos, animations, and movement to your presentation. These additions can be an incredibly effective way to develop, demonstrate, and emphasize a point. But overuse of this aspect of slideware, too, is rampant. For example, it is not uncommon for instructors to include clip art on every single slide. In fact, I attended a seminar where an expert recommended doing exactly that (name withheld to protect the mistaken, but innocent). If you want to include clip art, it should be directly and intuitively relevant to your presentation. Otherwise, students may spend their time trying to figure out the connection or become otherwise distracted.

Pictures are wonderful tools, however, when they are relevant and clearly linked to your presentation. In many cases, a good picture that clearly demonstrates the point you are making can have a tremendous and positive impact, and may be much more effective than text. For example, if I were to tell you that a particular politician looks like a monkey, it may have minimal impact or believability. Writing those words on a slide does not help. But, if I show you a picture of that politician next to a picture of a monkey, well …

It is important that clip art, pictures, or other visual material be clearly and obviously linked to your central message *from your students' point of view*. Students tend to notice pictures and try to make links to the lecture, whether or not they are the ones you intended. There have been several cases when I have shown a picture that I thought, in my warped little world, clearly made my point. In those instances, to my chagrin, I have had to backtrack from my main message to explain the link between the point and the picture. In short, if you have to explain your pictures you need to use different pictures, or none at all. A picture may be worth a thousand words, but, in the classroom, you want those words to be related to the topic at hand.

The Power and Pull of Video

The ability to insert video into presentation software can be liberating. I remember switching back and forth from the overhead projector to the VCR, fast-forwarding through a tape to get to the parts I wanted to show or showing an entire film when I really only wanted to show a part of it. Most slideware programs allow a teacher to insert video clips easily into their presentation and move seamlessly from slide to video and back. In fact, appropriate video can promote mastery of material better than pictures and text or narration alone (Daniel & Klacynski, 2005). Video is a powerful tool if used judiciously.

But even a good clip can have minimal impact if the instructor does not provide the proper context before showing it. If you watch a late-night talk show, the celebrity guest will set up a clip before it is shown. This tactic allows the audience to understand a bit of what is going on and better appreciate the fine acting they are about to witness. Video clips in the classroom can benefit from similar strategies. Tell your students what to look for or why what they are about to see is important or related to the subject at hand. Setting up the video clip will cause it to have more impact.

A growing number of instructors, however, are including in their presentations video clips that are entertaining but not necessarily elucidating. Just as with pictures and clip art, if a video does not clearly demonstrate the issue at hand, or requires significant explanation of its relevance, there may be a better way to get your point across (Mayer, Heiser, & Lonn, 2001). In many cases, a verbal explanation is more efficient, clear, and productive. Education and entertainment can go together. But if you have to choose between the two, I hope you choose wisely.

What About Flexibility?

Part of my initial reluctance to fully integrate slideware into my courses has been my worry that it would severely limit my flexibility. Some of my best classes have been a result of a few divergences, a choice to go into depth where I had not planned to, or a detour in response to student questions. Developing a slideware presentation, in contrast, requires planning. Preparing a lecture in that much detail seemed almost mechanistic to me. Once I had developed a lecture, I felt like I had to stick to the order and get through all of the content. It took me a long time to realize that this limitation was really self-imposed, both structurally as well as psychologically.

If you review the recommendations in this chapter, as well as the literature in the area of multimedia, you may come to the conclusion that less is better when it comes to slideware. You are astute. By creating guiding bullets as opposed to paragraphs of text, maximizing clarity, strategically including visuals for specific impact rather than merely because they may be cute, and minimizing distraction, the slideware becomes more of a guide than a script, allowing you to take charge of the flow and use the program to direct it.

There are times, however, when you may want certain resources available just in case students have a particular question or you want the option to talk about a topic at greater depth. Again, slideware does not have to be linear and can be made to accommodate many contingencies. Such flexibility can be attained, for example, by creating custom shows (groups of slides arranged by topic) or menus of links to specific slides that you can access if needed.

It Is All About Me: Egocentrism and You

As I argued earlier, keeping your audience in mind is especially important as you sit down to write your lecture. Many of us often create our slideware presentations as aids for ourselves more than guides to learning. Back in the olden days, lectures used to be developed independently of these programs, and we only sought out visuals to support a lecture after we had developed our points. We developed our thoughts on paper to deliver in a narration. Now, we click on program and develop our lectures in the same mediums in which we present them. We feel a compulsion to fill blank slides with what we used to put in our lecture notes — and then some. We then use this same presentation, developed for ourselves, to teach our students. This practice is all too common and is the root cause of most bad presentations. Recall my story of the faculty member who wrote everything on his slides for his own convenience. Do not confuse writing your lecture for yourself as being the same thing as writing a slideware presentation to supplement your lecture. Think about it as you develop your presentation: "For whom is this presentation intended?"

If you find that slideware programs help you organize your thoughts for a lecture, I encourage you to develop them this way: Go for it! When you are done, save the file and print it. These are your lecture notes. Then, reopen the file and delete all of the information that is there for you and not your students. Rename this file and use it as your classroom presentation. For your students, say what needs to be said and show what needs to be shown.

FINAL THOUGHTS

I wrote this chapter with the strong belief that the teacher's role in the classroom is valuable and central to the learning process. Inserting yourself into the process of teaching should encourage you to experiment with various pedagogical techniques and devices to the extent that they are helpful — and that includes presentation software. If done well, slideware can help create productive and stimulating presentations that lead to greater retention of material, greater ability to generalize, and higher performance on student assessments. If not done well, they can be a distraction from learning.

As the need for visual support varies as a function of content and objectives, the decision to use slideware should be made on a lesson-by-lesson basis. At each step in the process, you should ask yourself if the use of this technology is appropriate for your teaching style, the content, your audience, and your desired learning outcomes. If you decide that using slideware may have a positive effect on your teaching, it is important that you use it consciously, effectively, and strategically.

Once you have developed your vision for the lesson at hand, it is important that you reflect upon what material is best learned and supported by seeing it.

Although there are few universal rules applicable to all teachers in all contexts, Richard Mayer and his colleagues, among others, have developed productive lines of research that suggest best principles when using multimedia (see Mayer, 2001 for a review), several of which are consistent with the views shared in this chapter. In general, when it comes to text versus narration, I strongly encourage you to avoid text. When developing your presentation, less is better than more and plain is better than flashy. Remember, clarity is your primary objective.

I will leave you with the analogy that best guides my own use of slideware: that of a news anchor. As the term "anchor person" implies, I view myself as the central figure, or anchor, within the lecture. I can deliver the news in a way that graphics or text do not. The slideware is much like the graphics on a newscast — supplementary. If, for some reason, I need to throw it over to Jim for the weather, I will deflect attention to the slide long enough to get the weather report. Once the point is made, it is back to me. I encourage you to play with slideware, and other technologies, in the context of your own classroom. If things do not go so well, turn off the computer and go to a commercial.

IMPLICATIONS FOR TEACHERS AND STUDENTS

Having a vision of what you want to happen in your classroom before interacting with technology encourages its purposeful and guided use. For those of you who habitually use slideware to develop your lectures, preparing a course module without it can stimulate the thinking process behind laying out a course and help you make decisions about what content to present in class, and how to present it.

Depending on your teaching style and individual objectives, there are good reasons to use slideware, and good reasons not to. Be prepared to defend your minimal use of slideware, or your not using it at all. The literature is on your side — even if students, and many administrators, seem to expect it in all settings nowadays.

By minimizing the use of slideware, teachers often find that they use better, more powerful examples, and their teaching becomes more fluid. They may also find that student participation increases and that the atmosphere in their classrooms becomes more dynamic and reinforcing, when the slides are not the central focus.

This new world of opportunity means teachers can conceptualize their subject matter and style of teaching in a broader way. But along with this comes the responsibility of teachers to experiment with and thoughtfully develop pedagogical techniques that call upon their own expertise and experience.

Do not give up your strengths as a teacher, in other words. Accentuate them with technology. The use of slideware, in particular, can compromise your energy (including your physical movement about the classroom), your rapport with students, your storytelling, and your ability to explore ideas related to the topic (which can be a dynamic springboard to more depth). These are often the very things that make a teacher effective and create the spontaneous and unscripted moments that can be turned to your advantage. Make room in your presentations for you and your students to relate to the material in meaningful ways. Use slideware to punctuate foundational information and to explore concepts in a way that moves the listener beyond the confines of verbal descriptions. This is how slideware is best used. Conversely, do not be shy about turning off the slideware when it is superfluous, even in the middle of a presentation. *Tip*: If you hit the "B" key in the middle of a presentation, the screen will go black and everyone will have to find something else to look at, like you. When you are ready to proceed with slideware, hit the "B" key again and pick up where you left off (if you prefer a blank white background, the "W" key does the same thing).

REFERENCES

Bagui, S. (1998). Reasons for increased learning using multimedia. *Journal of Educational Multimedia and Hypermedia, 7*, 3-18.

Daniel, D. B., & Klacynski, P. A. (2005, April). *The effects of multimedia presentation of material on exam performance*. Poster presented to the SRCD Teaching of Developmental Science Institute, Atlanta, GA.

DeBord, K. A., Aruguete, M. S., & Muhlig, J. (2004). Are computer-assisted teaching methods effective? *Teaching of Psychology, 31*, 65-68.

Erwin, D., & Rieppi, R. (1999). Comparing multimedia and traditional approaches in undergraduate psychology classes. *Teaching of Psychology, 26*, 58-61.

Fletcher, J. D. (2003). Evidence for learning from technology-assisted instruction. In H. F. O'Neil, Jr. & R. S. Perez (Eds.), *Technology applications in education: A learning view* (pp. 79-99). Mahwah, NJ: Erlbaum.

Goolkasian, P., & Foos, P. W. (2002). Presentation format and its effect on working memory. *Memory and Cognition, 30*, 1096-1105.

Mayer, R. E. (2001). *Multimedia learning*. New York: Cambridge University Press.

Mayer, R. E., Heiser, J., & Lonn, S. (2001). Cognitive constraints on multimedia learning: When presenting more material results in less understanding. *Journal of Educational Psychology, 93*, 187-198.

Mayer, R. E., & Moreno, R. (1998). A split-attention effect in multimedia learning: Evidence for dual processing systems in working memory. *Journal of Educational Psychology, 90*, 312-320.

Mayer, R. E., Moreno R., Boire, M., & Vagge, S. (1999). Maximizing constructivist learning from multimedia communications by minimizing cognitive load. *Journal of Educational Psychology, 91*, 638-643.

Moreno, R., & Mayer, R. E. (1999). Cognitive principles of multimedia learning: The role of modality and contiguity. *Journal of Educational Psychology, 91*, 358-368.

Moreno, R., & Mayer, R. E. (2000). A coherence effect in multimedia learning: The case for minimizing irrelevant sounds in the design of multimedia instructional messages. *Journal of Educational Psychology, 92*, 117-125.

Moreno, R., & Mayer, R. E. (2002). Learning science in virtual reality multimedia environments: Role of methods and media. *Journal of Educational Psychology, 94*, 598-610.

Tufte, E. (2003, Nov. 9). PowerPoint is evil. *Wired*. Retrieved October 2, 2004 from http://www.wired.com/wired/archive/11.09/ppt2.html

CHAPTER ELEVEN

SUCCESSFUL EMPIRICAL SCHOLARSHIP OF TEACHING AND STUDENT LEARNING

Baron Perlman
Lee I. McCann

University of Wisconsin Oshkosh

UNTIL RELATIVELY RECENTLY, pedagogical scholarship was limited to a small subset of educational researchers from colleges of education and a small number of faculty in the different disciplines. Most teaching journals rarely published empirical work, just anecdotes and descriptions of what worked, and was exciting, in the classroom. Over time, a set of accepted "truths," based primarily on experience rather than empirical data, found their way into the canon of good teaching. This body of "pedagogical wisdom" is neither to be dismissed nor ignored, and to this day it may provide the most insight for the most people about good teaching. It can be found in books such as McKeachie's *Teaching Tips* (2002) or anthologies such as volumes 1 and 2 of *Lessons Learned* (Perlman, McCann, & McFadden, 1999, 2004).

The clarion call for a change in the academy came in 1990, when Ernest Boyer's *Scholarship Reconsidered: Priorities of the Professoriate* called for a redirection of faculty energy into other, more nontraditional types of scholarship — most specifically, scholarship of teaching and learning (SoTL). Boyer's writing provided the basis for the subsequent drumroll of support, publications, and activities by the Carnegie Foundation and the American Association for Higher Education, and more importantly for the avalanche of faculty attention to SoTL in the subsequent 15 years (Diamond & Adam, 1995; Halpern et al., 1998; Mathie et al., 2004; Richlin, 2001).

Boyer (1990) saw the challenge as redefining scholarship to include an emphasis on teaching and student learning, and to end the separation between the educational researcher and the teacher. He broadened the definition of traditional scholarship to include a SoTL that could be considered acceptable research for personnel purposes, and called for more and different ways that faculty could become scholars of teaching — something the traditional academy had previously had difficulty accepting. Teaching was to be integrated into, not separated from, the community of scholars (Shulman, 2004). For example, Angelo and Cross (1993) presented a wide variety of ways in which faculty can poll students to assess what the students are learning.

A SoTL was to help faculty take professional responsibility for their teaching (Shulman, 2004) in the face of increased outside attention to higher education by legislators and the public. Faculty needed to demonstrate accountability, and explain and assess their work, before others made them do so. A SoTL also would increase discussion of teaching among faculty, administrators, and others, thereby lessening the isolation of faculty in their teaching, opening classrooms to fresh ideas, and making teaching "community property" (Hutchings, 1993; Shulman, 2004). The SoTL's greatest success may be in encouraging more talk about teaching (Halpern et al., 1998: Mathie et al., 2004).

To define an acceptable scholarship, Hammack (1997) used a public outcome as the dividing line between self-inspection by the excellent teacher and a SoTL. In other words, a SoTL was more than excellent teaching and more than scholarly teaching (Hutchings & Shulman, 1999; Richlin, 2001). Accountable, professional faculty must have their SoTL assessed and publicly communicated. These processes are reflected in the literature on peer review (e.g., Chism 1999, Keig & Waggoner, 1994), and teaching portfolios (e.g., Hutchings, 1993, 1998; Seldin, 2004), mainstays of the SoTL. Portfolios are often lengthy and always documented, and thus are, to some degree, public.

Problems

There are three major problems with the scholarly nature of the current SoTL. First, many authors describe SoTL (e.g., Cross & Steadman, 1996) in terms of individual classroom research, in which faculty dissect, observe, attend to, get feedback about, and then institute changes in their own teaching. Such an approach can be invaluable in improving teaching and student learning. Much of it, however, violates many of the tenets of the empirical approach to knowing.

For example, there are limits to the reliability and validity of intuition and authority, and teachers may better remember those cases that fit their value system. They may recall a teaching technique that worked well and disregard others that were equally valuable or negative, or they may not recall other uses of this same approach that were less successful. Teachers may too readily accept their own personal judgment or a single episode or story about their own or someone else's experience in teaching, failing to question its validity or generalizability. They also may justify and rationalize what it is they do when they teach in order to protect themselves from the failures that all teachers experience, or may draw erroneous conclusions about cause and effect.

Scientifically acceptable scholarship follows certain guidelines, regardless of specific methodology. Sampling, generalizability of the data, bias, and the like are critical dimensions that should be considered in any SoTL, empirical or not, if we are to develop a worthwhile canon. Our experience is that faculty who do empirical SoTL do not forfeit the opportunity to also develop valuable perspectives on their teaching. For example, we are currently interested in how lower level courses differ from those at the upper levels. Although we can find nothing in the literature on this question, our colleagues affirm that there are differences, although each has a different idea on the matter. We have begun thinking more critically about our own courses and are learning new criteria and dimensions to apply to their design and to our own teaching of them as we develop a questionnaire for students to complete.

Second, proponents of SoTL (e.g., Boyer, 1990; Glassick, Huber, & Maeroff, 1997) hoped that a SoTL would make teaching more central in personnel decisions. Yet in talking with faculty we conclude that many find it difficult or impossible to have their SoTL respected for evaluative purposes (renewal, tenure, promotion, or pay increases). In part, this struggle may exist because many of those working to fit under the SoTL umbrella never quite dispel the feeling that behavior traditionally associated with the *gentleman scholar* is a satisfactory component of the SoTL (i.e., to read and know is sufficient as "acceptable" scholarship). This view, and the results it produces, often provides a basis for those who define scholarship traditionally to argue that SoTL is not "real" scholarship. We believe the more empirical approach that we describe below is harder to dismiss.

Third, scholarship must be public and disseminated, something that does not often happen with most SoTL except within one's home college or university, even if written documentation is provided on the Web (see Seldin, 2004, on placing teaching portfolios on the Web). Such departmental or institutional sharing is a valuable starting point for greater discussion of teaching and improved pedagogy, but may not meet the traditional scholarly criteria of "public-domain work," such as jury review.

Empirical work has the greatest potential to meet all the criteria of a strong SoTL and be more broadly accepted as "real" research, especially in faculty personnel decisions. Fortunately, empirical inquiry is well suited to psychologists, as it is a methodology with which most of us are well acquainted.

An Empirical SoTL

An empirical SoTL is a way of knowing that is different from the qualitative or anecdotal work so often reported in the SoTL literature, but it never excludes practical application. Whether using experimental, quasi-experimental, correlational, observational, survey, or case-study methodology, it values reliability and validity, and uses quantitative evidence for argument, deduction, and induction. It avoids overgeneralization from one's findings, emphasizes empirical "truth" as opposed to conjecture or conclusions based on limited or individual observations, and involves an approach that we often think of as "science" or "scientific."

Whenever possible, an empirical SoTL uses quantitative analysis to describe teaching and student learning and to summarize findings, allows others to confirm conclusions and speculation, and points the way for further work. Private insights into publicly available material are insufficient. For example, when we studied how faculty deal with students who miss exams (Perlman, McCann, Dettlaff, & Palladino, 2003), we developed a ranking of the most common to least common methods and reported mean faculty opinions on how well each worked.

Principles of Empirical Scholarship of Teaching and Learning

What is successful empirical SoTL? Based on talking with others, reading the literature, and our experience with empirical SoTL, we have some suggestions.

Why Collect Data?

All good teachers try to learn how well they are teaching, are concerned with students learning important course material, and make constant adjustments in their teaching. An empirical SoTL assists in these processes and improvements through the gathering and interpretation of numerical data. These data can provide a context for teachers' decisions, shed light on teaching effectiveness, and help teachers assist their students with their learning.

Getting Ideas

Collect data, rather than merely expressing your opinion (no matter how inspired that opinion may seem). Be alert to topics where everyone "knows" a procedure or particular approach is correct but there are no data to support the accepted opinion. Think about what you do in a typical semester (e.g., different types of final exams and why faculty use one or the other, and how much, how, and when students study for them). What are faculty's goals in giving comprehensive exams? (Faculty usually argue such exams are a good thing.) How do students view them?

Talk with colleagues. When you hear yourself arguing passionately with a colleague or a colleague arguing passionately with someone else about teaching, pay close attention — you may identify an idea for investigation. Will a little data shed light on the topic? For example, we often lament low levels of student performance in our courses, but what causes such lackluster achievement? If the college degree has mainly become a societal requirement, perhaps many students are being rational if they only want a C average, the minimum to earn the degree. We are in the process of learning what goals students have for grades in our courses and how that is related to the amount of work they do.

Talking with colleagues about teaching is often enlightening. A good example of the value of talking with others is our interest in student attendance. Why do students attend and not attend class? How would one gather valid and reliable data? They may be making good decisions about missing classes if they have a sick child, important assignments due in another course, find class a waste of time, and so forth. Would they have to be paged daily or reminded to e-mail their class attendance and reasons for missing each day? Would such research only be reliable and valid if students had to use an identification card that they swiped in a computer-terminal slot in order to gain class access? In the process of thinking about student attendance we talked with a colleague at a workshop we facilitated. Her proposed solution was simple and elegant. She will teach two sections of the same class each semester, identical except for the students and time of day. She will require student attendance in one section and not in the other, using an AB–BA design, with attendance required for only the morning section one semester and for only the afternoon section the next. The research is quasi-experimental in that she will not randomly assign students to sections. She will look at grades on course assignments (which will be identical in each section) and final grades, and ask students to complete a questionnaire about how attendance being required (or not) affected whether they came or not, the amount of work they did, and what they learned in class.

Talk with students. Students often are surprised and pleased to be able to talk about their education and course experiences with their teachers, and their insights can be powerful and useful. Often the best or most motivated students belong to honor societies and student clubs. Talk with such groups about their student experiences. They have much to say.

Be a student yourself. If you truly want to empathize with your students and experience what they are going through in your courses, attend a presentation in an area in which you know little or nothing and try to take notes. Your appreciation for the students' role may widen and increase, and all sorts of questions may come to mind.

Go to teaching conferences. Teaching conferences provide an opportunity to focus on the importance and process of pedagogy. It is almost impossible to leave without several ideas on which you could collect data. We talk with colleagues repeatedly at such venues and sometimes it is comforting to learn that some problems seem to beg for a good solution. For example, we still have not determined how to make the opening class period of our courses one that communicates information in a way that students retain. After all, students typically have several such class periods that day and their agenda is simply to find out how much work the course requires and, for some students, how well they think they will do. Aside from putting the course syllabus on brightly colored paper or giving a quiz on its content, we do not have any good ideas and we may gather data on what our colleagues do.

Review the literature. Before you undertake a SoTL study, review the relevant literature. Weimer (1993) called this strategy *informed practice*, placing one's SoTL within the context and history of what has gone before. In psychology, informed practice means consulting such data-based journals as *Teaching of Psychology* and *Psychology Learning and Teaching*. Read the reports of psychology's national taskforces. Consult the American Psychological Association's (APA) or the Association for Psychological Science's (APS) offices devoted to undergraduate education and teaching. Many books on teaching provide discussion and relevant information on what you want to study. Perlman (2005) provides a list of such books.

This strategy has the additional benefit of assisting you in identifying outlets for your scholarship. The annual meetings of the APA and APS both have teaching-related venues. The National Institute on the Teaching of Psychology held each January in St. Petersburg Beach, Florida provides poster sessions, as do regional teaching conferences. Two Web sites contain a variety of forums you can consider as outlets: the Office of Teaching Resources in Psychology (http://www.lemoyne.edu/OTRP/index.html) and the Society for the Teaching of Psychology (http://www.lemoyne.edu/teachpsych/div/divindex.html).

Keep a list of research ideas. When you think of a possible research idea write it down and jot down a few lines describing what the idea means. You may find common elements among several of your ideas and be able to blend what seemed like separate studies into a unified project.

Before You Begin: Goal Setting and Adequate Preparation

In *Scholarship Assessed*, Glassick, Huber, and Maeroff (1997) proposed criteria and procedures for assessing various types of scholarship, including SoTL. We describe them below. One usually thinks of assessment occurring after work has been completed and shared with peers for informal peer review, or as it is being considered for public-domain presentation or publication through a rigorous jury review. Our experience is that these standards also can help as you plan your research.

Have clear goals. Good scholars think clearly and ask good questions. For example, does your proposed SoTL project "show an examination of the assumptions in the teaching of the field ... or provide a framework for analysis of the issues, theoretical or otherwise?" (Chism, 1999, p. 104). If you read the results of the exact study you propose to carry out, what would you or your colleagues learn? If everything goes as planned, will your work achieve your goals, add consequentially to the field, and open additional areas for further exploration? Will the results help you or others to become more effective teachers or your students better learners?

Have realistic and achievable objectives. For some of the national surveys and catalog research we have done, the work required time we did not have. However, we accomplished the research in a timely manner by using student assistants. If you want to study the impact of something you are doing when you teach, can you "get at it" in ways that shed light on the issue? A good way to learn if your goals are clear is to try to state clearly the basic purposes of your work. If you cannot do that, you need to think more about what it is that you want to study and communicate to others.

Adequate preparation. All SoTL requires the necessary, practical research skills. Join the Society for the Teaching of Psychology (APA's Division 2) and learn what services and programs it supports. Martial the resources necessary to move the project forward — paper and printing costs, postage, and envelopes, or financial support (see below).

Appropriate methods. Careful consideration of control groups, sample size, bias, and the like gives research integrity and validity. Always ask colleagues and students to review your methodology prior to data collection, and modify your procedures based on their comments or in response to changing circumstances. It often is helpful to imagine the different ways your results might turn out, and then to consider whether your methodology will provide a strong basis for explaining these outcomes.

Effective presentation and reflective critique. Results must be effectively communicated. Use public-domain jury-review forums when possible; follow APA style and organize your work effectively when presenting it. Use the comments you receive from reviewers to improve the quality of the next manuscript draft or your future work.

Practical Methodological Advice

Pilot test. We always learn a great deal when we pilot test before sampling students, faculty, or both. Questions that seemed clear sometimes need to be reworded. We often get feedback like "what about _____?" and "add more variables to the study." You need not pilot test on your own students if you are studying something in one of the courses you are teaching, but can use students in your department's honor society or in other courses. Our experience is that colleagues are happy to fill out a questionnaire and provide (often painful, but gleefully given) feedback on what is unclear or missing. We do not ask this favor too often, however. It also is helpful to explain to them why you are doing the study.

Collaborate with others. When it comes to empirical SoTL, two heads often are better than one. Collaborators can provide more critical thinking and thus better ideas and help when difficult ethical or methodological decisions must be made. Consider working with someone outside your discipline. Their way of viewing problems and going about gathering data may be completely different from yours; the chances increase for a multi-methods project, or collecting data from a broader sample. If you are somewhat uncomfortable with empirical methods, work with someone well versed in them.

Obtain as broad and representative a sample as you can. If you want your research findings to generalize, the broader the sample the better. It is easy to get a good sample of student participants when doing survey research, and there are hundreds of them in various courses in your department. At other times, to obtain a sufficient sample you may need to sample majors over two or three years, or have colleagues assist you with using majors at their institutions.

Sampling faculty about their beliefs and teaching practices also is interesting, but it may be difficult to get a good-sized or diverse sample. We have tried to broaden and enlarge faculty samples at conferences, but our experience is that the *bystander effect* is powerful: Everyone assumes someone else will fill out the questionnaire you have left at the registration table or included in the notebook of conference materials. To get a good sample, one needs to cultivate relationships with faculty at other institutions and ask if they will distribute your questionnaire to their colleagues. When studying curricular issues, our experience is that we get at least a 40-percent response rate from chairs of departments nationally in our discipline, which is sufficient for reliable and valid results.

When gathering data from students, be overly explicit. Define your terms and spell out the criteria to be used. If you do not, it may be impossible to interpret your findings or you may have to start over with a new sample. For example, in doing a course portfolio, one of the authors had a group of students assess different texts. He did not specify criteria, but left them open — a big mistake. He wanted an evaluation of clarity of writing, clearness and boldness of examples, and depth of discussion. The students rated the texts on amounts of summary information, bold print, and pictures, and never mentioned content.

Student and faculty data on the same question are usually fascinating. If you can gather both faculty and student attitudes, beliefs, and perceptions on the same topic (e.g., what makes for a good text?) and compare them, you may have more robust and interesting data. You also may be able to make statistical comparisons between the groups.

Data must be accessible. The goal of empirical SoTL is that the final outcome or results of the work be public domain. This goal has a major impact on how such work is carried out. The rigorous criteria of empirical work and peer review must be met; it often necessitates more work than if the goal is simply to know the answer to a teaching problem. In brief, empirical scholarship is not a process in and of itself, but a process directed toward a public sharing of outcomes. Others must be able to replicate your work. Replication is an important SoTL issue, as all experienced teachers know that students respond differently, sometimes from semester to semester, to the same teaching style. It is essential to know what was done and how it was done, so subsequent studies can be accurately compared to your work.

Variables and the sample must be operationally defined. Systematic study means more than merely proceeding with forethought. For example, studying a small group of faculty or students in a single class or department may suggest powerful insights and solutions to teaching problems. However, if colleagues are to assess the validity of the findings and arguments, the sources of the data must be clearly defined. Small-sample or case-study scholarship may thus be useful as pilot studies for developing methods and hypotheses, but not adequate for public-domain work. Ideally, individual observation of our teaching and student learning takes place in classes or institutions that mirror many others in which our colleagues work. However, since we know that there are important distinctions among institutions and their faculty and students, the limitations of our samples must be acknowledged.

Those who use an empirical approach to the SoTL are concerned when demographics and methodology — which give context to findings and enable replication or comparison — are not reported. The operations or procedures we use define what was done, and limit our conclusions to the situations or types of cases studied.

Confounds must be avoided, or at least acknowledged. A SoTL requires recognition that correlation does not demonstrate causation. The third-variable problem — such as unusually motivated teachers or particular types of institutions and students accounting for outcomes instead of the teaching method under study — can be problematic.

Involve students. Involve students both as coauthors, and in refining and pilot testing your research when its focus will be students. SoTL data sets usually involve descriptive or simple parametric or nonparametric statistics. They can teach students a great deal about nonexperimental research. Invite students into the research from its onset, sharing the question you are trying answer and seeking their ideas. When studying teaching strategies and techniques in a course you are teaching, however, be careful that students' knowledge of your research goals, and the fact their behavior is under observation or study, does not bias the outcome.

Consider ethical problems. Always overtly consider any ethical problems your research may engender. It is easy to obsess too much about ethical problems, but close attention to them is important. Researchers are responsible for the welfare of their participants and those who engage in a SoTL must protect students, colleagues, and other research participants when doing their work. Whether your goal is to describe, infer relationships, or investigate causality, you must do so in an ethical manner.

Seek fiscal support. Look for fiscal support for your work. Doing so helps you become aware of who in the discipline supports such work, it may get you "free" pre-readings of your proposal, and it will improve the quality of your work by forcing you to think critically about it and formally present it to others. The

Society for the Teaching of Psychology awards grants each year. Do not consider only monetary support. Time is a faculty's most precious resource, and the release of time to do your work should be sought when possible. (We know it is paradoxical that dedicated teachers might teach less in order to do scholarship so they can teach better.) If your SoTL relates to student learning (e.g., general education issues) or behavior (e.g., retention in your institution) perhaps a dean or other administrator will provide funding.

Outcomes

Make your scholarship public. Plan to make your empirical SoTL public at a workshop at your college or university, or in a poster, symposium, presented paper, or a journal article. Consider newsletters and electronic forums, and learn which ones are the most prestigious and respected. If nothing else, such goals may set deadlines for you and keep you working on the project. The feedback you get from making your work part of the public domain improves future SoTL.

Exercise caution in drawing conclusions. Galguera (2002) correctly suggested the possibility of research bias and students giving socially desirable responses when faculty study students in classes they are teaching. Do not over-generalize from your results.

Work backwards. If you want the outcome of your work to be a journal publication, the rigor and nature of the research may differ from a non-jury-reviewed poster or from scholarship done just for yourself or for personnel purposes (e.g., a course portfolio). We have seen many interesting posters at national forums on the teaching of psychology that, because of sample size and methodology, would not be accepted as a journal article.

One study leads to the next. Typically your study will produce unanswered questions, and one study leads to the next. Findings are often counterintuitive or raise other questions. In talking to people about your results, you will probably end up with more ideas than you have time to pursue. If you have too many ideas, or some do not interest you, give them away to colleagues.

Personal Requirements for the SoTL Process

Practitioners of SoTL need to be patient. Good SoTL takes just as much time and critical thinking as any other form of scholarship. Gathering data can take several semesters. You also must be able to tolerate ambiguity and trust your feelings. If what you are studying is interesting and exciting, persevere. If it becomes tedious and boring, think seriously about whether you want to continue. Finally, you must value what you do. You are contributing to your discipline, student learning, faculty development and professionalism, and, one hopes, to your local community and larger society. If you do not value your SoTL, who will?

IMPLICATIONS FOR TEACHERS AND STUDENTS

SoTL often seems to have been defined in practice as faculty studying teaching and student learning in their own courses, mandating a "personal involvement." Empirical social science methodologies can contribute to more meaningful and deeper SoTL. Successfully practicing an empirical SoTL has several important implications for faculty and their students.

The Disconnect Between Research and Practice Is Lessened

Although research in the past may have been disconnected from the practice of teaching, there is no reason this separation must continue. Empirical SoTL can inform and help improve teaching, and the disconnect between the two seems to be lessening. For example, Chin (1999) reported that more evaluation research is appearing in the journal *Teaching Sociology*, and Weimer wrote (personal communication, March 16, 2004) that social-science research is more "prized and celebrated in pedagogical periodicals" than in the past.

Empirical scholarship of teaching can build knowledge and improve practice. For example, we recently completed a national study of how psychology undergraduate students practice psychological science (Perlman & McCann, 2005). Teaching psychology as a science has been agreed upon and encouraged by the discipline for the last 50 years, and faculty ranked thinking of and teaching psychology as a science first in importance as an expectation for the undergraduate psychology major (McGovern & Hawks, 1986). Although it is generally agreed that actually doing science is the best way to learn it, no one had ever described how often or in what ways our students learn it. We believe these findings have broad and important implications for how faculty teach psychology across the country, and we hope they will improve pedagogical practice.

Methodological Pluralism Increases Good Teaching and Student Learning

Methodological pluralism is an important component of a strong SoTL (Morreale, Applegate, Wulff, & Sprague, 2002; Wankat, Felder, Smith, & Oreovicz, 2002): "Faculty will have to learn and borrow from a wider array of fields and put a larger repertoire of methods behind the scholarship of teaching" (Hutchings & Shulman, 1999, p. 14). Huber and Morreale (2002) supported the value of breadth of methods and, more specifically, empirical social-science methods. We agree with them, but to acknowledge pluralism means just that. Social-science methods are not the only way to understand the nuances and day-to-day complexities of teaching and learning. These subjects are, by definition, not totally amenable to the experimental or survey methods.

Empirical Work Does Not Eliminate a Sense of Wonder and Excitement

In the SoTL writings, there is emphasis on "the wonderful sense of introspection, reflection, and community [among SoTL practitioners]" (Bilimoria & Fukami, 2002, p. 134) and a concern somehow that these will be destroyed if a SoTL becomes more rigorous in its standards. From personal experience, we know there can be as much excitement and wonder in empirical work as in the creation of an individual teaching or course portfolio. When we replicated four previous studies going back over 60 years (Perlman & McCann, 1999) that looked at the most frequently listed psychology courses in institutional course catalogs nationally and finalized the table comparing current to past data, we experienced a sense of history, continuity, and contribution that is difficult to put into words.

Empirical Scholarship of Teaching Complements a More Personal, Qualitative SoTL

Seitz (2002) provided a good example of a situation in which an empirical SoTL might complement a qualitative approach. In talking of narrative reporting he stated:

> Not only does it oversimplify the relationship between pedagogy and student achievement, but it also tends to efface differences among students in any given course, some of whom may well respond positively to a particular teacher or method at the same time that others remain detached, skeptical, and seemingly unaffected by the same approach the teacher's narrative celebrates. It is these latter, often unmentioned students whom I find myself wondering about whenever I read yet another tale of pedagogical success. (p. 65)

These unmentioned students can be heeded if we gather empirical data to complement qualitative methodology.

Empirical SoTL Yields Insight and Knowledge Although Teaching Is Complex

Just because complexity exists is not sufficient cause to give up empirical ways of investigating and knowing the effects of our teaching on learning. Such work often builds on the practical, thoughtful problem solving and narratives other colleagues have shared publicly. Because of the methods they use, colleagues who use an empirical approach can be valuable members of the teaching community.

Empirical SoTL May Be More Likely to Be Publicly Known

Everyone who writes about a SoTL agrees that scholarship of teaching must be shared with the teaching community. "The work of the professor becomes consequential only as it is understood by others" (Boyer, 1990, p. 23). We favor carrying such discussion beyond department or institutional groups. The dissemination, when possible, should be to as wide an audience as possible. An empirical approach may provide the greatest opportunity to participate in such public forums.

The more empirical SoTL is carried out and disseminated publicly, the more it benefits all teachers, even those not interested in doing such scholarship themselves. As consumers of such scholarship, they can improve their teaching based on findings important to them and their students. For example, a conference presentation (with data) on the teaching of Introductory Psychology prompted us to change how we teach the course.

Empirical SoTL Is Most Likely to Be Accepted as Scholarship

Publishing in pedagogical journals and writing about teaching are sometimes dismissed as not being legitimate scholarship (Weimer, 1993). We have talked with faculty members who have encountered such attitudes from department chairs, deans, and colleagues. Given the nature of much SoTL, these attitudes may be understandable or even at times deserved. However, the empirical approach is well known and has a long history as accepted scholarship, and may be perceived as more rigorous and systematic than personal anecdote, the "wisdom of practice" or "tips 'n quips" (Calder, Cutler, & Kelly, 2002, p. 49). The repeatedly stated hopes of SoTL authors are that such research will find greater favor over time. We think an empirical component increases the chances of this acceptance.

Although many disciplinary pedagogical journals were not empirical (Weimer, 1993) they may be moving in this direction (Weimer, personal communication, March 16, 2004). Weimer (1993) concluded that most of the writings in pedagogical journals generalizes to other disciplines, with the potential to increase cross-disciplinary discussions. Thus, much of such work in other disciplines could be useful in our own teaching and scholarship. Perhaps we need a journal that publishes the best of empirical SoTL, choosing the best works from a wide variety of disciplines and publishing them in one place.

Conclusion

An empirical SoTL answers questions about (a) what works in the classroom; (b) what is happening in the classroom, discipline, or curricula; and (c) how conceptual frameworks from subdisciplinary areas can be applied to teaching and student learning. It is a strong addition and supplement to other SoTL, is most likely to earn respect as scholarship in one's college or university, and provides the useful bonus of possible public dissemination in jury reviewed forums and journals.

References

Angelo. T. A., & Cross, K. P. (1993). *Classroom assessment techniques: A handbook for college teachers* (2nd ed.). San Francisco: Jossey-Bass.

Bilimoria, D., & Fukami, C. (2002). The scholarship of teaching and learning in the management sciences: Disciplinary style and content. In M. T. Huber & S. P. Morreale. (Eds.). *Disciplinary styles in the scholarship of teaching and learning: Exploring common ground* (pp. 125-142). Washington, DC: American Association for Higher Education.

Boyer, E. L. (1990). *Scholarship reconsidered: Priorities of the professoriate.* Princeton, NJ: The Carnegie Foundation for the Advancement of Teaching.

Calder, L., Cutler, W. W. III., & Kelly, T. M. (2002). History lessons: Historians and the scholarship of teaching and learning. In M. T. Huber & S. P. Morreale (Eds.). *Disciplinary styles in the scholarship of teaching and learning: Exploring common ground* (pp. 45-67). Washington, DC: American Association for Higher Education.

Chin, J. (1999). Is there a scholarship of teaching in *Teaching Sociology*? A look at papers from 1997-1999. Unpublished manuscript.

Chism, N. V. N. (1999). *Peer review of teaching.* Bolton, MA: Anker.

Cross, K. P., & Steadman, M. H. (1996). *Classroom research: Implementing the scholarship of teaching.* San Francisco: Jossey-Bass.

Diamond, R. M., & Adam, B. E. (1995). *Recognizing faculty work: Reward systems for the year 2000.* San Francisco: Jossey-Bass.

Galguera, T. (2002). Too close for comfort and/or validity? In P. Hutchings (Ed.). *Ethics of inquiry: Issues in the scholarship of teaching and learning* (pp. 55-64). Menlo Park, CA: Carnegie Publications.

Glassick, C. E., Huber, M. T., & Maeroff, G. I. (1997). *Scholarship assessed: Evaluation of the professoriate.* San Francisco: Jossey-Bass.

Halpern, D. F., Smothergill, D. W., Allen, M., Baker, S., Baum, C., Best, D., et al., (1998). Scholarship in psychology: A paradigm for the twenty-first century. *American Psychologist, 53,* 1292-1297.

Hammack, F. M. (1997). Ethical issues in teacher research. *Teachers College Record, 99,* 247-265.

Huber, M. T., & Morreale, S. P. (Eds.). (2002). *Disciplinary styles in the scholarship of teaching and learning: Exploring common ground.* Washington, DC: American Association for Higher Education.

Hutchings, P. (1993). *Making teaching community property: A menu for peer collaboration and peer review.* Washington, DC: American Association for Higher Education.

Hutchings, P. (1998). *The course portfolio: How faculty can examine their teaching to advance practice and improve student learning*. Washington, DC: American Association for Higher Education.

Hutchings, P., & Shulman, L. S. (1999). The scholarship of teaching: New elaborations, new developments. *Change, 31*(5), 10-15.

Keig, L., & Waggoner, M. D. (1994). *Collaborative peer review: The role of faculty in improving college teaching*. (ASHE-ERIC Higher Education Report No. 2.) Washington, DC: The George Washington University School of Education and Human Development.

Mathie, V. A., Buskist, W., Carlson, J. F., Davis, S. F., Johnson, D. E., & Smith, R. A. (2004). Expanding the boundaries of scholarship in psychology through teaching, research, service, and administration. *Teaching of Psychology, 31*, 233-241.

McGovern, T. V., & Hawks, B. K. (1986). The varieties of undergraduate experience. *Teaching of Psychology, 13*, 174-181.

McKeachie, W. J. (2002). *McKeachie's teaching tips* (11th ed.). Boston: Houghton Mifflin.

Morreale, S. P., Applegate, J. L., Wulff, D. H., & Sprague, J. (2002). The scholarship of teaching and learning in communication studies, and communication scholarship in the process of teaching and learning. In M. T. Huber & S. P. Morreale (Eds.), *Disciplinary styles in the scholarship of teaching and learning: Exploring common ground* (pp. 107-123). Washington, DC: American Association for Higher Education.

Perlman, B. (2005). Books to enhance your teaching and academic life. In W. Buskist, B. C. Beins, & V. W. Hevern (Eds.), *Preparing the new psychology professoriate: Helping graduate students become competent teachers*. Syracuse, NY: Society for the Teaching of Psychology (Download from http://teachpsych.lemoyne.edu).

Perlman, B., & McCann, L. I. (2005). Undergraduate research experiences in psychology: A national study of courses and curricula. *Teaching of Psychology, 32*, 5-14.

Perlman, B., & McCann, L. I. (1999). The most frequently listed courses in the undergraduate psychology curriculum. *Teaching of Psychology, 26*, 177-182.

Perlman, B., McCann, L. I., Dettlaff, D. M., & Palladino, J. J. (2003). Teacher evaluations of make-up exam procedures. *Psychology Teaching and Learning, 3*, 36-39.

Perlman, B., McCann, L. I., & McFadden, S. L. (Eds.). (1999). *Lessons learned: Practical advice for the teaching of psychology* (Vol. 1). Washington, DC: Association for Psychological Science.

Perlman, B., McCann, L. I., & McFadden, S. L. (Eds.). (2004). *Lessons learned: Practical advice for the teaching of psychology* (Vol. 2). Washington, DC: Association for Psychological Science.

Richlin, L. (2001). Scholarly teaching and the scholarship of teaching. In C. Kreber (Ed.), *The scholarship of teaching: New directions for teaching and learning, no. 86* (pp. 57-68). San Francisco: Jossey-Bass.

Seitz, J. E. (2002). From private to public classrooms: "Inadequate" student texts in the scholarship of teaching and learning. In P. Hutchings (Ed.), *Ethics of inquiry: Issues in the scholarship of teaching and learning* (pp. 65-73). Menlo Park, CA: The Carnegie Foundation for the Advancement of Teaching.

Shulman, L. (2004). *Teaching as community property: Essays on higher education*. San Francisco: Jossey-Bass

Seldin, P. (2004). *The teaching portfolio: A practical guide to improved performance and promotion/tenure decisions*. Bolton, MA: Anker.

Wankat, P. C., Felder, R. M., Smith, K. A., & Oreovicz, F. S. (2002). The scholarship of teaching and learning in engineering. In M. T. Huber & S. P. Morreale (Eds.), *Disciplinary styles in the scholarship of teaching and learning: Exploring common ground* (pp. 217-237). Washington, DC: American Association for Higher Education.

Weimer, M. (1993). The disciplinary journals on pedagogy. *Change, 25*(6), 44-51.

We thank the Society for the Teaching of Psychology and the University of Wisconsin Faculty Development Program for support for this work.

CHAPTER TWELVE

LOW-TECHNOLOGY, HIGH-IMPACT TEACHING TECHNIQUES

Lester A. Lefton

Tulane University

I NSTRUCTORS OF COURSES in psychology — especially introductory psychology — are often called to the classroom in the same way that ministers are called to the church. It takes extraordinary commitment and dedication to be the instructor of introductory psychology. Nonetheless classes are often too large, resources too few, and respect too little.

There are some real obstacles. We often find that classrooms are too noisy. Occasionally students are spread out in a large classroom despite the fact that there are only 30 people. Classrooms often have distractions like windows that overlook highways. If you are teaching a large section of introductory psychology, knowing everyone's name and keeping track of the students presents another challenge. Too often we are placed in classrooms without up-to-date technology and many classrooms do not even have chalk in them. Remember chalk? The learning environment must be comfortable for both the instructor and students in order for learning to be maximized; seats can be uncomfortable and students are forced to sit in them for an hour or hour and a half, which rates high on anyone's annoyance dimension.

Despite such challenges, most instructors recognize that teaching the introductory class affords wonderful opportunities. On the most basic level, it makes our department chairs and deans happy because teaching introductory psychology is often cost efficient: Introductory classes tend to be larger than in upper-division ones. Teaching these classes also gives you an opportunity to present a positive view of our discipline — one based on theories and facts — and to dispel popular-press misconceptions of what psychology is about. You also get to present divergent points of view on many different topics. And finally, as an instructor of introductory psychology, you get to touch many individuals' lives.

Two Types of Instructors

I think instructors fall into two broad types: *pullers* and *pushers*. Pullers are traditional instructors who have a well-honed lecture in which they ask students to pull the material from their well-organized, coherent, well-thought-out — indeed brilliant — lectures. Well-honed lectures are terrific, but today's students are used to fast-paced music, games, and computers. They click their way through the Internet at breakneck speeds. A consequence is that they have little patience for the logic of a well-developed, lucid style.

So, many of us have become pushers. We use the force of our personalities, occasional histrionics, and clever examples to push the material into our students' consciousness, to stimulate them whether they wish to be stimulated or not. Regardless of whether you are a pusher or a puller (and the likelihood is greater that you are a pusher if you teach introductory psychology), you need to be structured and well organized. Students respond well to instructors who are in charge and in control, accountable and accessible, regardless of their individual teaching style.

Best Teaching Practices

The best instructors focus on what needs to be accomplished in the class. They recognize that they cannot teach everything — the topics are many and the class hours few. The truth is we generally only have 35 hours or so to teach dozens of key concepts in a subject that spans more than 100 years. Accordingly, the best introductory psychology teachers teach with a clear viewpoint that they wish to convey, recognizing that textbooks and ancillary materials can usually fill in the blanks. The best instructors understand that content has to be explained in a variety of ways for all students — not just the top 10 percent. The top 10 percent will always get it; it is the other 90 percent that we have to worry about. In the introductory psychology class, students are usually quite heterogeneous. There are some students who may have taken a psychology course before and others for whom this may be their first university course. It often is hard to predict who will do well and who will struggle.

Use a Behavioral Contract

As a preventive measure to ensure good decorum, enter into a behavioral contract with your students that states what you consider appropriate decorum. You should put the behavioral contract in your syllabus and discuss it on the first day of class. For example, I promise my students that I will always start class on time and never go beyond a certain time if they are quiet when I want to begin class.

Organizing Course Content

The most effective instructors methodically determine before they get to the classroom the objectives for the course and the concepts that are essential for mastery. Additionally, these instructors explain how this information will serve students in their continuing studies and beyond. This contextual framing provides the students with a foundation for what needs to be learned and what needs to be achieved both in the classroom and through homework.

A terrific, basic technique used by many instructors to help students master course content is *learning points*: bullet points or sentences that say to the students,

"This is what I want you to know." So, for example, a learning point might be the idea that "Reinforced behaviors tend to occur again." You may then spend the next 15 minutes explaining the nature of reinforcement while all the time, on the blackboard, overhead, or PowerPoint presentation, you have the sentence, "Reinforced behaviors tend to occur again."

Many Students Are Visual Learners

A simple diagram, flowchart, or list of key points can be more important than a text or a lecture because today's students tend to be visual learners (Ackerman, Kyllonen, & Roberts, 1999). They think in terms of pictures, creating mental images to retain information, and learn best through visual aids like graphs, pictures, and videos. But they also need to see the instructor's body language and facial expressions — not just the visual aids — so do not keep the room too dark. An overhead typically is much more legible than hand-written notes or the chalkboard and allows you to insert figures, diagrams, or photos. You can also do as I do and use short video clips as part of a PowerPoint presentation. And you can list key points and then later include questions relating to them on every exam, thus rewarding students for learning and retaining material and applying what they have learned.

Generalizations

Another key technique of the best instructors is that they use *generalizations*. Through generalizations, unique bits of information can be structured, ordered, and better understood; as a result, students can make better sense of their intellectual world. It is important to recognize that generalizations provide the fabric and texture of a lecture. Generalizations without details are hollow, but at the same time details without generalizations are barren. Generalizations and applications of a general principles are the things that make a lecture interesting and memorable. Teaching students that reinforcement is not just a laboratory procedure but that it operates in the classroom (verbal recognition), home (weekly allowance), workplace (bonuses), and in the community (recognition through achievement awards) is a way of generalizing the concept to many situations. Instructors should ask students to generalize from their experience to produce widely applicable principles. But remember to give details to support your generalizations.

A Model of Excellence

The best instructors also present a model of *excellence*. Excellence refers to true merit in the classroom. Such instructors demand a great deal of their students. Many people can be excellent and many can succeed and get As. Maintaining high standards will motivate student learning, and it also will help students to feel good when they meet those standards. My experience is that expecting students to perform well becomes a self-fulfilling prophecy; when I have high expectations for my students, they have them as well. The truth is that no matter how hard we try, our preconceived ideas about students show in our teaching behavior — we subtly convey those expectations and students tend to respond to our behavior by adjusting their own behavior to match these expectations. The result is that the original, often unspoken, latent expectation comes true. Our expectations need to be ones of excellence.

Respect Students' Viewpoints

The best instructors protect minority opinions, keep divergent points of view civil, and make connections between various opinions and ideas. This responsibility means reminding a class of the variety of explanations to a social or personal problem. The instructor thus becomes like an orchestra conductor of a variety of opinions.

Instructors must be careful not to isolate particular students and potentially embarrass them by putting them on the spot, especially with regard to their ethnicity, sexual orientation, age, disability, or other individual characteristics. Instructors must also recognize that students see the world from their own point of view and sometimes have trouble recognizing that theirs is not the only possible vantage point. A student who has strongly held religious beliefs may tend to believe that his or her own viewpoint is more advanced or superior to others and that his or her congregation/church/group — whatever that group might be — is the standard or reference point against which other people and religious beliefs should be judged. The importance of maintaining an open mind and recognizing multiple cultural views should be kept in mind. Instructors should encourage students to keep an open mind, just as they themselves do.

TURNING OBSTACLES INTO OPPORTUNITIES: DISH THE DIRT

Teaching is a dynamic tension between the obstacles and liabilities students present and the opportunities and power of teaching. The question teachers often face is, "How do I turn obstacles into opportunities?" I have always argued that as an instructor you have to learn to dish the DIRT. You have to create *Desire, Interest, Relevancy*, and use *low-Technology*.

How do we do this? It begins with the resources that are available to us. The truth is that the most valuable resource is almost always the teacher. It is the teacher who makes the difference. Fifteen years after taking an introductory psychology course, students do not remember the book or the Web site that they used; if the teacher was skilled, they remember the instructor. Other resources are important too, of course. Most textbook publishers provide computerized test banks, four-color textbooks, videos, slides, CD-ROMS, as well as Web sites. All of these things are truly rich resources to help the main resource, the instructor.

Desire

We have to instill student desire to learn, to be open to different ideas, to come to class, to do the homework and readings, and most especially, to become excited about and see the relevance of psychology in their daily lives. It is our own enthusiasm, excitement, and belief in the discipline, and our energy for teaching, that drives this quest for learning on the part of students. Simple behaviors on our part show it — are we energetic, organized, on time, and prepared? Teachers need to display their passion for the subject matter. Do whatever is necessary to get students excited: Move about in a classroom (do not stand fixed in place at the front of the room), change your voice inflection, wave your arms.

To help generate student desire, it is important to know who your students are and what they bring with them educationally and experientially — this knowledge will help you to design the format, content, and especially the style of your presentation. At the beginning of the semester, preferably on the first day of class, instead of just calling roll, ask the students to complete a brief survey that includes their name, hometown, major, intended career plans, previous experience with the subject of psychology, and most importantly, their expectations for the course (of course, this information is voluntary and your instructions should make that explicit). This student profile provides the stealth weapon every effective instructor needs: information. What students expect from the course, and some of the background experiences that shape those expectations, can add critical content to an otherwise flat class discussion. Review the surveys as soon as you leave the class the first day and create your own database of information, from hometowns to majors. Build a profile of the class and work the information into class discussion. "Is anyone here from the Midwest? From Youngstown? How do you see this theory play out in your community?"

Likewise, address the expectations you read in the surveys right away and state the objectives of the course in the context of the students' comments. Many students in an introductory course expect to be able to solve their relationship problems with their mother, father, sister, cousin, or to cure their roommate of depression and generally be able to dispense credible psychological advice to anyone — including themselves. By acknowledging these expectations and addressing them early in the course, the instructor can eliminate potential disappointment, and ethical problems, down the road. The instructor can use this opportunity to reemphasize the course objectives.

Interest

The instructor needs to create interest in class. Do not assume students will be interested in what you have to say. Even if some students are, the best students' minds can still wander. From the first moment of class you have to create interest, and continue doing so throughout class.

The content, how that content is delivered, and the activities that students will participate in all contribute to creating student interest. The content must be made relevant: Students want and need to see how what they will learn is relevant to psychology, to their other studies, and potentially to their lives. So present the material in a way that is provocative, and highlights this relevance. Reading from old, yellowed notes is quickly noted by students — and not appreciated. Do not start with facts. Instead, open with an issue. Pose a question. Ask students, "Do you think day care is deleterious to the emotional development of children?" or, "Do you think prison really works to rehabilitate criminals?" If students can somehow relate the material to something they already know, the likelihood of their learning the new material is greatly improved. Last, use words like *you, we, us, and our* to suggest that you are interested in the subject, are a participant in the discovery process, and that you relate to them and think of them and yourself together as a cohort, a community of learners.

Relevancy

It is important to prepare students for what they are going to hear and learn. Setting a clear agenda for the class in a handout, on a slide, or on the chalkboard keeps their attention focused and gives you the chance to make your key points in context. By starting off with a question to frame the discussion — a question to which any student can respond — you break the ice and lead into the topic of daycare or the effect of punishment on behavior. Likewise, returning to that same question as you close the lecture will help the students see the link between learning and applications and the link between the real world and psychological data.

It is easy to ask students whether they think therapy for alcoholics works, or what the impact of culture on a person's worldview might be. In my teaching, I have found that many college students today seek learning experiences that might help them cope with life — for example, marriage, a new job, or losing a grandparent. One way to give them such learning experiences is to ensure that opportunities to answer questions are neither too easy nor too difficult. If questions are too easy, students' minds wander because they feel the material is trivial. If the questions are too complex or difficult, they may tune out because they feel that they have no chance of answering them. Posing questions that are challenging — not too hard or too easy — hits the sweet spot that engages students to think critically. Questions that are "just right" facilitate learning. Although every class is different, you might ask questions like, "What would be Vygotsky's key complaint about Piaget's theory?" or, "What is the central argument against Gilligan's views?" or perhaps, "What event or events made Freud so biased in his views about women?"

Another way to give students relevant learning experiences is to take them with you to hear guest lecturers or to visit laboratories on your campus or other campuses. Activities that get students out of the classroom interest and engage them, create excitement, and thus facilitate more learning and generalization.

You can even use music in class. I often begin class with music from a relevant play, musical, or movie that students may have seen and link the music to the topic at hand. Take requests. Students seem to like the idea of a boom box playing something different to begin each class.

In the end, you want students to be active learners. Relevant material facilitates active learning. Active learners engage in activities that force them to think about and comment on the information presented. If developing active learning means group work, collaborative learning, or reflective writing, so be it. Active learning forces students to develop a deeper understanding of general course content or specific principles and their application than when the material is treated as knowledge to be learned by rote. As a consequence, students are more likely to study, develop their own questions, and make generalizations.

Another way to foster academic learning is to sometimes break the class up into smaller groups. In my experience, learning about psychology takes place especially well when the students are permitted to work in small groups. The purpose of such an arrangement can be to encourage collaborative or cooperative learning, or just to let students have a quick chat among themselves. They can refer to their text and notes, as well as ask questions of each other and you, while working on the task at hand.

To take the learning process even further, consider developing a private discussion forum for your class through devices like WebCT or Blackboard, so that they can communicate and share ideas with one another (and you) outside the classroom.

Develop Low-Technology, High-Impact Teaching Techniques

When teachers develop low-technology, high-impact techniques they are not necessarily using equipment, but rather using concepts and ideas that are easily remembered, that aid in teaching, and that focus on key concepts. In my opinion, our goal as instructors is to inspire critical thinking, to encourage oral skills, and to foster written skills. By presenting clear key ideas with only minimal use of technology, we make the highest impact on learning.

The syllabus. The syllabus is the foundation of your course. It does not involve technology, but it is critical to your success. The syllabus serves three major purposes: It (a) shapes your expectations for students, (b) presents your organization in terms of substance and style, and (c) it lays out for students the rules, regulations, and schedule of your class. The syllabus should inform students about you, your priorities in the course, and how the course will be organized. It tells the students who you are, what your training is, and how they can contact you. Overall, the goal of your syllabus is to inform students of the nature of the course, lay out your expectations, and form a contract between you and them. Through the syllabus, you tell the students, "This is what you are expected to do in this course, and I will hold you to all of this." Simultaneously, you agree not to ask for more than, or anything different from, what is specified in the syllabus. Make every effort to stick to the syllabus, especially the schedule, homework dates, and test dates. Announce any changes well in advance and put them in writing.

Critical thinking. When I refer to critical thinking I mean being open-minded but evaluative. Good teachers reject glib generalizations; they determine the relevance of information and look for biases and imbalances, as well as for objectivity and testable, repeatable results. A critical thinker identifies central issues, draws careful conclusions, and maintains a skeptical and questioning attitude. A critical thinker also has to tolerate some uncertainty and be patient — and to accept that all the answers do not come at once.

When thinking critically about research, psychologists sort through information the way a detective does, trying to be objective, questioning the hypotheses and conclusions, avoiding oversimplification, and considering all the arguments, objections, and counterarguments. Like detectives, psychologists evaluate all assumptions, actively seek out conflicting points of view, and revise their opinions when the data and conclusions call for it. To ask students questions that require higher-order thinking, pose such questions as:

♦ What evidence can you cite for support of this view?
♦ How does _____ compare or contrast with _____?
♦ How would you create or design a new study to test this view?
♦ What criteria would you use to assess this problem?

Avoid the tendency to "profess" too much. Our duty is to help students to learn and become critical thinkers, but the truth is, we talk a lot — probably too much. Asking questions, and keeping in mind relevancy, interest, and desire, helps us as teachers to eschew overuse of electronic technology for the more difficult, roll-up-your-sleeves teaching, and to avoid the mistake of teacher as orator. Teachers in classroom talk most of the time (we *profess*, after all!). Students rarely respond (although we hope they learn). In fact, of those who respond, only about 20 percent tend to dominate the discussion (see for example, Skidmore, Perez-Parent & Arnfield, 2003).

Be aware of gender differences in class. Of students who respond in class, men take up more of the time than women, even when there are more women present. Women behave differently in the classroom. We know from the literature (Turkel, 2004; Lee et al., 2002; Boatwright & Egidio, 2003) that, as children, girls are often focused on interdependence and develop cooperative learning styles. Both women and men desire active involvement in the classroom, though, so you should ask questions that everyone can answer. Encourage cross-student dialogues by using relational questions — "Well, Bob, you argued this approach is not going to work in your home, but Julia feels . . ."

Use signals and silence. Brief exclamations are terrific. Say things like "Wait, wait, wait" — and then actually wait a bit. You can elicit longer, more meaningful, and more frequent responses from students by maintaining silence in the classroom. Wait time is positively related to student achievement, and I have found that silence for at least 5 seconds after a question is asked is a great thing (see Atwood & William, 1991; McKeachie, 2002; Rowe, 1974). Say something like, "Let's think about Juanita's response before going further"; or "These comments, together with other things members of the class have said, suggest there are strong feelings about [fill in topic here]. Let's spend some time discussing it." Then give the students time to formulate their ideas.

Take a hands-on approach. Walk out into the class, use interesting slides, reach out to students, and learn their names (or at least the names on their tee shirts). Ask students to be volunteers in any demonstrations that you do. As I suggested earlier, use words like *we* and *us* to demonstrate that you connect with your students and that you are engaged in a common, shared undertaking: learning and teaching psychology. The end of a lecture should not come as a shock to a class but needs to be arrived at sensibly. Say something like "At this stage I would like to go over, again, the main learning points …"

The 1-minute paper. One of the most effective techniques to help students reflect on the day's lecture is to ask them to do just that. Ask them to take literally 1 minute and rip a piece of paper from their notebooks to write a comment or a question about the lecture (Angelo & Cross, 1993). For example, they might write what else they wanted to know or identify an unresolved question. It is feedback for you, and it is a focus on learning for them. Alternatively, you can ask students to write questions that require critical thought about the material being studied. Or ask, "What point from the lecture was least clear?" It is amazing the kinds of comments that students will provide that can help you refocus your lecture as well as to get them to solidify the material in their own minds. Some examples of such 1-minute focus questions that I have received over the years are the following:

"If a person makes it belatedly through a stage of development — say at age 45 — can he continue to grow?" "Can a bad experience at one stage be negated by a good experience at the next?" "Are Freud's idea and theories shown cross-culturally? At all?"

IMPLICATIONS FOR TEACHERS AND STUDENTS

♦ Teachers should be genuine and authentic with students and show these qualities in how they teach.

♦ Teachers should be cautious about technology and fads, replacing them with high-quality, well-prepared classroom teaching.

♦ Good teaching — and we all know it when we see it — takes energy, commitment, and lots of preparation.

♦ Instructors teach in many ways — sometimes by saying nothing and waiting, sometimes by wading into the thick of a discussion.

♦ Effective teaching often means talking less, engaging students more, and taking some intellectual risks. One way to do these things is to have a top-notch and complete syllabus that eliminates many of the questions that new students might have. Do not waste valuable class time explaining how make-up tests are done.

♦ At the end of the day, low-technology, person-to-person interactions will reach out and touch students and make them want to be educated. Establishing relationships with students is fundamental. In the minutes before class, greet students at the door and say hello. Explain to students that one-on-one meetings with you are an important way to help them fully engage with the class material. Explain that you have set aside time for them. Also think about setting up a buddy system so students can get in touch with each other about coursework.

♦ Teach fundamentals, laying guideposts for students' later learning in more advanced courses. Be prepared to skip a few topics; we do not have to teach everything. Make students (and yourself for that matter) bridge the gap between psychological theory and application.

♦ Relax. Teaching introductory psychology is supposed to be fun. You know more than the students do, and your confidence and enthusiasm will win the day. Be self-deprecating from time to time and do not take yourself too seriously.

REFERENCES

Ackerman, P. L., Kyllonen, P. C., & Roberts, R. D. (Eds.). (1999). Learning and individual differences: Process, trait, and content determinants. Washington, DC: American Psychological Association.

Angelo, T. A., & Cross, K. P. (1993). Classroom assessment techniques: A handbook for college teachers (2nd ed.). San Francisco: Jossey-Bass.

Atwood, V. A., & William, W. W. (1991). Wait time and effective social studies instruction: What can research in science education tell us? Social Education, 55, 179-181.

Boatwright, K. J., & Egidio, R. K. (2003). Psychological predictors of college women's leadership aspirations. Journal of College Student Development, 44, 653-669.

Lee, R. M., Keough, K. A., & Sexton, J. D. (2002). Social connectedness, social appraisal, and perceived stress in college women and men. Journal of Counseling & Development, 80, 355-361.

McKeachie, W. J. (2002). McKeachie's teaching tips: Strategies, research and theory for college and university teachers (11th ed.). Boston: Houghton Mifflin.

Rowe, M. B. (1974). Wait-time and rewards as instructional variables, their influence on language, logic, and fate control: Part one — wait-time. *Journal of Research in Science Teaching, 11*, 81-94.

Skidmore, D., Perez-Parent, M., & Arnfield, S. (2003). Teacher-pupil dialogue in the guided reading session. *Reading: Literacy & Language, 37*(2), 47-53.

Turkel, R., The hand that rocks the cradle rocks the boat: The empowerment of women. (2004). *Journal of the American Academy of Psychoanalysis & Dynamic Psychiatry, 32*(1), 41-53.

CHAPTER THIRTEEN

PROFESSING PSYCHOLOGY WITH PASSION

Lessons I Have Learned

David G. Myers

Hope College

HAVING RECENTLY COMPLETED three and a half decades professing psychology, and having just turned 60 years of age, this seems a fitting time to reflect again on some lessons I have learned in my career. Perhaps this self-disclosure can stimulate some of you to reflect on the lessons you have learned while professing psychology. Can you articulate what Bob Sternberg calls your "tacit knowledge" — the implicit, experienced-based principles that facilitate your work life?

CAREER AND LIFE LESSONS

Lesson #1: One Cannot Predict the Future

As an undergraduate chemistry major who had taken only introductory psychology during my first three years, I never would have guessed that I would become a social psychologist. When entering graduate school, aiming to become a college teacher, I never would have guessed that I would become engaged by research. When doing research during my assistant professor years, I never would have guessed that I would become a writer.

The awakening of my interest in social-psychological research illustrates why I have come to expect the unexpected. When I arrived to begin Iowa's graduate program in 1964, having declared my interest in personality, my advisor explained that the department's one faculty member in personality had just left. "So we've put you in social psychology" — that is how I became a social psychologist.

During my second year, I assisted social psychologist Sidney Arenson by engaging 40 small groups in discussing story problems that assessed risk taking. We replicated the phenomenon of increased risk taking by groups, dubbed the "risky shift," and before long this college-teacher wannabe had, to his surprise, also become a research psychologist. Moreover, the research mutated unpredictably — from risky shift to a broader group-polarization phenomenon to studies of the subtle influence on attitudes of mere exposure to others' attitudes.

Lesson #2: Contrarian Professional Investment Can Pay Big Dividends

Major contributions often occur when people invest in a research problem at an early stage — when, as Bob Sternberg says, the intellectual stock is still undervalued. Unless you are uncommonly brilliant, which most of us are not, a good way to contribute to psychology is to pick a research problem that has received little study. This strategy offers the chance to master the available literature before it proceeds to third-order interaction effects. Stay with the stock — become a world-class expert. The risky-shift/group-polarization literature was visited by dozens of people who dabbled with a study or two and then moved on to do a study or two in other areas. The people who really enlarged our understanding were not these researchers, but those who stayed around long enough to dive deep, often by offering a single idea that they pushed to its limits.

Lesson #3: Scholarship Can Be a Lonely Enterprise

When you have freshly mastered a literature and know it about as well as anyone in the world, few other people may know or care. Unless one is working on a team project, to be a scholar is often to feel alone and ignored. Once we have done our research, written it up, endured the publication lag, had your work cited in secondary sources, and gone on to other things, *then* people will take us to be an expert and may invite us to give talks and write reflective chapters. Meanwhile, the fresh minds working at the cutting edge will be languishing for such opportunities.

Lesson #4: Success, Even If Serendipitous, Builds on Itself

Life is not fair. Success biases new opportunities toward those who have already been given other opportunities. Although the skills required for research and for writing overlap only modestly, it was my good fortune to happen onto what turned out to be a fruitful research problem that led to an invitation to write my social psychology text, which led to an invitation to write an introductory psychology text, which lent credibility to my approach to a literary agent about writing *The Pursuit of Happiness*, which opened doors for other opportunities to communicate psychological science to the lay public. Although the process begins with solitary hard work, fortunate outcomes can lead to more opportunities, whether you are the most deserving person or not. Success feeds on itself. So it pays to start well.

Lesson #5: To Be an Effective, Contributing Professional, One Need Not Be Uncommonly Brilliant or Creative

With dogged work, I was able to master a literature and connect some dots, despite not having the genius to invent the theories. You need not be as theoretically creative as Nobel-laureate cognitive psychologist Daniel Kahneman to work at winnowing truth from falsehood, at consolidating what we have learned, or at communicating it to college students and the lay public. That is what Dean Simonton (1994) has discerned from the curvilinear relationship between intelligence and leadership ability. Up to a point, intelligence facilitates leadership. However, an excessive intellectual gap between leader and follower can hamper their communication. Good teaching and science writing likewise require enough intelligence to comprehend what the pioneering theorists are saying and discovering, but not so much intelligence that one is out of touch with how ordinary people think and talk.

If you are not brilliant or expert on every aspect of a problem, it also helps to gain the support of people whose competencies complement your own. I suspect every text author has at times felt mildly embarrassed by people who are too impressed — people who think we just sat down and wrote what they are reading, assuming they never could. Such folks should not be so intimidated. It actually took a whole team of reviewers and editors to shape, over several drafts, a work that surpasses what the author, working alone, was capable of writing.

Lesson #6: You Do Not Get Pellets Unless You Press the Bar

Life has us on partial reinforcement schedules. What one reviewer thinks is pointless research, another will think is pioneering. What one reader finds "too cute," another will find refreshingly witty. The poet Pennington was once rejected by a magazine that explained, "This is the worst poem in the English language. You are the worst poet in the English language." So he sent the poem to another magazine, which accepted it "with glowing praise," and chose it as its year's-best poem.

Given the unreliability of others' judgments of our work, it pays to try and try again. Our colleagues who are athletic coaches live with the publicity given both their victories and their defeats. Those of us who are scholars only announce our victories. However, let me admit to one of my strings of unpublicized defeats. Several years ago, *Today's Education* rejected my critique of the labeling and segregation of "gifted" children from the 95 percent of children deemed, by implication, "ungifted." I then submitted it to six other periodicals, all of which rejected it. Noticing that *Today's Education* by now had a new editor, and thinking the piece slightly improved, I resubmitted it to *Today's Education* without reminding them that they already had rejected a previous draft. They accepted it immediately, published it, later gave permission for its reprinting in newspapers and magazines, and invited me to write more.

Lesson #7: If You Feel Excited by an Idea or a Possibility, Do Not Be Deterred by Criticism

We have all heard stories of great books that were rejected countless times before publication, or works of art or music that went unappreciated during the creator's lifetime. People derided Robert Fulton's steamboat as "Fulton's Folly." As Fulton later said, "Never did a single encouraging remark, a bright hope, a warm wish, cross my path" (Sale, 2002). Much the same reaction greeted the printing press, the telegraph, the incandescent lamp, and the typewriter. John White's book, *Rejection* (1982), is one story after another of all the scorn and derision that greeted the work of people from Michelangelo and Beethoven to the American poet A. Wilber Stevens, who received from his hoped-for publisher an envelope of ashes. Dr. Seuss initially was rejected by some two dozen publishers. "There is no way to sell a book about an unknown Dutch painter," Doubleday explained before Irving Stone's (1934/1989) book about Van Gogh survived 15 rejections and reportedly sold 25 million copies. In a possibly apocryphal story, one of the seven publishers that rejected *The Tale of Peter Rabbit* said that the tale "smelled like rotting carrots."

If you pick up brochures for anyone's textbook and read all the nice quotes, you may feel a twinge of envy, thinking it must be nice to get all those glowing reviews — those are not all the reviews. Let me tell you about some reviews that you will never see quoted. One long-retired reviewer of my introductory psychology text offered the following in his chapter reviews:

> The use of the English language in this book is atrocious. Faulty grammar and syntax, imprecise meaning and incorrect terminology etc. etc. are abundant. When I'm reading the book I have the feeling that it is written by one of my undergraduate students; when reviewing this edition it is at times like correcting an undergraduate term paper.

In response to another chapter he wrote:

> I find the tone and even content paternalistic, value laden and maybe even demeaning. Especially the section on "work" is very poor; it left me angry that one would want to present such "crap" to learning young adults. Did Dr. Myers really write this vague, stereotypical, poorly worded, unclear and confusing section on work?

Yet another chapter: "At times this text reads as if it has been a translation from the German language." (Incredibly, this reviewer, who also had helpful suggestions, shortly thereafter adopted the book.)

Then there was the reviewer who noted that the book "is very biased and opinionated. I don't think the author is very competent. I have thought of writing a text and perhaps now moreso," whereupon he proceeded to offer his services.

While preparing that book's first edition, there were days when, after being hammered on by editors — one of whom scribbled criticism all over several chapters with but *one* still-remembered compliment: "nice simile" — I longed for a single encouraging word. One of my most difficult professional tasks — perhaps yours, too, as you cope with mentors' criticisms, professional reviews, or student evaluations — is being open to feedback without feeling defeated by it. The lesson I have learned from this is: Listen to criticism, but if you have a vision, hold to it. Keep your eye on the goal. In retrospect, I am glad I submitted to the process, but I am also glad I did not let it intimidate me into submission.

Lesson #8: As Praise and Criticism Accumulates, Its Power to Elate or Depress Lessens

Compliments provoke less elation and criticisms less despair, as both become mere iotas of additional feedback atop a pile of accumulated praise and reproach.

That helps explain why emotions mellow as we age. I have spent hours in sleepless anguish over my children's ups and downs, but rarely, of late, over professional criticism. As Albert Ellis keeps reminding people, not everyone is going to love what we do. The more feedback I receive, the more I can accept that.

Lesson #9: Achievement Comes With Keeping Focused and Managing Time

Our basketball coaches say their teams play well when they keep their focus, without being distracted from their game plan by the referees' calls, the opposing fans, or the other team's spurts. A successful entrepreneur friend speaks of achieving success by keeping his focus — knowing his niche, where he is needed, what he is good at. We all get asked to do all sorts of things that other people can do as well or better. My experience is that the world is a better place when each of us identifies and then focuses on our best gifts. When a service club wants a talk on a topic where I have no expertise, or when a caller needs a counselor, I decline, with thanks, or offer a referral, remembering that every time I say "yes" to something I am implicitly saying "no" to some other use of that time. Sometimes I want to say yes to that use of time, which is what led me to spend time preparing these reflections. Other times, the alternative uses of the time feel like higher priorities.

When my house needed repair work, I tried, even when supporting a family solely on an assistant professor income, to emulate my father, who would pay craftspeople to do what they could do better and more efficiently, which gave them work and freed his time for his profession. In the long run, it has paid off. I am not advocating a workaholism that competes with investing in family relationships, relaxing hobbies, and an equitable sharing of daily domestic work, if I can focus all those other hours on the professional work that I most enjoy, I will have more to give. It is a point I make to younger colleagues when I see them doing clerical work, which both deprives someone else of a job and steals time from their own profession.

Time management also pays dividends. Several years ago I noticed one of my colleagues writing down something in his desk calendar as someone left his office. What was he doing? He was logging his time, he explained, to see how closely his use of time mirrored his espoused priorities. I decided to do the same. What a revelation! Not only did I learn how long it took me to write a textbook — 3,550 hours for the first edition of *Social Psychology* — I learned how poorly my actual priorities matched my proclaimed priorities. More minutes adding up to more hours than I would have believed were frittered away uselessly — not counseling students, not teaching, not doing research or writing, not in meetings, just doing nothing useful. While still allowing time for spontaneous connections with people, that very realization made me more conscious of wasted time.

Another time-management strategy is to set big goals, then break them down into weekly objectives. Before beginning work on a new textbook, I would lay out a week-by-week schedule. My goal was not to have the whole 600-page book done by such-and-such date — that is too remote and formidable — but writing three manuscript pages a day — a relative cup of tea. Repeat the process 400 times and, presto!, you have a 1,200-page manuscript. It is really not so hard, nor is reaching many goals when attacked day by day. Although we often overestimate how much we will accomplish in any given day, we generally underestimate how much we can accomplish in a year, given just a little progress every day. Moreover, as each mini-deadline is met, one gets the delicious, confident feeling of personal control.

Lesson #10: Success Requires Enough Optimism to Provide Hope and Enough Pessimism to Prevent Complacency

Feeling capable of but one task at a time partly reflects a nagging lack of self-confidence, the sort of "defensive pessimism" that, ironically, can enable success — when it goads us to believe that only by utter diligence will we ever do work on a par with that done by all those more brilliant people at more famous places. It was because I knew I was not a gifted writer (my worst college grade was in a writing class) that I focused on developing my writing skills — by reading great writers such as C. S. Lewis and Carl Sagan; by studying style manuals such as Strunk and White's *Elements of Style* (Strunk & White, 2000), Jacques Barzun's *Simple and Direct* (2001), and William Zinsser's *On Writing Well* (2001); by subjecting my writing to a computer grammar checker; and, especially, by engaging a writing coach — a poet colleague who has closely edited some 5,000 of my manuscript pages while patiently teaching me what it means to develop a voice, to order words to maximize punch, to write with rhythm. It pays to have enough self-confidence to risk undertaking a project, and enough self-doubt to think you will fail if you do not focus enormous effort on it.

IMPLICATIONS FOR TEACHERS AND TEACHING

Each of these lessons, born of experience, has implications for teachers and teaching.

The future's unpredictability provides a rationale for liberal education. You cannot know your future, I explain to new and prospective students. Your interests on entering college will likely change during college, and change again during your working life. Most students end up majoring in something they didn't have in mind on entering college, and end up in a vocation unrelated to their major. That is why a broad education for an unpredictable future — a liberal education — serves most students better than a purely vocational education.

Contrarian investment sometimes pays dividends, not only when placed in undervalued financial and intellectual stocks, but also in undervalued or undeveloped students. We teachers take joy in spotting and encouraging potential talent in students whose minds are just now awakening to the world of learning. I came to college with an above-average but undistinguished high-school record and interests that barely ranged beyond sports, salmon fishing, and the family business. Thanks in part to Whitworth College faculty, who opened my mind to interesting ideas and encouraged me to believe in my own potential, my interests expanded and, much to my surprise, four years later I found myself in graduate school.

Teaching, like scholarship, can be a lonely enterprise. When preparing classes and facing students, we're usually on our own. My college has responded to this reality with a weeklong August "teaching enhancement" workshop for new faculty. Not only are they exposed to some effective teaching strategies, they gain a senior faculty mentor (who plays no part in assessing them for tenure), and they immediately gain a support group of friends who are part of their pledge class of newcomers.

Teaching success, like scholarly success, feeds on itself. With success comes increased comfort and confidence, which breeds further success, which builds one's reputation, which heightens students' expectations as they enter your class. Students often begin courses having heard "Professor Smith is interesting" and "Professor Jones is a bore." Robert Feldman and Thomas Prohaska (1979; see also Feldman & Theiss, 1982) found that such expectations can affect both student and teacher. Students in a learning experiment who expected to be taught by a competent teacher perceived their teacher (who was unaware of their expectations) as more competent and interesting than did students with low expectations. Furthermore, the students actually learned more. In a follow-up experiment, Feldman and Prohaska videotaped teachers and had observers later rate their performance. Teachers were judged most capable when assigned a student who nonverbally conveyed positive expectations.

To see whether such effects might also occur in actual classrooms, a research team led by David Jamieson (Jamieson, Lydon, Stewart, & Zanna, 1987) experimented with four Ontario high school classes taught by a newly transferred teacher. During individual interviews they told students in two of the classes that both other students and the research team rated the teacher very highly. Compared to the control classes, the students given positive expectations paid better attention during class. At the end of the teaching unit, they also got better grades and rated the teacher as clearer in her teaching. The attitudes that a class has toward its teacher are as important, it seems, as the teacher's attitude toward the students.

Effectiveness does not require uncommon brilliance or creativity. Some of our colleagues have the genius to invent great ideas and do pioneering research. If others of us lack the smarts or resources to match their intellectual accomplishments, we may nonetheless be smart enough to take the bread that's baking up in the ivory towers and bring it down to the street where folks can eat it. Moreover, some of us may have gifts of warmth, enthusiasm, and passion for teaching that enable us to communicate psychology more effectively than can our most distinguished psychological scientists. Many leading scientists understand this, and therefore appreciate those who effectively give their work away to the public.

Teachers, too, get partial reinforcement for bar pressing. Some demonstrations, some jokes, some media, some lectures, some discussion topics flop. Others *really* work. The point is effectively made. Students are engaged and participating. As we try new activities and get rewarded for the things that do work, our courses gradually mutate to greater and greater effectiveness (assuming we maintain our freshness and enthusiasm).

Great teachers are informed but not deflated by criticism. Feedback — the more specific the better — is part of the process by which students reinforce and strengthen what we do well, and inform us what needs redoing. Even very good teachers get wounded by stinging criticism from a few anonymous students. So do all of us. Here, from my files, is an example from one student's end-of-course evaluation:

What did you find beneficial about this course: *Nothing*

If you think that the course could be improved, what would you suggest? *End the course*

What advice would you give to a friend who is planning to take this course? *Don't*

Because we hold such comments to ourselves, we may be unaware that our esteemed colleagues occasionally get similarly stung.

As student feedback accumulates, its power to elate or depress wanes. If the nasty feedback above had been in response to my first teaching effort, I might have contemplated my father's invitation to come home to Seattle and join the family insurance agency. Coming after many semesters of teaching, after receiving feedback from many hundreds of students, a single statement of praise ("this is the best class and best teacher I have ever had") still feels good, and a single hostile statement ("the course was dull and the tests unfair") still feels bad. But one's head doesn't swell over the former (we know not all students responded so warmly) nor does the sting of a single criticism cause a sleepless night.

Teaching success comes with focus and time management. It comes with identifying and harnessing our gifts (are we especially good at lecturing? facilitating discussion? engaging students with activities and media?). It comes with teaching multiple sections of a few courses (as opposed to single sections of many courses). Noting that it took emotional energy to gear up for class and to descend after class, I bunched my classes together into Tuesdays and Thursdays — leaving the other days emotionally freer to concentrate on research and writing. Having multiple sections of the same course — teaching, if possible, all my social psychology sections one semester, all my introductory psychology sections another — further reduced the workload without compromising the teaching load. By clustering our year's sections of a given course in one semester, we reduce the number of preparations (and of sets of lectures, exams, media hassles, and trips to the Xerox machine) in any one semester.

Teaching success grows from a mix of confidence-enabling optimism and defensive pessimism. To feel comfortable and in command of our material and presentation, we have got to believe in our competence and teaching skill. Yet a dash of anxiety both motivates preparation and lends a certain edge. Just before meeting my first class of the day I would always find my autonomic nervous system requiring a last-minute visit to the bathroom (a phenomenon that other colleagues experience as well). That pre-class arousal is part of the edge, the energy, and the enthusiasm that enables our best teaching.

CONCLUSION

There is one final lesson I have learned, which is that *professing psychology is a wonderful vocation.* Consider: What more fascinating subject could we study and teach than our own human workings? What teaching aims are more worthy than restraining intuition with critical thinking and judgmentalism with understanding? What subject is more influential in shaping values and lifestyles than our young science of psychology? There are "two sorts of jobs," wrote C. S. Lewis in *Screwtape Proposes a Toast* (1965):

Of one sort, a [person] can truly say, "I am doing work which is worth doing. It would still be worth doing if nobody paid for it. But as I have no private means, and need to be fed and housed and clothed, I must be paid while I do it." The other kind of job is that in which people do work whose sole purpose is the earning of money: work which need not be, ought not to be, or would not be, done by anyone in the whole world unless it were paid. (p. 114)

I am thankful that I am blessed with a vocation that is decidedly in the first category. A vocation that is mind expanding, full of fresh surprises, and focused on humanly significant questions.

REFERENCES

Barzun, J. (2001). *Simple and direct.* New York: Perennial Currents.

Feldman, R. S., & Prohaska, T. (1979). The student as Pygmalion: Effect of student expectation on the teacher. *Journal of Educational Psychology, 71*, 485-493.

Feldman, R. S., & Theiss, A. J. (1982). The teacher and student as Pygmalions: Joint effects of teacher and student expectations. *Journal of Educational Psychology, 74*, 217-223.

Jamieson, D. W., Lydon, J. E., Stewart, G., & Zanna, M. P. (1987). Pygmalion revisited: New evidence for student expectancy effects in the classroom. *Journal of Educational Psychology, 79*, 461-466.

Lewis, C. S. (1965). *Screwtape proposes a toast.* London: Fontana.

Sale, K. (2002). *The fire of his genius: Robert Fulton and the American dream.* New York: Free Press.

Simonton, D. K. (1994). *Greatness: Who makes history and why.* New York: Guilford.

Stone, I. (1989). *Lust for life.* New York: Plume Books. (Original work published 1934)

Strunk, Jr., W., & White, E. B. (2000). *Elements of style* (4th ed.). Needham Heights, MA: Allyn & Bacon.

White, J. (1982). *Rejection.* Boston: Addison-Wesley.

Zinnser, W. (2001). *On writing well, 25th anniversary.* New York: HarperResource.

AFTERWORD
Good Ideas and Good Teaching

Baron Perlman
Lee I. McCann
University of Wisconsin Oshkosh
William Buskist
Auburn University

WE HOPE THAT the chapters in this book help you to think critically and productively about your teaching and, at least in some small way, to teach more effectively. Teaching is an evolutionary, iterative process — the proverbial three steps forward and two steps back. The wisdom and ideas extolled in this volume are only a starting point. The goal of superb teaching and student learning is hard won, and not often won for long.

As this book's editors, we have learned a great deal from reading our authors' essays. Not only did we read, reread, and edit these chapters, we also talked with each other, and corresponded by e-mail over the course of the book's development. The authors' ideas stimulated our thinking about our teaching, just as we hope their ideas will stimulate your thinking about your teaching. One of the joys of teaching is talking about it with others who know the successes and tribulations of educating students. We want to share three threads of our conversations with you. As we worked on this book and chatted with each other about our authors' ideas, we began to wonder even more about where good ideas for our teaching come from, what makes for good teaching, and how we track our teaching's effectiveness.

WHENCE GOOD IDEAS FOR TEACHING?

There are many wellsprings for ideas for the courses we teach, many of which are intimately related to who we are as people and what we bring to the classroom as unique individuals. If we are willing to make use of our interests and experiences, we enrich our students' educations.

Do Some Reading

Although few of us will ever visit the types of archives that Ludy Benjamin described in his chapter, we all have our own favorite literary resources that we occasionally revisit. For example, in the past few years, one of us (Perlman) has begun rereading his favorite books on psychology from graduate school and early in his career, at least the ones he kept. He looks at them now with a more seasoned and mature eye, and is now better able to articulate for his students and himself what drew him to these authors' ideas in the first place. For example, *How Can I Help?* (Dass & Gorman, 1985) and *If You Meet the Buddha on the Road, Kill Him!* (Kopp, 1972) continue to play a special role in his work with undergraduates who are considering graduate school in the helping professions. These books capture the nature of helping, and the personal attributes needed, far better than undergraduate counseling texts. Asking students to write assignments based on these books helps them discover their own identities and aspirations.

Of course, many good teachers regularly read the literature on teaching that is found in such journals as *Teaching of Psychology* or the British journal *Psychology Learning and Teaching* or in the numerous outstanding books that are currently available on college and university teaching in general (e.g., Dominowski, 2002; McKeachie, 2002) and the teaching of psychology in particular (e.g., Forsyth, 2003; Lucas & Bernstein, 2005; Perlman, McCann, & McFadden, 1999, 2004). Although teaching journals typically contain a blend of content and teaching technique, books tend to emphasize primarily teaching technique and style (see Davis & Buskist, 2002). Specialty journals in all of psychology's manifold subfields also are rich sources of ideas, especially for demonstrations and to provide empirical support for many of the points we make in class.

Talk With Colleagues

We also know that colleagues are a superb source of good ideas for improving our teaching. Good teachers actively seek out colleagues for advice on both teaching content and teaching technique, and for encouragement and support. We often find it useful to run an idea past our colleagues about a risk we want to hazard in class — perhaps a new demonstration or metaphor. None of us could ever keep up with all of the important new findings in psychology relevant to our upper-division courses, let alone our introductory courses, were it not for the advice and counsel of our colleagues. Most good teachers surround themselves with a network of peers who alert them to a journal, newspaper article, book, or book review that is interesting and may add to the content of their courses.

Colleagues also are wonderful sources of critique. Sure, we may have to endure humorous suggestions on how to improve our teaching (get a personality transplant, hire a real teacher to take your place, etc.), but we usually can count on a sympathetic ear and a number of useful examples of what colleagues have tried in similar circumstances.

Get Out of the Office and Go to a Teaching Conference

Good teachers often regularly attend teaching conferences to "steal" their colleagues' expertise, knowledge, and teaching techniques. As you can tell from this volume's collection of essays, a lot of highly interesting and practical information is shared at NITOP. Keep in mind, though, that although NITOP is the most substantive conference of its kind, other teaching conferences abound throughout the United States. The Association for Psychological Science, as part of its annual conference, sponsors a daylong preconference teaching institute and features a teaching track within the conference itself. Likewise, the Society for the Teaching of Psychology (STP; Division 2 of the American Psychological Association, APA) sponsors an expansive teaching track during the annual meetings of the APA. In addition, STP sponsors an annual "Best Practices" conference in the Atlanta area that focuses on a different teaching area each year.

In our experience, attending teaching conferences has broadened our circle of teaching friends and colleagues, exposed us to a vast array of practical suggestions for improving our teaching, and refueled our passion for teaching. Indeed, good teachers, even the best ones, leave teaching conferences inspired to improve their teaching and to set the bar a tad higher for the next semester.

Draw Upon Your Personal Interests

Good teachers also draw on their hobbies, interests, and life experiences. For instance, one of us (Perlman) has a fondness for historical and mystery stories, and uses ideas and examples taken from these sources in his teaching of both Introductory Psychology and Abnormal Psychology. Tony Hillerman's mysteries on the Four-Corners region and the Native Americans who reside there provide a wealth of examples of health psychology, personal identity, and the role culture plays in who we are and how we cope. Eliot Pattison's series about a Chinese man who is released from the Chinese gulag in Tibet and becomes a "detective" in a Buddhist world is a treasure of examples of cross-cultural ideas and how our Western society and its mores promote many of the pathologies students study.

WHAT IS GOOD TEACHING?

Good teaching starts long before a course begins, residing to some extent in the context for learning that your department and even your institution provide for students. An initial consideration, of course, is whether the department's curriculum is designed well enough that, when you walk into your class, you know the students have been well prepared in prerequisite courses and that your course is placed at the proper level in their course of study (freshman, sophomore, etc.).

Preparation

However, good teaching is primarily influenced by variables, such as preparation, over which you have more direct control. Taking time before the semester begins to set goals, organize your courses, review past evaluations of your teaching, item-analyze exams from the previous versions for the course, prepare overheads or slideware, and so on, is another cornerstone of good teaching. Most of us have probably gone to class unprepared and discovered what a mistake we made when we had to rely too heavily on our notes (if we brought them with us) or could not field students' questions very well.

To be sure, our preparation is only as good as our knowledge base. It is difficult to explain a concept to students if you do not first understand it yourself, or if you have been caught off guard and attempted to fake it. Undoubtedly, you have found this situation to be as uncomfortable as we have and likely vowed never to put yourself in it again.

Knowledge, Communication, and Relevance

From your students' point of view, being a knowledgeable teacher is one thing, but being able to convey that knowledge at a level they can understand is something entirely different. Good teachers seem to have their own unique ways of building bridges between what psychological scientists have discovered, how practitioners apply that knowledge to solving important human problems, and how students perceive these dimensions of psychology as relevant in their lives. In one way or another, good teachers make clear to students why they should care about psychology. In more concrete terms, consider this: If Pavlov's work had been only relevant to salivation in canines, it would have been dropped from introductory psychology long ago. Because Pavlovian conditioning lies near the heart of our emotional lives, his work continues to have relevance today. Good teachers help their students see this connection vividly by enlivening the class with examples to which students easily relate. Not-so-good teachers do not, which leaves their students wondering why they need to know about Pavlov's drooling dogs other than for passing an exam.

Organization

Closely linked to preparation and knowledge is how teachers organize their presentations. Good teachers organize their material so that basic or background knowledge essential for understanding a point is provided *before* that point is made, increasing the likelihood that students will understand it — and remember it. One of us (McCann) puts a lecture outline on the board before each class, forcing him to have developed a good organization, and helping students to follow the lecture and understand which sub-points relate to which major points in the discussion.

A good teacher always seems one step ahead of students, anticipating their questions and answering those questions in the warp and weft of their teaching. A good teacher need not be dramatic, but students enjoy being in the presence of teachers passionate about their subject matter, about students, and about teaching itself.

Another key to effective organization is transitioning from one point to the next. Good teachers link their main points by creating interesting, humorous, or just-plain-clear segues. As Daniel noted in his chapter, slideware use seems to hinder this important facet of teaching. Clearly, as a lecture or discussion proceeds, good teachers go out of their way to identify the most important points, repeating and perhaps re-explaining those points until their students "get it."

Good teachers also tie their entire lecture or discussion together with a summary at the conclusion of the class period. Think about how useful a good summary is: It reinforces the major points that you have made, gives students a chance to fill in any blanks in their notes, and helps both you and your students stand back from the details and gain a little perspective on the day's lesson. It also offers students the chance to ask you any questions they had not thought to ask earlier or to clarify a point that they thought they understood earlier in the presentation but now find they do not.

When considering how to pull your lecture or discussion together by way of a summary, you may want to adopt the "rule of one." What one thing do you want your students to walk away with from that particular day — an idea, an example, a principle? Something new, interesting, or useful? Whatever that one thing might be, use it as the centerpiece of your summary and connect all of your corollary points to it.

Rapport

As Joseph Lowman (1995) pointed out, our classrooms are emotionally charged environments for students. Thus, establishing a supportive, even nurturing connection with them would appear integral to good teaching. How might we develop such connections? Buskist and Saville (2004) offered several suggestions, including arriving early to class and staying late to chat with students; learning your students' names; taking time to learn something about your students' interests, hobbies, and goals; being enthusiastic about teaching and your subject matter; and using humor every now and then to lighten the class mood. We have discovered that a little rapport goes a long way in having students see us as approachable and personable.

Good teachers know how to tinker with the affective dimensions of the classroom to maximize the likelihood that students become engaged or excited about the subject matter. They turn students on to the discipline, and that is especially important in the introductory and other lower-level courses. Students enjoy being in the presence of a teacher who knows the subject matter so well that the class period seems to be over almost as soon as it started. We are sure you can remember the feeling of being a student and enjoying the perception that you were mesmerized — hanging on the teacher's every word, and feeling almost disappointed when class ended. For what seemed to be a nanosecond, you were transported into your teacher's world, only to have to return to your own when it was over.

In the final analysis, good teaching is a blend of personal attributes of the teacher and the teacher's technique. You may be tempted, like most good teachers are, to ask: "Which part of this mix is more important?" Many teachers — especially the inexperienced and mediocre — immediately determine that technique is the key becoming a good teacher. However, in considering this question, we ask you to contemplate Parker Palmer's (1998, p. 10) idea that "Good teaching cannot be reduced to technique; good teaching comes from the identity and integrity of the teacher" and consider its implication for your development as a good teacher.

HOW DO WE KNOW IF WE ARE GOOD TEACHERS?

Head Counts

Some of the ways we track our teaching quality are obvious and simple, yet often overlooked. For example, what is the trend in enrollment in our classes? Are we seeing the same number of students or a few less each semester, or is the waiting list to get into our classes growing? If the size of a class is gradually declining, and the number of majors in our department is not, all may not be well in that course. Similarly, if we go to the first day of an upper-level course and see familiar faces of students who have completed other courses we have taught, we can be reasonably sure that, at least for those students, our teaching is hitting the mark — assuming, of course, that the current class is not required for these students to graduate, or that seats are not so scarce they would take any course with anyone!

Student Reaction

As our courses get underway, the day-to-day reactions of our students tell us a great deal about how our teaching is going. Are there lots of questions? Is discussion lively? Does it indicate that students have mastered the material and are interested in it? Other obvious signs, for good or ill, are student comments and complaints about the assignments and exams. Let us not forget the feedback that students' nonverbal behavior provides us — if students make eye contact with us, smile when we look at them during class, and have relatively few confused — or worse, dazed — looks on their faces, then we tend to feel that our teaching is at worst okay, and at best, pretty darn good.

Student Performance

Another indicator of how things are going in a course can be found by paying close attention to student performance on exams and other assignments. To what extent do students appear to be mastering the subject matter? Although having few or no low grades in a class might be a sign that your course is too easy, it may also mean that your students actually understand the material. Student learning is perhaps the most important immediate outcome of good teaching.

Student Evaluations

Of course, the most common tool that teachers use to determine how well we are teaching is student evaluations. Although there remains debate about the uses to which such evaluations are put (particularly by administrators), psychometrically sound and properly administered student evaluations can be rich with useful feedback about our teaching (McKeachie, 2002). The three of us have independently found that such evaluations from any of our courses can be divided up into three non-overlapping piles: those from students who love us, those from students who hate us, and those from students who fall somewhere in between. We generally "chuck" the first two piles and pay attention to those students who mostly like our teaching but also offer some specific criticisms of it or gentle suggestions for improving it.

Teacher Foibles and Student Feedback

Many good teachers avoid getting student evaluations *only* at the end of the academic term. These teachers have discovered that receiving feedback this late in the semester (or sometimes not until after the semester ends) provides no help in improving their teaching for the particular group of students who completed the evaluation. Instead, good teachers offer students multiple opportunities during the academic term to evaluate their teaching. Sometimes these teachers provide students with their standard institutional teaching evaluation. At other times, they provide their students with a "home-grown" evaluation that they tailored especially for their own use as it relates to their development as teachers (i.e., a purely formative feedback device).

As teachers work to improve their craft, they become acutely aware of their personal teaching foibles and the outright mistakes they tend to make. We may profess too much at times, have too much energy in the classroom, or get off on tangents. Some of us also may talk too rapidly or have indecipherable handwriting on the overhead or blackboard.

To counteract such weaknesses in our teaching, it is often a wise idea to seek frequent and specific student feedback that goes well beyond the standard student evaluation of our teaching. Indeed, students are an often-overlooked source of ideas and feedback. You may be pleasantly surprised by the thoughtfulness of their replies when you ask them, verbally or in writing, to tell you what went well in a class, what they misunderstood, whether they have any suggestions on how something might be done differently, or what they liked or did not like. For example, two of us (Perlman and McCann) were delighted to discover that our upper-level students, when asked what they liked to have covered on the first day of class, wanted us to say something about our background and how we ended up teaching that particular subject.

In-Class Assessment

You also may find that querying students directly about what they are learning provides useful feedback regarding the extent to which you are getting your points across. For example, one handy technique toward this end is simple: Organize students into pairs and have them quiz each other on important concepts that you put on a slide or on the overhead. This strategy often generates plenty of student questions about the material and gives teachers a golden opportunity to clarify and reinforce important concepts and principles. Other in-class assessment strategies are also useful (see Angelo & Cross, 1993, for a detailed discussion).

Teacher Reaction

These sorts of day-to-day classroom experiences can be a bountiful source of ideas for improving our teaching. Obviously, when things go well it is useful to consider why they went so well, and whether that approach or those circumstances could be generalized to other teaching situations. Alas, even more valuable ideas come from those occasions when our teaching fares less well and we are compelled to find ways to fix it. Furthermore, in our experience, we have found that in some risky teaching situations, it is best to reserve judgment on our teaching effectiveness until after we have "tinkered" with the new situation at least a few times.

How we personally feel about our teaching is another important source of knowledge about the teaching quality. We feel like we are good teachers when we sense that we are excited about the material and look forward to being in class and sharing it with our students. We feel like we are not such good teachers when we feel less enthusiastic about our teaching — when we feel disconnected from our students. Such self-perception should be taken as a signal that we need to reevaluate what we are doing in the classroom and ponder what factors in our professional or personal lives may be hampering our classroom performance. Such situations may be ripe with insight for helping us become better teachers. For example, when one of us (Buskist) gets down about his teaching, he often turns to his statement of his teaching philosophy, or to old student evaluations, and in reading these things is reminded of the many reasons he loves to teach. He often discovers new insights into the ways his philosophy is evolving. Such reviews often suggest new ideas for experimentation in the classroom — and they revitalize his energy level at the prospect of such risk taking.

One of us (McCann) recently developed a new course. It was an incredible amount of work, much more difficult than the creation of a new course was when he first started teaching. When he was done preparing and teaching the course, and sought to discover why it seemed to be so much hard work, he concluded that the problem was that as he created the new lectures, assignments, and exams, he was compelled to include all of the bells and whistles he had gradually added to his existing courses over the years. His self-serving conclusion was that he must have been doing something right over the years to have altered and (he hoped) improved his current classes that much.

A Final Thought

This volume of collected talks from NITOP is about good ideas for good teaching. It represents a blend of topical content and pedagogical technique as it applies to the effective teaching of psychology. Our chief aim in assembling this volume has been to recapture some of the excitement we, as attendees of NITOP, experienced as we sat in the audience and listened to the authors give fascinating and often inspirational talks. These talks have given us pause to contemplate our past, present, and future as teachers of psychology; we hope that the written versions of them have done the same for you.

References

Angelo, T. A., & Cross, K. P. (1993). *Classroom assessment procedures: A handbook for college teachers* (2nd ed.). San Francisco: Jossey-Bass.

Buskist, W., & Saville, B. K. (2004). Rapport-building: Creating positive emotional contexts for enhancing teaching and learning. In B. Perlman, L. M. McCann, & S. H. McFadden (Eds.), *Lessons learned: Practical advice for the teaching of psychology* (Vol. 2, pp. 149-155). Washington, DC: Association for Psychological Science.

Dass, R., & Gorman, P. (1985). *How can I help?: Stories and reflections on service*. New York: Knopf.

Dominowski, R. L. (2002). *Teaching undergraduates*. Mahwah, NJ: Erlbaum.

Davis, S. F., & Buskist, W. (Eds.). (2002). *The teaching of psychology: Essays in honor of Wilbert J. McKeachie and Charles L. Brewer*. Mahwah, NJ: Erlbaum.

Forsyth, D. R. (2003). *The professor's guide to teaching: Psychological principles and practices*. Washington, DC: American Psychological Association.

Kopp, S. (1972). *If you meet the Buddha on the road, kill him!: The pilgrimage of psychotherapy patients*. Palo Alto, CA: Science and Behavior Books.

Lowman, J. (1995). *Mastering the techniques of teaching* (2nd ed.). San Francisco: Jossey-Bass.

Lucas, S. G., & Bernstein, D. A. (2005). *Teaching psychology: A step by step guide*. Mahwah, NJ: Erlbaum.

McKeachie, W. J. (2002). *McKeachie's teaching tips* (11th ed.). Boston: Houghton Mifflin.

Palmer, P. (1998). *The courage to teach: Exploring the inner landscape of a teacher's life*. San Francisco: Jossey-Bass.

Perlman, B., McCann, L. I., & McFadden, S. H. (1999). *Lessons learned: Practical advice for the teaching of psychology* (Vol.1). Washington, DC: Association for Psychological Science.

Perlman, B., McCann, L. I., & McFadden, S. H. (2004). *Lessons learned: Practical advice for the teaching of psychology* (Vol. 2). Washington, DC: Association for Psychological Science.

CONTRIBUTORS

LUDY T. BENJAMIN, JR. holds the Fasken Chair in Distinguished Teaching at Texas A&M University, where he is Professor of Psychology and Educational Psychology. Benjamin's teaching honors include awards from the American Psychological Foundation and American Psychological Association and designation as Presidential Professor of Teaching Excellence at Texas A&M. Trained as an experimental psychologist, his principal area of scholarship is the history of American psychology, especially the applications of psychology in business, education, and clinical settings and the nature of popular psychology in the 19th and 20th centuries. He has written 14 books and more than 125 articles, most of those on historical subjects.

LAURA E. BERK is Distinguished Professor of Psychology at Illinois State University, where she has taught many undergraduate courses, including child and adolescent development, lifespan development, introductory psychology, and research methods. She has published widely in the field of child development, focusing on the effects of school environments on children's behavior and learning, the social origins and functional significance of children's private speech, and the role of make-believe play in the development of self-regulation. Berk's books include *Private Speech: From Social Interaction to Self-Regulation* (Erlbaum, 1991), *Scaffolding Children's Learning: Vygotsky and Early Childhood Education* (National Association for the Education of You, 1995), and *Awakening Children's Minds: How Parents and Teachers Can Make a Difference* (Oxford Univ. Press, 2001). She has also authored three widely distributed textbooks: *Child Development* (Allyn & Bacon, 6th ed., 2002), *Infants, Children, and Adolescents* (Allyn & Bacon, 5th ed., 2004), and *Development Through the Lifespan* (Allyn & Bacon, 3rd ed., 2003).

DOUGLAS A. BERNSTEIN is currently Professor Emeritus at the University of Illinois, Courtesy Professor of Psychology at the University of South Florida, and Visiting Professor of Psychology at Southampton University. A Fellow of the American Psychological Association and the Association for Psychological Science (APS), Bernstein serves as program committee chair for the annual National Institute on the Teaching of Psychology, and he founded the APS preconference Institute on the Teaching of Psychology. He has won numerous teaching awards and has contributed chapters to many teaching-related volumes. He has also coauthored several textbooks and occasionally offers workshops on textbook writing for prospective authors. As a hobby, he collects student excuses.

KENNETH S. BORDENS is Professor of Psychology at Indiana University-Purdue University at Fort Wayne (IPFW), where he has taught for the past 25 years. Bordens' main research area is psychology and law, and he has published several studies on juror and jury decision making. His most recent research is on the on how jurors and juries process evidence from complex, multiple-plaintiffs civil trials. He has coauthored four textbooks: *Research Design and Methods: A Process Approach* (McGraw-Hill, 6th ed., 2004), *Psychology: An Introduction* (Harrison Press, 8th ed., 2005), *Psychology of Law: Integrations and Applications* (Addison Wesley, 2nd ed., 1997), and *Social Psychology* (Erlbaum, 2nd ed., 2001). He is currently writing texts on the history of psychology and statistics. Bordens teaches courses in social psychology, law and psychology, child development, research methods, the history of psychology, and introductory psychology. He has taught introductory psychology, social psychology, and history of psychology on the Internet.

WILLIAM BUSKIST is Distinguished Professor in the Teaching of Psychology at Auburn University. His research interests center on identifying and understanding the qualities and behaviors involved in "master teaching" and on designing training programs that promote effective undergraduate teaching. He is a member of the National Institute on the Teaching of Psychology Planning Committee. He serves as the editor for The Generalist's Corner section of *Teaching of Psychology*. Together with Steve Davis, he has edited two volumes on the teaching of psychology. He has received over two dozen awards for his undergraduate teaching, including the 2000 Robert S. Daniels Teaching Excellence Award from the Society for the Teaching of Psychology (STP). He is a Fellow of Divisions 1 (General Psychology) and 2 (STP) of the American Psychological Association.

DAVID B. DANIEL is an Associate Professor of Psychology at the University of Maine at Farmington. Currently, he is a visiting scholar in the field of Mind, Brain and Education at the Harvard Graduate School of Education; coordinator of the Society for Research in Child Development's Teaching of Developmental Science Institute; and Chair of the Society for the Teaching of Psychology's task force on pedagogical innovation. Daniel was also the recipient of his campus's Teacher of the Year award for several consecutive years and is now "retired" from contention. His research on the evaluation of effective pedagogy has informed his current efforts to develop effective pedagogical and teaching techniques. As coordinator of his campus's team-taught General Psychology course, he has had the opportunity witness a variety of effective, and not-so-effective, teaching strategies by instructors of various styles.

JOSH R. GEROW, Professor Emeritus of Psychology at Purdue University, is currently an adjunct faculty member at the Manatee Community College South Campus in Venice, Florida. An instructional psychologist, Gerow taught for 32 years at Indiana University-Purdue University at Fort Wayne (IPFW), where his research focused on factors that influence performance in introductory psychology. He has made several presentations at past meetings of the National Institute on the Teaching of Psychology, having attended the first session at the University of Illinois, Champaign 26 years ago. His text, *College Decisions: A Practical Guide to Success in College* (Atomic Dog Publishing, 2004), coauthored with his wife, Nancy, is currently in its third edition, and his *Psychology: An Introduction* (Harrison Press, 2005), coauthored with Kenneth S. Bordens, is in its eighth edition.

SUSAN B. GOLDSTEIN is Professor of Psychology at the University of Redlands in Southern California where she has been involved in a number of curriculum-transformation projects. She received her PhD in Psychology from the University of Hawaii while a grantee of the East West Center. Her research has focused on stigma, cross-cultural conflict resolution, and intercultural attitudes. She has been teaching courses on culture and psychology for nearly two decades.

PETER GRAY is a Professor of Psychology at Boston College, where he has served his department as Department Chair, Undergraduate Program Director, and Graduate Program Director. He is author of an introductory psychology textbook, which is now going into its fifth edition, and he has published many research articles in the areas of neurobiology, developmental psychology, and educational psychology. His current research focus is on the evolutionary functions of children's play. His avocations include long-distance bicycling, kayaking, and backwoods cross-country skiing.

SAUL KASSIN is the Massachusetts Professor of Psychology at Williams College, in Williamstown, Massachusetts. He is the author of the textbooks, *Psychology 4e* (Prentice Hall, 2004) and *Social Psychology 6e* (Houghton Mifflin, 2005). He has also authored and edited a number of scholarly books, including: *Confessions in the Courtroom* (Sage, 1993), *The Psychology of Evidence and Trial Procedure* (Sage, 1985), and *The American Jury on Trial* (Hemisphere, 1988). Kassin's research focuses on police interrogations and confessions and their impact on juries; he has also studied eyewitness testimony, including questions pertaining to general acceptance within the scientific community. Kassin is a Fellow of the American Psychological Association and Association for Psychological Science and has served on the editorial board of *Law and Human Behavior* since 1986. He has testified as an expert witness; lectures frequently to judges, lawyers, psychologists, and law enforcement groups; and has appeared as a media consultant for several news programs.

STEPHEN M. KOSSLYN is the John Lindsley Professor of Psychology at Harvard University and Associate Psychologist in the Department of Neurology at the Massachusetts General Hospital. His research has focused primarily on the nature of visual mental imagery, visual perception, and visual communication; he has published 7 books and over 250 papers on these topics. Kosslyn has received the APA's Boyd R. McCandless Young Scientist Award, the National Academy of Sciences Initiatives in Research Award, the Cattell Award, a Guggenheim Fellowship, the J. L. Signoret Prize (France), an honorary Doctorate of Science from the University of Caen (France), and election to Academia Rodinensis pro Remediatione (Switzerland), the Society of Experimental Psychologists, and the American Academy of Arts and Sciences.

LESTER A. LEFTON is Professor of Psychology and Senior Vice President for Academic Affairs and Provost of Tulane University. Before joining Tulane in 2001, Lefton was Professor of Psychology and Dean of the Columbian College of Arts and Sciences at the George Washington University from 1997 until 2001. Prior to that, he was at the University of South Carolina from 1972 until 1997, serving in several capacities, including Dean of the College of Liberal Arts and Director of Graduate Studies in General-Experimental Psychology. He is a Fellow of the American Psychological Association and a teaching award winner. Noted for his energetic teaching style and his widely used introductory psychology textbook in its ninth edition, Lefton is known for his active involvement with undergraduate students and his interests in issues in higher education.

LEE I. McCANN is a Professor of Psychology and both a Rosebush and University Professor at the University of Wisconsin Oshkosh. McCann is a Fellow of the American Psychological Association and has served as a consulting editor for the journal *Teaching of Psychology*. He is coauthor (with Baron Perlman) of *Recruiting Good College Faculty: Practical Advice for a Successful Search* (Anker, 1996) and coeditor (with Baron Perlman and Susan McFadden) of *Lessons Learned: Practical Advice for the Teaching of Psychology*, volumes 1 and 2 (Association for Psychological Science, 1999, 2004), and the Teaching Tips column in the APS *Observer*. With Baron Perlman, McCann is the coauthor of several articles and book chapters dealing with teaching psychology and the psychology curriculum, and has presented numerous papers, posters, workshops, and invited presentations at regional and national conferences.

DAVID G. MYERS has spent his career professing psychology at a place called Hope (Michigan's Hope College). His scientific writings, supported by National Science Foundation grants and fellowships and recognized by the Gordon Allport Prize, have appeared in two dozen periodicals, including *Science*, the *American Scientist*, the *American Psychologist*, and *Psychological Science*. Myers has digested psychological research for the public through articles in more than three dozen magazines, from *Scientific American* to *Christian Century*. His 15 books include textbooks for introductory and social psychology, and general-audience trade books on happiness, social change, hearing loss, and intuition.

BARON PERLMAN is a Distinguished Teacher, and a Rosebush and University Professor in the Department of Psychology at the University of Wisconsin Oshkosh and a Fellow in the Society for the Teaching of Psychology in APA. He is coauthor of three books: *The Academic Intrapreneur* (with Jim Gueths and Don Weber; Praeger, 1988), *Organizational Entrepreneurship* (with Jeffrey R. Cornwall; Irwin, 1990), and *Recruiting Good College Faculty: Practical Advice for a Successful Search* (with Lee McCann; Anker, 1996). He is editor of the Teaching Tips column in the APS *Observer*. The columns are published in book form in *Lessons Learned: Practical Advice* for the Teaching of Psychology, Volumes 1 and 2 (Perlman, McCann, & McFadden, Eds.; Association for Psychological Science, 1999; 2004). He facilitates workshops on empirical scholarship of teaching and learning, peer review of teaching, faculty recruitment, and the course portfolio.

ROBIN S. ROSENBERG is a clinical psychologist in private practice and has taught introductory psychology at Lesley University. In addition, she is coauthor (with Stephen M. Kosslyn) of *Psychology: The Brain, the Person, the World* (Allyn & Bacon, 2nd ed., 2003). She is certified in clinical hypnosis and is a member of the Academy for Eating Disorders. She received her PhD in Clinical Psychology from the University of Maryland, College Park. Rosenberg did her clinical internship at Massachusetts Mental Health Center and had a postdoctoral fellowship at Harvard Community Health Plan before joining the staff at Newton-Wellesley Hospital's Outpatient Services, where she worked before leaving to expand her private practice. Rosenberg specializes in treating people with eating disorders, depression, and anxiety and is interested in the integration of different therapy approaches. She was the founder and coordinator of the New England Society for Psychotherapy Integration.

LESTER M. SDOROW is a member of the Department of Psychology at Arcadia University and has served as Chair of both the Department of Behavioral Science at St. Francis College (where he was named Outstanding Educator) and the Department of Psychology at Allentown College (where he was named Teacher of the Year). Sdorow cofounded (with the late Richmond Johnson of Moravian College) the Annual Lehigh Valley Undergraduate Psychology Conference and served as President of the Pennsylvania Society of Behavioral Medicine and Biofeedback. Sdorow's research interests are in psychophysiology, sport psychology, and health psychology. Sdorow has made numerous presentations on the teaching of psychology at local, regional, and national conferences.

INDEX

Active learning, 12-13, 114-115, 150.
See also Demonstrations and in-
class exercises

Allport, G., 8, 25

Amrine, M., 27

Anti-Semitism and psychologists, 7-8

Archives, 17-32; description, 17-19,
29; Library of Congress, 24-25,
27, 31; teaching, use in, 30-31;
University of Akron, 18, 21, 26,
27, 31

Arenson, S., 155

Asch, S., 5, 12

Attention: student inner and outer, 84

Bandura, A., 9

Bartoshuk, L., 8, 23

Beach, F., 22

Beers, C., 5

Benchley, R., 111

Berger, H., 2, 7

Best teaching practices, 145-154;
behavioral contract, 146;
challenges to 145; generalization,
147; interest, create, 149; learning
points, 146-147; low-technology,
high-impact, 151-153; organize,
146-147; profess less, 151-152;

questions, 150; visual aids, 147

Binet, A., 12

Biographical vignettes, 1-17. *See also*
Active learning

Boring, E. G., 42

Bouthilet, L., 26

Boyer, E., 131

Brain, 72-79. *See* also Neuroscience

Brethren. See Psychological Round
Table

Brown v. Board of Education, 5;
APA's role, 24-28

Brozek, J., 29

Bruner, J., 22

Calkins, M. W., 1, 2, 8, 18

Cannon, W., 34, 35

Cartoons, 115-116

Cattell, J. M., 8, 18

Chein, I., 27

Clark, K. B., 5, 24-28

Clark, M. P., 5, 24-28

Classic: studies, 33-44; theories in
psychology, 64-67

Cognitive development: Piaget, 67

Colleagues, 166

Cook, S., 26-27

Common sense: about psychology,

Marshall, T., 25, 28
Maternal deprivation: Harlow, 37-38
McClelland, D., 22
McDougall, W., 4
McIntosh, P., 48-49
Mental images, 72-73
Miles, W., 8, 18
Milgram, S., 5, 101
Miller, N., 22
Moniz, E., 12
Morgan, C., 8-9, 22
Mulcaster, R., 40
Murray, H., 7, 8-9
Music: use in teaching, 116, 150

National Institute on the Teaching of
    Psychology: history, v-vii
Neuroscience, 71-82; teaching
    guidelines, 80
NITOP. *See* National Institute on the
    Teaching of Psychology
Novello, D., 112

One-minute paper, 152-153
Overheads, 120

Pathologizing: avoiding in
    psychology, 62-63
Pattison, E., 167
Pavlov, I., 12
Peer review, 132
Penn, W., 12
Penne, C., 12
Pennfield, W., 4, 5-6, 12
Perloff, R., 26
Perls, F., 4-5
Pfaffman, C., 8
Piaget, J., 12, 67
PowerPoint. *See* Presentation software
Presentation software, 119-

130; changing classroom
    characteristics, 121-122; effective
    use, 120-128; teaching better,
    124-128
Psychoanalytic theory, 65-66
Psychological: anthropology, 48;
    phenomena, existence of, 72-75,
    and explanations of, 76-78
Psychologists: life experiences, 3-5;
    lives outside psychology, 5-6
Psychology Round Table, 21-23
Public image and psychology, 24-
    28; psychology not a legitimate
    science, 28

Ramón y Cajal, S., 6, 12
Rapport, 169
Rayner, R., 9
Rodin, J., 5, 12, 23
Rogers, C., 66-67
Rorschach, H., 3, 12

Sagan, C., 160
Sanford, E. C., 1
Sanford, F., 26
Scarr, S., 6, 8
Scavenger hunt, 12-13
Scholarship of teaching and learning,
    131-143; definition, 132;
    empirical, 133; principles of, 134-
    139; history, 131-132; reasons for,
    132; scholarly nature, problems,
    132-133
Secret society. *See* Psychological
    Round Table
Secret Six. See Psychological Round
    Table
Sears, R., 22
Self-actualization, 66-67
Self, 66

Seligman, M., 23, 108

Sensory deprivation, 41-43

Seuss, Dr., 158

Sheldon, W., 36

Shneidman, E., 7

Silence, use in teaching, 152

Sleep: Function of, 61-62. *See also* Evolutionary theory

Slideware. *See* Presentation software

Society of Experimental Psychologists (SEP). *See* Experimentalists.

Society for the Teaching of Psychology, 118

Somatypes: Sheldon, 36

SOTL. *See* Scholarship of teaching and learning

Spaulding, D. A., 38

Sperry, R., 10

Spitz, R., 37

Startle, 76-77, 79

Steinberg, R., 156

Stereotyping, 52

Stevens, A. W., 158

Stevens, S. S., 22

Storytelling in teaching, 83-96; life-story narratives, use of, 92-94

Students: attendance in class as a barometer of teaching, 169-170; construing meaning, 86-87; cultural awareness, gaining, 52-53; engaging and interesting, 112; evaluations of teaching, 170-171; expectations of 147, 161; instill desire, 148-149; presentation software, response to, 122-123; respect viewpoints, 148; small groups, 150. *See also* Presentation software

Sullivan, H. S., 9

Summer, F., 5

Syllabus, 151

t-test, 6

Taste: bitter, function of, 62

Teaching: assessments of, in-class, 171; challenges, 97; conferences, 166-167; innovations, teaching diversity, 53; portfolios, 132 presentation software, 124-128; quality, dimensions of, 167-169; and faculty assessment of, 169-172. *See also* Best teaching practices, Presentation software

Terman, L., 8

Texts: change in, 33-34

Titchener, E. B., 8, 19

Therapy: *Consumer Reports'* research, 106-108; obsessive-compulsive disorder, 76-79

Titchener's private club of experimentalists. *See* Experimentalists

Tryon, R. C., 41

Urch, G., 19

VanGogh, V., 158

von Helmholtz, H., 12

Walk, R., 3

Washburn, M. F., 8

Watson, J. B., 9, 72

Women psychologists: not welcome in psychology, 8-9, 19-20, 24

Wolpe, J., 3

Wundt, W., 19

Yerkes, R., 8, 20